Judgement and
Choice

Judgement and Choice

The Psychology of Decision

Robin M. Hogarth

University of Chicago
Graduate School of Business
Center for Decision Research

A Wiley—Interscience Publication

JOHN WILEY & SONS
Chichester · New York · Brisbane · Toronto

British Library Cataloguing in Publication Data:

Hogarth, Robin M
   Judgement and choice.
   1. Decision-making
   I. Title
   153.8′3   BF441   79–42822

ISBN 0 471 27744 4

Photoset in India by The Macmillan Co of India Ltd., Bangalore
and printed in the United States of America

To
Hilly and the CDR

Contents

APPENDICES

Preface

Although it sounds trite, decision making is one of the most important recurrent human activities. Nonetheless, three observations about decision making strike me as paradoxical: (1) people are generally unaware of *how* they make decisions and often *why* they prefer one alternative to others; (2) they show little concern for the quality of their own decision making processes (although the failures of others are often indicated with haste); and (3) the scientific study of decision making has not in my view attracted the attention it merits.

One argument could resolve these paradoxes, namely: people are effective decision makers. However, although it is true that people have been observed to be effective at making some kinds of decisions, the available empirical evidence also indicates important deficiencies across a range of problems with both trivial and important consequences.

A major goal of this book is to help people make better decisions. The orientation, however, is quite different from the standard texts on decision making methodology, statistical decision theory and related subjects. I write as a psychologist who recognizes that almost all decisions are based on the anticipations people make about the immediate and/or distant future. Anticipations, or predictive judgements as I call them, lead to choices, i.e. decisions. I further recognize that the basis of predictive judgements is largely intuitive; however, I believe, and indeed show in the book, that intuition can both be studied and educated. Although formal decision making methods are also discussed, the emphasis is on the unstructured, natural way people make judgements and exercise choice. Since this accounts for almost all real decision-making activity, the emphasis is more than justified.

The book is written for an audience that consists of neither professional psychologists nor decision theorists. It is written for decision makers, people who manipulate their specialist knowledge in making choices, be it in industry, commerce, government service, medicine or indeed any other professional activity. Consequently the book is written at a non-technical level. Footnotes placed at the end of each chapter do however provide references to the specialized literature and a detailed bibliography, or guide to further reading, is contained in an appendix. Many of the examples chosen for illustration actually concern business applications; however, this should not diminish either the appeal or usefulness of the book for other classes of decision makers. The choice simply reflects the kind of decision makers to whom I have been most exposed.

PLAN OF THE BOOK

The book consists of nine chapters and four appendices. It is organized as follows. Chapter 1 discusses the nature of human judgement emphasizing limitations on human ability to process information. In Chapter 2 an important normative implication of these limitations is explored, viz., the necessity to treat the environment as probabilistic. Experiments describing difficulties in thinking probabilistically are discussed and means suggested to overcome these shortcomings. Chapter 3 continues this theme but generalizes to situations where people have to combine multiple sources of information for prediction.

Chapter 4 discusses choice: models of how people make choices, principles of rational choice and paradoxes indicating how, in their actual behaviour, people fail to follow normative principles that they do accept at an intellectual level.

Two important issues in judgement concern how people learn the relationships they use in making predictions and the role of memory. These topics are discussed in Chapters 5 and 6 respectively.

Chapter 7 recognizes that the quality of judgement and choice are crucially dependent upon imagination and creativity. For example, I argue that without imagination, free choice is impossible. A conceptual model of creative processes is outlined and related to an overview of creativity techniques.

In Chapter 8, decision aids and methods of structuring problems are presented and discussed within the framework of *decision analysis* with its emphasis on the two key questions of rational choice: (1) assessing the consequences of alternative actions (i.e. utilities); and (2) estimating the probabilities of future events. Whereas I acknowledge that decision analysis is no panacea, I do believe it to be superior to other methodological approaches that have been suggested for making decisions. Choosing a method of analysing decisions is itself a decision. Therefore, one should choose the best even if it falls short of perfection. Appendices A, B, and C can be considered as supplements to Chapter 8. Appendix A outlines the rules of probability theory (and can also be usefully referred to with respect to Chapters 2 and 3); Appendix B provides a tutorial on probability assessment and is based on previously unpublished material that has been used successfully with a wide group of people over a period of about six years. Appendix C outlines a method proposed by Ward Edwards for assessing the utility of outcomes that can be characterized on many dimensions.

Chapter 9 integrates the various findings discussed in the book and provides a conceptual overview of human judgement. It also contains some speculations about the origins of the judgemental deficiencies noted in the preceding chapters. Finally, Appendix D provides a guide to further reading in the form of a bibliography organized by topics.

ACKNOWLEDGEMENTS

Since this book essentially surveys and documents the work of a fairly new and active field of psychological enquiry, my first debt is clearly to all those whose common efforts have created this body of knowledge. They communicate, naturally enough, through professional journals and at conferences, but also by means of 'The List' administered by Sarah Lichtenstein. Without such a network, this book would simply not exist. No doubt many of these decision researchers will disagree with my choice of specific topics and the emphasis given to different aspects. However, such choices are the prerogative and responsibility of any author.

The manuscript has benefited from conversations, critical comments and the encouragement of several colleagues, notably Carlo Brumat, Hillel J. Einhorn, Spyros Makridakis, Dennis Lindley, and Paul Slovic. In addition, the students in my elective course at INSEAD in 1979, and particularly Derek Nutt, gave much useful, detailed feedback. My various handwritten and corrected drafts have been expertly processed by several people: Marie-José Rouault at London Business School, Lindsey Hill at INSEAD, and Charlesetta Nowels at the University of Chicago. I am grateful to all of them. Permission to reproduce material that has appeared in print elsewhere was granted by several publishers and specific acknowledgements are made in the appropriate places in the text.

At an emotional level, my wife, Hélène, and our three children have supported me in both the high and low moments of writing this book and my indebtedness to them is probably far greater than I myself realize.

Finally, at both an emotional and intellectual level, I owe a tremendous debt to my friend, colleague, and former teacher, Hillel J. Einhorn. His intellect, humanity and infectious enthusiasm have both encouraged and sustained my work in this field. I consequently dedicate this book to him and the new Center for Decision Research that he has brought into existence.

Chicago, USA ROBIN M. HOGARTH
September 1979

CHAPTER 1

The nature of human judgement

Judgement and choice are pervasive activities. For example, as you read this text you will probably be making a judgement concerning the quality of the book and/or its usefulness to you. Right now you may also be anticipating how long it will take you to read this chapter, or indeed the whole book. These examples illustrate two kinds of judgement which are common to almost all choice situations.

First, people make value judgements by which they express preferences, for example: concerning the quality and usefulness of this book, for more as opposed to less money, for one job over another, for the relative beauty of works of art, for one kind of holiday compared to another, etc. Second, people make predictions which reflect what they expect to happen: for example, how long it will take to read this chapter or the book, how someone might react to what you say or do, whether a particular person will be successful in a given job, the extent to which the sales of your company will exceed a given figure next year, whether President Giscard of France will be re-elected in 1981, etc.

In short, judgement is an inevitable aspect of living. However, for the most part judgements are made intuitively—that is, without apparent reasoning and almost instinctively. And indeed, for much that affects us, intuitive choices are adequate. Either the outcomes of judgement are relatively unimportant, for instance your choice of which shirt to wear on a particular day, or they involve skills acquired under conditions that have allowed you to test their adequacy, as in driving a car for example.

However, the increasing interdependency and complexity of modern life mean that judgement now has to be exercised on matters with more important consequences than was ever the case in the past. Furthermore, the frequency with which people are called upon to make important judgements in unfamiliar circumstances is growing.

Consider, for example, advances made only this century. The development of modern transportation systems, e.g. air travel, large urban transit systems and motorways, imply that many judgements have to be made which daily affect the safety of millions. The growth of large corporations implies that the decisions of a few persons can affect the livelihoods of many more people than would have been the case several years ago. For example, in the UK, the decision by some 140 engineers at Heathrow Airport (London) to strike at Easter 1977 paralysed the massive British Airways, affected thousands of travellers and cost the corporation some £30 million in lost revenue.

The debate over nuclear power is another striking example. People make judgements about its relative advantages and disadvantages and public officials have to make decisions involving both enormous sums of money and risks that no one has ever experienced. In the realm of economics, recent history indicates a striking lack of agreement concerning which policies can most effectively deal with inflation and unemployment, and indeed the causes of those social ills. However, decisions have to be made on economic issues and such decisions are based on judgement. Development of modern means of warfare has also increased the need for good judgement, since the consequences of mistakes in this area are too horrible even to contemplate.

It could be argued that tools exist today to help decision makers make more reasoned choices and that this offsets the increased risks and stakes which have accompanied technological advances. It is, of course, true that many tools exist.[1] However, it is not true to say that such decision aids are equal to their task. First, one cannot eliminate the need for judgement. Even with the most sophisticated computer system someone has to make decisions concerning design, choice of variables and mode of use, etc. Second, most tools lack the flexibility to capture the essence of many important problems. Third, decision making takes place in situations involving people and judgements have to be made about those situations and the people in them whether they are in the board room, parliament or on the shop floor. Formal decision aids frequently cannot handle these important contextual considerations.

Despite the increasing complexity of modern technology and life, it might also be claimed that our organizations have adapted to facilitate decision processes. However, this is patently not true. The writings of both Peyrefitte in France and Crossman in the UK are quite explicit concerning the fact that cabinet members have neither the time nor information necessary to make reasoned judgements on the wide range of issues with which they are confronted.[2] Ministers must either delegate decisions to civil servants (which of course also implies making judgements about their competence), or decide themselves on an intuitive basis. The same could be said of chief executives. For example, evidence suggests that managers are sometimes incapable of understanding the situations in which they have to make crucial judgements concerning the survival of their organizations.[3]

Whereas most people reading this book will probably never be called upon to make decisions of the magnitude described above, it is true that the technological, economic and social environment in which they must now operate have also changed considerably in recent decades. Today even the humblest of us must make choices affecting others, and frequently under time pressure. Consider, for instance, the series of judgements exercised when driving a car.

However, what is common to both the more humble and eminent persons in our society is the increasing necessity to handle and process information for judgemental purposes. Indeed, it has been said that we are now living a second industrial revolution; but instead of steam, the new revolution is being propelled by *information*. And, as in the first revolution, relative success will be determined by the ability to handle the propelling force. In the not so distant past human survival and progress depended upon physical skills, e.g. for hunting, fighting, fishing, etc.; there can be little doubt that the need today is for *conceptual* skills, that is the ability to process information and make judgements.[4]

Despite the above, it is a curious fact that although most professionally trained persons (for example, engineers, lawyers, doctors, managers), have both followed courses and received on-the-job training concerning the subject matter of their expertise, almost none has given serious thought, or received instruction concerning conceptual skills and, in particular, the intuitive processes they use to manipulate their substantive knowledge.

Intuition, flair and judgement are, it seems, sacrosanct. Indeed, the questioning of a person's judgement can be likened to an attack on his or her moral and professional character. Furthermore, despite the fact that most people recognize that nonsense fed into a computer will result in nonsensical output (i.e. 'Garbage in—garbage out'), few question the notion that good information given to a human brain will result in anything but good judgement.

The issue to be faced is whether the intuitive choice processes that have apparently served the human race well until the present date are adequate for the rest of this century and beyond. Recent research suggests that they are not and, what is more disturbing, that people are unaware of this situation.

The purpose of this book is to bring the psychological study of judgement and choice to the attention of a wider, non-specialist audience. As indicated above, two forms of judgement are considered, evaluations and predictions. Evaluations, or as we shall say evaluative judgements, reflect individual preferences. Thus, it cannot be categorically said that they are 'wrong' in any case although a series of such judgements could be inconsistent. Similarly, in a free world it cannot be said that a person's opinions in the form of *predictive* judgements are wrong at the moment they are expressed. On the other hand, reality can subsequently show that the predictions were inaccurate.

The theme of this book is that since choice reflects both evaluative and predictive judgements, the quality of choice depends upon the extent to which (1) evaluative judgements really translate true preferences, and (2) predictive judgements are accurate.

On the subject of evaluative judgement the book will have relatively little to say except to discuss briefly situations where choices are to be made between outcomes which have to evaluated on several, and sometimes conflicting dimensions. For example, consider the choice between two jobs where one is better paid than the other, but the latter is in a more desirable location. In such a situation it is important to investigate the extent to which one is willing to 'trade-off' pay against location and so to explore one's true preferences.

The main topic of the book is predictive judgement. We shall be particularly concerned with exploring: (1) the basis of intuitive, predictive judgements; (2) systematic biases in predictive judgement; and (3) normative principles of judgement.

The book has two underpinnings: (1) the findings and theories of judgemental psychology; and (2) probability theory or, as it has been more aptly named, the 'logic of uncertainty'.

THE BASIS OF PREDICTIVE JUDGEMENT

Intuitive judgements are made on the basis of information which has been processed and transformed by the human mind. Consequently it is appropriate to consider the characteristics of the human mind as an information-processing system. Unfortunately, the techniques of neither neurology nor psychology have reached the stage where one can observe what happens to information as it passes through the human mind. However, recent decades have seen considerable interest and advances within cognitive psychology, an area which encompasses the study of perception, problem solving, judgemental processes, thinking, memory, concept formation and human information processing in general.

These studies have produced at least two firm conclusions: first, people have limited information-processing capacity; and second, they are adaptive. Therefore, the nature of the judgemental task with which a person is faced determines to a large extent the strategies that can be used for dealing with the task (these notions will be explained below). Consequently, to understand the bases of judgement it is necessary to have a clear notion of human possibilities and limitations as well as of the structure of judgemental tasks.[5]

Limited information-processing capacity

There are four major consequences of limited human information-processing capacity. These concern: (1) perception of information; (2) the nature of processing; (3) processing capacity; and (4) memory.

(1) Perception of information is not comprehensive but *selective*. For example, it has been estimated that only about 1/70th of what is present in the visual field can be perceived at one time. Thus since we are literally bombarded with information we have to select; however, to select it is necessary to know what to select. *Anticipations* therefore play a large part in what we actually do see. Physical as well as motivational reasons account for why 'people only see what they want to see'.

(2) Since people cannot simultaneously integrate a great deal of information, processing is mainly done in a *sequential* manner. This can, of course, be misleading in the sense that the actual sequence in which information is processed may bias a person's judgement (an issue explored in Chapter 3). However, it should be realized that our normal way of acquiring information is across time and that the sequence of events observed is important in making anticipations leading to actions. For example, the simple act of walking several yards along a busy street involves a constant series of minor adjustments to some initial anticipations. That is, when walking we constantly adjust our path to avoid bumping into objects or people we may not have seen when starting. We acquire

information across time (e.g. where people are relative to us on our path), and we are constantly making minor adjustments on the basis of this information.

It should be emphasized that this kind of judgemental 'strategy' will be quite successful in many circumstances. Consider, for example, short-term anticipations of sales returns, stock-market prices, the weather, etc. Anticipations of the immediate future are usually made on the basis of the last information you have just observed. If the weather is fine today, it will more probably than not be fine tomorrow (weather comes in spells). If the stock-market price of a particular company is high today, although it will almost certainly be different tomorrow, it will usually still be high. In a relatively stable environment, predictions based on the most recent observations of a series will be fairly accurate. Indeed, this is almost guaranteed by the sheer inertia of human and natural activity. Furthermore, research on learning indicates that when people observe events occurring closely in sequence (for example, a rise in sales following an advertising campaign), this is an important cue for inferring causality[6] (this notion is explored further in Chapter 5).

However, when the environment is unstable, such judgemental strategies are clearly deficient. Consider, for example, what happens when a sudden change in events causes larger changes between successive observations than are normally expected. People are unable to adjust their predictions to a different level of 'stability' and confusion reigns. A striking example of this was the economic chaos engendered by the Arab oil embargo of 1973.

(3) People do not possess intuitive 'calculators' which allow them to make what one might call 'optimal' calculations. Rather, they use fairly simple procedures, rules or 'tricks' (sometimes called 'heuristics') in order to reduce mental effort. For example, if you were asked to predict how well someone was likely to do in a particular job, you would not make a detailed mental investigation and calculation of the predictive ability of the person's characteristics (e.g. by combining information such as the track-record of people of his or her age, schooling, and past performance). It is more probable that you would use a simpler procedure, for example by considering how similar the person was to people who had already succeeded in the kind of job envisaged. The use of such heuristics will be examined in several chapters.[7]

(4) People have limited memory capacity. Although there is considerable uncertainty as to how memory processes actually work, current theories support the viewpoint that memory works by a process of associations which reconstruct past events.[8] Thus, unlike a computer, which can access information intact in its original form (i.e. as input), human memory is an active reconstruction process. Therefore, depending upon which association is used to reconstruct, memory can change. A nice example of this is the case of two scientists who were trying to remember the dates of a conference which they both remembered as having been announced to last 4 to 5 days. One scientist maintained that the dates were from March 30 to April 3, the other from April 30 to May 3. The first scientist was sure because he specifically remembered March 30 in the circular announcing the conference. The other was equally sure since he specifically recalled the date of

May 3. They consulted the circular letter to settle the dispute. The letter, to their mutual surprise, gave the dates as March 30 to May 3. This was obviously a mistake but it illustrates the point that memory is formed by reconstructing fragments of information. In this case, the cause of the disagreement was that the scientists reconstructed from different bits of information.[9]

Reconstruction can, however, be of considerable use as demonstrated in an experiment by de Groot.[10] He asked both master and ordinary chess players to memorize chess positions on a board. There were two experimental conditions. In one, the pieces were placed on the board at random; in the other, the positions were taken from actual chess games. Both master and ordinary players had similar, poor powers of recall for the random placements. However, the masters outperformed the others in reconstructing positions from actual chess games. It appears that reconstruction is important in memory not only from the viewpoint of recreating situations for 'recall', but also in processing information as patterns rather than as distinct units. In the experiment described, the masters were apparently able to recognize patterns from real games as units and to reconstruct them, subject to a few exceptions relevant to particular situations. In the random situation, they were unable to do this.

The meaning of information

From the above, one might conclude that people, whom I have depicted as selective, sequential, limited-capacity information processors, can be likened to ineffective computers. However, the computer analogy is inappropriate. People have emotions, they can reverse thought chains in ways that computers cannot and have powers of imagination and creativity that would be extraordinarily difficult to program into computers.[11] Furthermore, people attach *meaning* to information and such meaning is often the clue to understanding how human thought processes work.

That is, the selection of specific items of information and anticipations concerning them are based on the meaning given to that information in particular environments. Through experience, people build up an understanding of the world they live in and they use that understanding to select information, to interpret it and to anticipate events.

I shall argue throughout the book, that to understand the basis of a person's predictive behaviour, it is necessary to understand the way that person conceptualizes the world and the meaning he or she gives to information.[12] An economic example illustrates this point. Imagine you believe that the rate of inflation in a country is inversely related to the level of unemployment. Furthermore, you have been told that there has recently been a substantial drop in inflation in that country. If you were asked to make a forecast of economic trends in the country you would probably anticipate an increase in unemployment. However, consider someone who does not believe there is a relationship between the rates of inflation and unemployment. On receiving the same information as yourself, this person will not make the same inference. You give different meanings to the same information since it is interpreted within different conceptualizations, or models of the world.

Despite this emphasis on meaning per se, it should still be recognized that the meaning people give to information and their interpretations are, of course, effected within their limited information-processing systems described above.

The context of judgement

Before reading this section, attempt to answer the following questions:

(1) What will be the revenue (in dollars, pounds or francs as appropriate) of your organization (viz., company, school, institution) in the next calendar year?
(2) How tall is the Queen of England?

Now think about the process by which you generated your responses. It is most unlikely that you could have answered the questions other than by making some comparisons with known points of reference. For example, consider the revenue of your organization. You probably started to answer this question by thinking of points of reference such as the level of this year's revenue, economic trends in your branch of activity and in general, etc. In other words, your judgement was made on the basis of points of reference you believe to be related to the target predicted (i.e. next year's revenue) or, in the terminology to be used in this book, *cues*. It was not made in any absolute sense. Similarly your judgement of Queen Elizabeth's height was probably made by reference to your memory of her size relative to other people (e.g. the 'average' male or female with whom you have seen her pictured).

Most judgements are the result of a number of comparisons with such points of reference or cues. This process was conceptualized by the psychologist Brunswik in his so-called 'lens model' illustrated in Figure 1.1.[13] In that conceptualization Brunswik and his followers have been concerned with understanding the interrelationships between two systems. One system is the 'real' network of relationships between cues in the environment and the event to be predicted; the second system is the network of relationships between cues in the individual's mind and his or her predictions. For example, consider judgements in the form of your prediction of next year's revenue of your organization. The first system is the economic environment in which the organization operates (including the actions taken by your organization, competitors, etc). This system can be said to generate (i.e. produce) the outcomes you are trying to predict, that is revenue. The second system represents your mind. It indicates the relationships you perceive or imagine between cues in the environment, e.g. anticipated trends and competitive reactions, and your prediction of revenue. In other words, the first system is the environment, the second the representation of the environment in your mind which you use for prediction. Accuracy of prediction clearly depends on the extent to which the 'model of the environment' is matched by the 'model of the person', i.e. in terms of cues, relationships between cues, and between cues

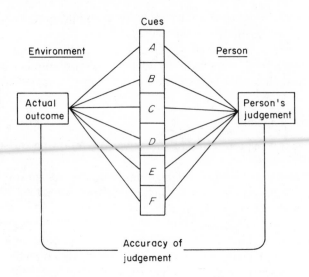

Figure 1.1 Brunswik's lens model. The model is to be understood as follows: The person makes judgements about an uncertain event (e.g. next year's revenue) on the basis of 'cues', *A, B, C, . . ., F* (e.g. this year's revenue, competitive reactions etc.). The relationship between the person's judgement and the cues are represented by the lines between the 'person' box and the cues; the relationship between the cues and the uncertain event are shown on the environmental side of the lens model. Accuracy of judgement depends on the extent to which the relationships on both sides of the lens are the same

and the target event, as well as the relative importance of the cues.

It must be emphasized that Brunswik's conceptualization is only a model. That is, it cannot claim to describe actual thought or environmental processes accurately although it can be said to represent them. The importance of Brunswik's lens model is to stress:

(1) judgement results from a series of operations on information which is related to other items of information or events;
(2) such interrelationships in the human mind have an analogue in nature;
(3) judgement will be accurate to the extent that the individual's picture of reality and judgemental rules match those of reality;
(4) Brunswik also stressed that judgement takes place in a *probabilistic* environment. That is, the relationships between cues in the environment and the target outcome can not be represented by strict functional rules. Rather the rules are probabilistic—which roughly means that they are not exact in 100 % of cases. This notion is explored in detail in Chapter 2; and

(5) judgemental accuracy is a function of both individual characteristics and the structure of the task environment.

In this book, examination is made of the kinds of rules people have been found to use in particular task environments. This will lead to an evaluation of the appropriateness of those rules and to seek remedial action where necessary.

SUMMARY

Judgement and choice are essential and pervasive activities. Two kinds of judgement are involved in choice: evaluations and predictions, i.e. judgements of preference and belief. This book is primarily concerned with predictive aspects of judgement. It was argued that intuitive judgemental processes are no longer adequate to deal with the modern world and that it is incumbent upon decision makers to examine their judgemental processes.

However, such an examination entails an understanding of judgemental processes. The nature of the human mind as a selective, sequential information-processing system with limited information processing and memory capacity was described. Nonetheless, the apparent analogy with the computer is inappropriate. People give meaning to information and it is necessary to understanding that meaning within a person's limited information-processing system.

It was further pointed out—through the conceptual device of Brunswik's lens model—that accuracy of judgement depends upon the extent to which the mind mirrors the environment it attempts to predict. Human judgemental ability is a function of both the person and the task.

NOTES AND REFERENCES

1. Developments in decision theory and particularly multi-attribute utility theory are good examples of progress made in recent years—see R. L. Keeney and H. Raiffa. *Decisions with multiple objectives: Preferences and value trade-offs.* New York: Wiley, 1976; and D. E. Bell, R. L. Keeney, and H. Raiffa (Eds.), *Conflicting objectives in decisions.* Chichester, England: Wiley, 1977. These approaches will be discussed in Chapter 8.
2. See A. Peyrefitte, *Le Mal Français*, Paris: Plon, 1976 and R. H. Crossman. *The Diaries of a Cabinet Minister*, Vol. 1 London: Hamilton and Cape, 1975. The plethora of books about the Watergate crisis are also most revealing in this respect.
3. An illuminating example of this is contained in R. I. Hall, A system pathology of an organization: The rise and fall of the Old Saturday Evening Post. *Administrative Science Quarterly*, 1976 (June), **21**, 185–211.
4. See also R. F. Sinsheimer, The brain of Pooh: An essay on the limits of mind. *American Scientist*, 1971, **59**, 20–28.
5. Supporting evidence for this paragraph as well parts of the succeeding section can be found in H. A. Simon and A. Newell, Human problem solving: The state of the theory in 1970. *American Psychologist*, 1971, **26**, 145–159; and P. Slovic and S. Lichtenstein, Comparison of Bayesian and regression approaches to the study of information processing in judgment, *Organizational Behavior and Human Performance*, 1971, **6**,

649–744, as well as in the references contained in these two works.

6. A. Michotte. *The perception of causality*. London: Methuen, 1963.

7. More evidence on this point will be presented in Chapter 3.

8. U. Neisser, *Cognitive psychology*, New York: Appleton-Century-Crofts, 1967. The classic work on memory by reconstruction is F. C. Bartlett, *Remembering*, Cambridge, England: Cambridge University Press, 1932.

9. B. Fischhoff, P. Slovic and S. Lichtenstein, Knowing with certainty: The appropriateness of extreme confidence. *Journal of Experimental Psychology: Human Perception and Performance*, 1977, **3**, 552–64.

10. A. D. de Groot. *Het denken van den schaker (Thought and choice in chess)*, The Hague: Mouton, 1965.

11. U. Neisser, The imitation of man by machine, *Science*, 1963, **139**, 193–97.

12. The role of *meaning* in judgement has, incidentally, been largely ignored in judgement research, although there are signs that this situation is changing.

13. A useful description of Brunswik's model and research related to it is provided in Slovic and Lichtenstein, Ref. 5 Brunswik's own writings are far from easy to digest. However, his views of psychology have been summarized by L. Postman and E. C. Tolman, Brunswik's probabilistic functionalism. In S. Koch (Ed.), *Psychology: A study of a science*, Vol. 1, New York: McGraw-Hill, 1959.

CHAPTER 2

Randomness and the probabilistic environment

A statement was made in the preceding chapter that we live in a probabilistic environment. In fact, this is not true. A more accurate statement is that the world is perceived by us as being probabilistic since we are unable to see and comprehend the myriad of factors that cause events to occur. To illustrate, consider the familiar exercise of tossing a coin. What does it mean to say that it has 1 chance in 2 of coming down 'heads' and 1 chance in 2 of coming down 'tails'?

The meaning is simply that we are uncertain whether it will be heads or tails on any particular throw. Furthermore, the chances of 1 in 2 reflect that uncertainty. Note that this statement does not mean that there are no causes for the coin to fall on one or the other side on a particular throw. Indeed, there must be causes. The statement simply implies that we are unaware of the force of various causes and so are prepared to assess chances of 1 in 2. The probabilistic statement expresses our degree of knowledge and is not a property of the coin per se (although the statement can be made in light of the coin's properties, e.g. it is not bent).

However, this admission of uncertainty lying within ourselves, rather than being a property of events in the environment, is something people have much difficulty in accepting. Indeed, there is considerable evidence to suggest that even in the 'rational' world of business, businessmen tend to deny the presence of uncertainty and when they do accept it, to think of it as some kind of physical property of the environment rather than attributing it to themselves.[1] However, if you think about it, it is absurd to make a statement of the kind that one situation or venture is more uncertain than another; it is simply you who are more uncertain in one of the situations. Nonetheless, this is not the way our society teaches us to think about uncertainty and our use of language obscures this basic point. A prominent investigator has put it this way:

> The usual tests and language habits of our culture tend to promote confusion between certainty and belief. They encourage both the vice of acting and speaking as though we were certain when we are only fairly sure and that of acting as though the opinions we do have were worthless when they are not very strong.[2]

Why should you accept that uncertainty lies in yourself? After all, suppressing our uncertainties is both more comfortable and a considerable simplification.

The reasons are important: First, explicit recognition of uncertainty can save you from deluding yourself.* Second, although there is often an emotional block in accepting uncertainty, in that one feels a loss of control over the environment, accepting uncertainty may paradoxically help you gain greater control over your environment. In this chapter, these and related issues will be explored by discussing concepts from the discipline developed to deal with uncertainty: probability theory.

In particular, three key concepts from probability theory are examined and an assessment made of the extent to which humans have an intuitive appreciation of them. The concepts are randomness, statistical independence and sampling variability. Experimental evidence is reviewed which indicates how people's untutored appreciations of these basic concepts is deficient. Subsequently, the kinds of judgemental errors resulting from such misunderstandings are discussed, as are possible ways of overcoming such deficiencies.

Finally, I do not underestimate the emotional difficulty of accepting uncertainty, both because of the uncomfortable feeling it often engenders and because of the consequent possible delays in action. However, there can be little doubt that people who accept uncertainty and yet are not paralysed in action will be more successful in the long run.[3]

RANDOMNESS AND STATISTICAL INDEPENDENCE

Roughly speaking, in any predictive context one can think of the ability to predict as being governed by the amount of unexplainable irregularity or randomness you can observe. For example, we accept that the outcomes (heads or tails) of tosses of a fair coin are random in that it is impossible to predict heads or tails accurately on each of a long series of tosses. That is, although *on average* we may expect to see about as many heads as tails, the exact sequences of heads and tails is irregular and thus unpredictable. Similarly, we can think of the event 'next year's sales' as being random in the sense that although we may 'know' precise bounds within which next year's sales will lie, the actual level of sales within those bounds is uncertain. However, whereas people can accept these ideas at an intellectual level, most have great difficulty in dealing with randomness in the real world. People want to treat the world as though it were more predictable than it ever could be for them.

An important statistical concept related to randomness is the notion of statistical independence. Two events, for example the outcomes of successive throws of a die or turns of a roulette wheel, are said to be statistically independent if knowledge of the occurrence of one event gives no information concerning the outcome of the second, or vice versa.

However, independent, random observations are not limited to games of chance such as coin-tossing or roulette. Many real-life processes have these characteristics and we all have considerable experience in dealing with them. For

---

* You may wish to delude others, but deluding yourself is usually not to be recommended.

example, extensive evidence exists that daily changes in stock market prices (i.e. up or down compared to the previous day's price) are of this nature.[4] Similarly, the output of many industrial processes can be considered to vary randomly around some average value. Consider, for example, a machine that is set to produce bolts of a certain width. Not all bolts will be precisely the required width; rather there will be small, irregular variations around the required width. As long as the bolts are within certain tolerance limits, this is all that most would worry about. Indeed, almost any time series (i.e. observations generated across time such as sales figures, export statistics etc.) will have a random component due to the fact that what one actually observes on any given occasion is the result of many different factors which would be impossible to enumerate. For example, in considering the monthly sales of a company, one may be able to attribute certain rises and falls to specific factors such as a time trend or seasonal effects: however, a myriad of other factors also 'cause' monthly sales and thus induce irregularities or randomness.

Despite extensive experience with independent, random observations, people are extraordinarily inept at recognizing and dealing with the concept. Consider the following evidence.

A well-known phenomenon is the so-called *gambler's fallacy*. This refers to the behaviour of many people who, despite knowledge that they are dealing with gambling devices with fixed and known properties (e.g. roulette wheels), behave as though those properties—for example, the chance of observing a Red on the next throw—change. In particular, after a long sequence of, say, Reds in roulette, there is an almost compulsive belief that Black will become more likely.

Some investigators have sought the explanation to these types of phenomena by considering development across the life cycle. For example, a study by Cohen and Hansel aimed to discover how children aged 6 to 15 + acquire the concept of statistical independence.[5] The experimental task required the children to guess which of two outcomes would occur in a sequence of outcomes generated at random (i.e. similar to a coin-tossing experiment). Results indicated that the younger children frequently made their choices in order to balance the outcomes of the series (in other words, similar to making sure in a coin-tossing experiment that there are as many heads as tails). Indeed, according to Cohen and Hansel, the concept of independence does not even seem to start to form until children reach the age of 12 + to 15 + . The behaviour of the children in these experiments was, of course, similar to the 'gambler's fallacy' described above.

As mentioned above, adults also have difficulty with the concept of independence and particularly with respect to random sequences. To illustrate this point, see whether you are able to generate a random sequence yourself. For example, imagine a series of 20 tosses of a fair coin and write down, in sequence, the outcomes of each of the 20 tosses.

Now compare your results with those of Figure 2.1. There I have reproduced two series of 20 tosses, series *A* and series *B*. One of these series, like yours, was generated intuitively; the other resulted from an actual coin-tossing experiment.

14

Series A	Series B
H	H
T	H
T	T
H	H
T	H
T	T
H	H
H	T
T	T
T	H
T	T
T	H
T	T
T	H
T	T
H	T
T	T
H	H
T	H
T	H

Figure 2.1   Two series of coin tosses: one imaginary, and one real

Which series resembles most the one you generated? Which series was artificially generated and which was the result of the actual coin-tossing experiment?

How can you judge? Most people use two criteria. First, since the coin is presumed fair one should observe roughly as many heads as tails. Based on experience with giving this task to people, I can tell you that it is highly unlikely that either your series or that of the person whose series is reproduced in Figure 2.1 would have anything other than 9, 10 or 11 heads in the series.[6] However, a quick calculation based on probability theory tells us there is only about 1 chance in 2 of actually observing 9, 10 or 11 heads in a real sequence of 20 tosses of a fair coin. That is, in 20 tosses there can be anything from 0 to 20 heads and these possibilities are spread out far more than most people imagine. People have a natural and understandable tendency to judge things as more likely the closer they represent what they believe the ideal should look like[7]—in this case the ideal is clearly 10 heads in 20 throws.

Second, it is unlikely that one would observe, say, 10 heads followed by 10 tails, or at the other extreme, to see heads and tails alternate in sequence, viz. H, T, H, T, H, ... The observed pattern should be somewhere between these two extremes. Statisticians have devised a method for assessing whether such intermediate patterns correspond to random sequences. The idea is the following: define a sequence of the same outcomes, e.g. heads, as a *run*, and count the number of runs in the series. For example, in Series A (the outcome of the real experiment), there are 10 runs; in Series B, there are 13 runs. In 20 tosses of a fair coin one should expect to see approximately 11 runs, and reasonable limits of variation would be between 7 and 15 runs.[8] The difference between the number and type of runs observed in artificially generated human series is that, compared to random sequences, individual runs tend to be too short (i.e. there are too many runs). Wagenaar has explicitly investigated the ability of adults to detect random from nonrandom sequences. He summarizes his experiments by stating that

> Subjects are unable to produce a randomized sequence of two, three or more alternatives even if they are explicitly instructed and motivated to do so. Generally S's show a tendency towards too few repetitions and too many alternations.[9]

Wagenaar also investigated people's ability to detect the amount of randomness in sequences of data.[9] Subjects observed sequences of black and white dots under varying conditions of dependence between successive observations of the same colour. That is, unlike fair coin-tossing experiments, the observation of outcomes affected the chance of succeeding outcomes. For example, to continue the analogy with a coin-tossing experiment, if heads were observed, heads would not be equally likely as tails on the subsequent throw. Heads could be more or less likely depending on how the scheme was arranged to depend on the observation of heads. In Wagenaar's experiments, the schemes tested varied the chances that successive observations would be of the same colour from 1 in 5 to .4 in 5. It turned out that schemes where the chances were set at 2 in 5 were judged by the subjects to be 'the most random'.

These experiments illustrate two points. First, people have a tendency to expect what they observe, i.e. sequences of data, to be *representative* of the process generating them: for example, in 20 tosses of a fair coin one expects to see 10 heads—the tendency of the children in the Cohen and Hansel experiments to balance the series. Second, people have little appreciation of the concept of randomness. In particular, they underestimate the extent to which deviations from what they expect to see in random processes are quite normal.

VARIABILITY AND SAMPLING VARIABILITY

An important point related to the preceding discussion is that prediction is difficult because we rarely have all the necessary information. For example, imagine that you are observing a production line and that the items produced can be classified as acceptable or defective. You see, say, 100 items which include 5 defectives. Is this reasonable? How many defectives should you expect to see?

In this example, as in most judgemental activity, you are involved in a process of sampling; that is, observation of part of all possible information on the basis of which you need to make an inference or judgement about the whole—in the example above the proportion of defectives produced by a particular machine. As should be apparent from the discussion of human information-processing capacity in Chapter 1, sampling is a fundamental activity. Almost all that we learn is by way of samples and our actions are based on sample information. For example, you, the reader have already sampled part of this book. You are probably trying to anticipate whether it will be worth the effort to finish it. However, as illustrated above, samples are rarely wholly representative, and this is particularly true of small samples. Most of what we can observe exhibits variation and, as will be illustrated below, an understanding of variation is important in judgement.

Two basic principles

There are two basic principles for estimating variability when observing outcomes that are random and independent:

(1) *The amount of variability is positively related to the degree of randomness.* For example, tosses of a fair coin will exhibit more irregularity than tosses of a bent coin where the chances of observing heads are fixed at say 4 in 5. Observations made from measuring instruments (e.g. psychological tests, thermometers, cardiographs, seismic recorders or reports by humans concerning, *inter alia*, stock levels, trading statistics, etc.), usually reflect two sources of variation: variation in the underlying traits or dimensions being measured, and variation due to unreliability of the instruments: other factors being equal, the more reliable an instrument, the less the variability one will observe in actual measurements.

(2) *Averages* of observations show less variation than the observations that have been averaged. Furthermore, variation is reduced as the number of observations that are averaged increases.* As an example, consider a factory producing cars and concentrate on the number of cars produced per day. Across a year, the average number of cars produced per day will show less variation on a weekly basis than the actual numbers produced per day. Similarly, the average per month will show less variation than the average per week, and the average per quarter less than the average per month.† Another way of looking at this principle is to realize that if

---

* By average is meant 'arithmetic mean'.

† For the sake of this illustration, assume that there are no seasonal effects.

you want to estimate the average daily production of the factory, a weekly average is liable to be more accurate than a day picked at random, the average for a month more accurate than the average for a week, etc. In other words, you can be more confident in your average, the more days you used to estimate it.

The above two principles seem quite straightforward and one would expect that people apply them in a relative if not absolute sense. The ability of people to do just this was tested in an ingenious series of experiments by Kahneman and Tversky.[7] Subjects in their experiments were faced with problems of the following kind:

(1) There are two programs in a high school. Boys are a majority (65 %) in program A, and a minority (45 %) in program B. There is an equal number of classes in each of the two programs. You enter a class at random, and observe that 55 % of the students are boys. What is your best guess—does the class belong to program A or to program B?[7]

(2) A certain town is served by two hospitals. In the larger hospital about 45 babies are born each day, and in the smaller hospital about 15 babies are born each day. As you know, about 50 % of all babies are boys. The exact percentage of baby boys, however, varies from day to day. Sometimes it may be higher than 50 %, sometimes lower.

For a period of 1 year, each hospital recorded the days on which (more/less) than 60 % of the babies born were boys. Which hospital do you think recorded more such days? The larger hospital? The smaller hospital? About the same (i.e. within 5 % of each other)?[7]

(3) A medical survey is being held to study some factors pertaining to coronary diseases. Two teams are collecting data. One checks three men a day, and the other checks one man a day. These men are chosen randomly from the population. Each man's height is measured during the checkup. The average height of adult males is 5ft 10in, and there are as many men whose height is above average as there are men whose height is below average.

The team checking three men a day ranks them with respect to their height, and counts the days on which the height of the middle man is (more/less) than 5ft 11in. The other team merely counts the days on which the man they checked was (taller/shorter) than 5ft 11in. Which team do you think counted more such days?

The team checking 3? The team checking 1? About the same (i.e. within 5 % of each other)?[7] (Reproduced by permission of Academic Press Inc)

To answer these three questions correctly requires an understanding of the two principles enumerated above. The first problem concerns the first principle. That is, sampling from a population where 65 % are boys (program A) produces less variation than when sampling from a population where 45 % are boys (program B). Thus although the majority of students in the class sampled (55 %) were boys—and thus the class seemed more representative of program A—it is in fact slightly more probable that the class sampled came from program B.

Incidentally, if you answered 'program *A*', you too are 'representative'; 67 of Kahneman and Tversky's 89 subjects also gave that answer.

Second, consider the hospital problem. This problem tests your appreciation of the second principle. That is, the larger the size of sample you observe, the more confidence you can have that a statistic (e.g. the mean or a proportion) is close to the true value.* With small samples you should expect high variability in such estimates, in larger samples less variability. Indeed this principle has been given the name of 'the law of large numbers' and does seem quite intuitive. More information should lead to greater confidence. However, this principle was not evident to Kahneman and Tversky's subjects. Only 10 out of 50 subjects realized that in the smaller hospital there would probably be a larger number of days where over 60 % of babies born were boys; furthermore, only 9 out of 45 realized that in the larger hospital, there would be less than 60 % male births on more days than in the smaller hospital.

If you understood the hospital problem, then you should also appreciate the third problem. Taking the mid-value of three heights will reduce observed variability relative to recording a single height only. Consequently you would observe more observations over 5ft 11in by the team checking 1 person, and more mid-values less than 5ft 11in by the team checking 3 persons. Once again, a majority of Kahneman and Tversky's subjects failed to answer these questions correctly.

The subjects whose responses are indicated had not been formally trained in statistical methodology. Consequently, it is legitimate to ask whether 'experts' would fall prey to the same kinds of questions. Tversky and Kahneman developed analogous problems which they presented to trained scientists and which concerned the interpretation and design of experiments.[10] They found that these statistically sophisticated scientists made the same kinds of judgemental errors as the naïve subjects in the other experiments. In particular, they overestimated the extent to which they should have confidence in data. Tversky and Kahneman dubbed this failing 'the law of small numbers', i.e.

The law of large numbers guarantees that very large samples will indeed be highly representative of the population from which they are drawn. If, in addition, a self-corrective tendency is at work, then small samples should also be highly representative and similar to one another. People's intuitions about random sampling appear to satisfy the law of small numbers, which asserts that the law of large numbers applies to small numbers as well.[10]

To summarize the essence of this chapter so far, I have argued that people have little appreciation for the concepts of randomness, statistical independence and sampling variability. However, given that they have extensive real-world experience of these phenomena, it is clearly legitimate to ask why. Two reasons are suggested here both of which relate to the discussion in Chapter 1. First, in

---

* Incidentally, note that in this problem, contrary to the first problem the true proportion (50 %) is the same in both populations (i.e. hospitals) so lack of differences in the proportions is not a factor.

order to learn from our environment it is necessary to receive appropriate feedback. However, many judgemental tasks are so structured that the nature of feedback is considerably biased. This topic is explicitly developed in the next section as well as in different parts of the book. Second, given limited information-processing capacity, people have a great need to structure and interpret their environment. Findings from the psychology of perception show that what we are able to perceive is often structured by so-called 'Gestalt' forces. Such forces, however, are not restricted to perception. Other branches of psychology have shown, for example, how people seek to find patterns in music as well as in rather banal letter-series completion tasks. Indeed, it has been said,

Patterns, temporal as well as spatial, occur in many spheres of life besides music. People appear to have strong propensities, whether innate or learned, to discover patterns in temporal sequences presented by the environment, and to use these evidences of pattern for prediction. The ability and desire to discover temporal patterns undoubtedly has had great value for the survival of Man: in predicting the seasons for example, or the weather. The urge to find pattern extends even to phenomena where one may well doubt whether pattern exists (e.g. in the movements of the stock market).[11]

PRACTICAL IMPLICATIONS

What are the consequences of failing to appreciate the nature of random fluctuations? There is clearly no precise answer to this question. However, in the following examples, I intend to show that the major consequence concerns the meaning we attach to what we observe. This can by itself engender self-delusion as well as other undesirable consequences.

Managing by exception[12]

Imagine that you have the responsibility of a department where a number of people have periodic targets to meet (e.g. weekly sales targets, daily output or production rates). Since you are conscientious, you always check each person's performance against target at the end of each period. When doing so, you frequently find that at least one individual has performed well below target. Consequently, you speak to that person. Your experience is that your interventions are justified in that the performance of the individual concerned usually improves in the next time period. What inference can you draw from this situation? When confronted with this kind of situation most people tend to believe that their interventions justify their actions. However, consider the structure of the task more carefully.

A possible representation of the above situation is given in Figure 2.2. Here the target performance of one individual is represented by a straight line. The crosses represent actual performance achieved. As can be seen, and indeed as would be expected, performance does not match target exactly on every occasion. Rather, performance is sometimes more, sometimes less than target, although on average

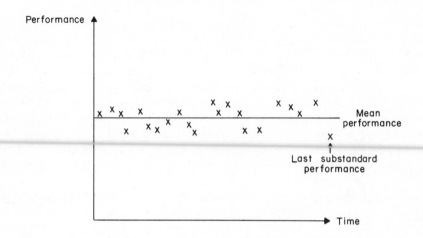

Figure 2.2   Performance plotted across time. (Reproduced by permission of
CEDEP)

target is being achieved. The actual performance of this individual can be
described by irregular fluctuations around some average value, in this case the
target. Now consider the last cross (i.e. performance level) of the series shown.
This is some way below target performance and thus you would wish to speak to
the individual after this occasion.

However, consider what would happen if you did not intervene. If the
individual's performance can be represented by a series of irregular fluctuations
around some average value, then it is highly probable that it will be closer to that
average (i.e. improve) in the next time period. That is, irregular—or random—
fluctuations in performance will always produce the occasional substandard
performance; furthermore, it is highly likely that performance will improve on
the next occasion *without intervention on your part.*

There is a reverse side to this situation too. What is likely to happen after
someone has produced an exceptionally high level of performance? On the next
occasion, performance is likely to be closer to the mean level, that is *decrease.*
Consequently, if you were to praise your outstanding performers, you might
observe that your praise leads to deterioration in their performance. After both
forms of extreme performance (high or low), the next observation will probably
be closer to the mean level.

The point being made here is the following: In many situations, observed
performance (e.g. production rates, sales statistics, athletic performance) varies
irregularly around some average level. Thus the most likely prediction for a yet to
be observed performance is in the region of the average of the series.
Consequently, exceptionally good performances are liable to be followed by
lower (i.e. average) ones, and exceptionally bad performance will be bettered. We
all have our good and bad days and these are sometimes accentuated or offset by

specific circumstances. From a judgemental viewpoint, the danger is over-reaction. For instance, in the example given above, the manager acts in an entirely 'reasonable' manner: he is busy and manages by 'exception', he speaks to bad performers (to keep them 'on their toes'). However, the feedback he has from the environment is misleading: the manager is led to a false attribution concerning the efficiency of his interventions, and thus on his ability to manage. Performances do not improve *because* he has spoken to those with substandard performance. Performance would have improved anyway.

Other examples

Another example of this type of phenomenon comes from an experience of flight school instruction in Israel.[13] Psychologists had advised instructors that each successful execution of a flight manoeuvre should be positively reinforced by the instructors (with praise). However, the instructors' experience with the approach was that praise for successful completion of complex manoeuvres was counter-productive. Praise typically led to reduced performance on subsequent occasions. However, performance in flight manoeuvres is not reliable and one should expect irregular fluctuations. Nonetheless, the flight instructors failed to realize this and attributed decrements in performance to the policy of praising previous good performance.

Kahneman and Tversky comment on this incident as follows (parentheses added for clarity):

> This true story illustrates a saddening aspect of the human condition. We normally reinforce others when their behavior is good and punish them when their behavior is bad . . . therefore (artificially), they are most likely to improve after being punished and most likely to deteriorate after being rewarded. Consequently, we are exposed to a lifetime schedule in which we are most often rewarded for punishing others, and punished for rewarding.[13]
>
> (Reproduced by permission of the American Psychological Association)

It was indicated above that lack of reliability is a cause of irregularities in observations. This is particularly the case in economic data, as the following story illustrates. In a book published in 1974, a noted French economist attempted to analyse the relation between the rate of inflation and the level of industrial investment since 1962. Basing his analysis on figures issued by INSEE, the official French government statistics body, he noted a positive relationship between levels of investment and increases in the rate of inflation. This observation led him to develop the thesis that the rate of increase in inflation was caused by the demand stimulated by increased investment. Furthermore, to diminish the rate of inflation it would be necessary to reduce the level of industrial investment. However, when the empirical basis for these conclusions is examined more closely in the light of subsequent statistical investigations, it turns out that (a) industrial investment in France between 1962 and 1970 was over-estimated by amounts of up to 35 %, and (b) inflation was initially under-estimated in the period under consideration. In other words, the intriguing thesis of a leading economist (and others) was based on a spurious empirical relationship induced by errors of measurement.[14] The story therefore again illustrates how people do not consider the vagaries of irregular fluctuations when interpreting information. Awareness that economic statistics are inherently unreliable would, in this case, have been sufficient to forewarn the economists from attempting unwarranted, causal explanations.

Failure to think of unreliability of records is often a cause of mistaken attributions. In 1965, for example, a crime wave was proclaimed in New York City. It subsequently turned out to be due to an improvement in record keeping.[15]

The above examples all indicate how individuals can and do make false attributions because they fail to understand the concept of random fluctuations. In a somewhat different vein, Campbell has discussed the problems of inferring causation in the evaluation of 'social experiments', for example assessing whether a reduction in traffic accidents follows from lowering speed limits or the introduction of breathalyser tests.[16] In such situations, which involve recording observations across time periods both before and after introduction of the social measure, the attribution of causation is difficult precisely because of the nature of random fluctuations. In elaborating on these issues, Campbell points out that an understanding of sampling fluctuations can also help '*trapped* administrators whose political predicament requires a favorable outcome whether valid or not'.[16] If such politicians want to be seen to have had successes, Campbell's advice concerns both when to start a social experiment and to whom the treatment should be given: '. . . the advice is pick the very worst year, and the very worst social unit. If there is inherent instability, there is no where to go but up, for the average case at least'.[16]

AVOIDING THE TRAPS

Above I have discussed the nature of randomness, statistical independence and variability. Furthermore, I have presented experimental evidence indicating that people have difficulty in recognizing and dealing with phenomena which have these properties. In particular, since people are motivated to order and make sense of their world, they have tendencies to seek patterns where none exist and to make unjustified causal attributions. How does one avoid these traps?

There are two defences, one attitudinal, the other technical. *At the attitudinal level it is necessary to recognize that we live in a probabilistic environment.* However, the environment is not probabilistic because of its inherent properties; it is probabilistic because our representation of it is necessarily imperfect. That is, the *source of the uncertainty lies in us rather than in the environment.* One way to think about this is to note that random fluctuations are usually caused by a large number of factors. It is impossible for the human mind to identify and assess the effects of these sources of variation. Consequently, the mind must accept the apparently random nature of the environment. At the attitudinal level, therefore, it is necessary to be humble and accept 'the probabilistic environment'. This is, of course, not easy since we have a natural tendency to anticipate and seek simple explanations. Perhaps one way to induce an appropriately humble attitude is to keep a 'track record' of occasions when you make causal attributions about people or events, and observe the number of times you were right or wrong. Another is to ask yourself systematically each time that you impose a causal explanation on a situation whether the 'random' hypothesis is not equally or even more likely. Experiments indicate that people have a strong need to feel that they control situations. However, by giving up 'illusory control' and concentrating on the non-random aspects of a situation you may, in fact, exercise greater control over your environment.[17]

At a technical level, one needs tools to be able to recognize when one is dealing with random observations (or more accurately 'apparently random' irregularities). Tools are in order since, as discussed above, when left to our own devices we are inept at recognizing randomness.

Two simple tools

Two 'quick and dirty' tools are available when you are simply trying to determine whether observations are varying at random around some level of performance. Reconsider, for example, Figure 2.2. How would you know whether this series is produced at random, and what are reasonable limits of variation? The first necessity is to record the observations in sequence on a graph such as Figure 2.2. When this is done, calculate the arithmetic mean and draw a straight line through the data passing through the average you have calculated, as illustrated in Figure 2.2. Now assess limits of variation by drawing lines on either side of the average line which include most of the observed points and yet are parallel to the average line. Such lines are indicated by the dotted lines in Figure 2.3. The distance

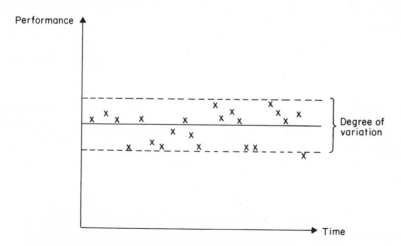

Figure 2.3   Performance across time and degree of variation

between the dotted lines will give you a fair idea of the amount of variation you can expect.

Figure 2.3 represents irregularities around a mean performance level. However, performance might be improving or deteriorating across time. In this case it is necessary to estimate such a trend by a straight line, and to follow the process indicated above.

The parallel line test will help you estimate the limits of variation; however, it will not show you whether the observations themselves are statistically independent of each other. An easy way to do this is to use the so-called 'unfolding test'.[8] Take a sheet of paper and cover all observations in Figure 2.3 except the first (in time). Now try to predict, given the first observation, where the second point will lie. Uncover, and observe the second point—but keeping the other points hidden from view. Now try to predict the third point; uncover; predict the fourth point; uncover—and so on. If you do have a series of independent observations you should find it impossible to predict where the points will lie. This unfolding test is both simple and effective (try it with the data in Figure 2.3 or better still with data from your own experience).

Handling complex series

The two above aids can be used effectively without technical knowledge and are useful for simple series of the type illustrated here. In many situations, however, series are more complex. They can have trends coupled with seasonal and/or cyclical components. For example, consider Figure 2.4, which shows shipments of petrol to service stations in France. This series is clearly difficult to interpret: there are wide fluctuations, possibly seasonal factors and some kind of upward trend across time. In such cases you should either consult someone with statistical knowledge or attempt an analysis yourself using a time-series computer package.[18] In either case, however, you have to be aware of the questions to be posed. Is there really pattern in the data? Or are all irregular fluctuations within reasonable limits? For instance, Figure 2.5 presents the data of Figure 2.4 after elimination of seasonal and random components. (Incidentally, Figure 2.5 took less than two hours to produce with the aid of a computer package—including entering the raw data, checking for mistakes, adjusting months for comparability, drawing the figure, etc.) The real underlying trends that were not apparent in Figure 2.4 are clear in Figure 2.5. The drop in 1973 corresponds to the Arab oil embargo; decreases in 1976 and afterwards coincide with large increases in the price of petrol.

SUMMARY

This chapter has argued that our limited information-processing capacities oblige us to accept the environment as probabilistic. However, the source of the uncertainty lies in us rather than in the environment. Three important statistical concepts related to interpreting probabilistic phenomena were discussed—

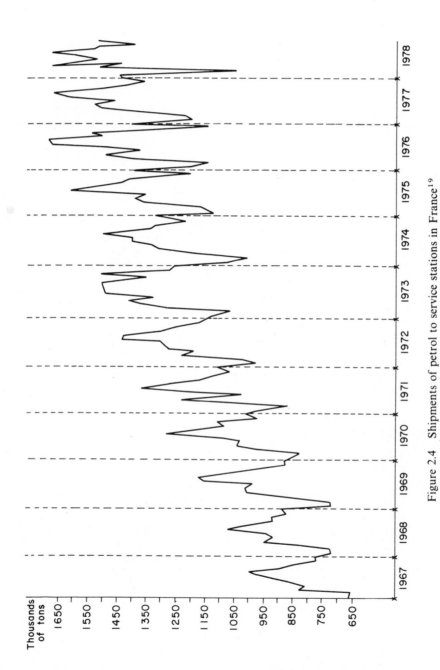

Figure 2.4   Shipments of petrol to service stations in France[19]

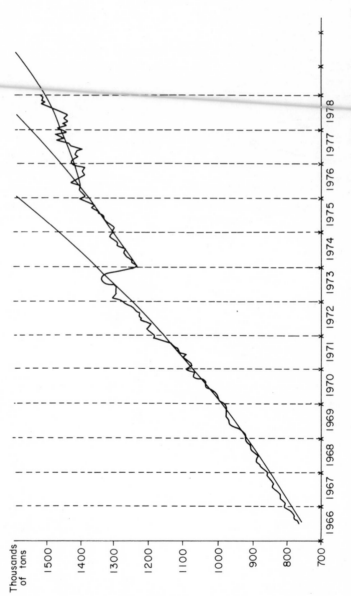

Figure 2.5   Shipments of petrol to service stations in France (after eliminating seasonality and randomness)[19]

randomness, statistical independence and sampling variability—together with evidence of intuitive human misunderstanding of these concepts. It was pointed out that the acceptance of randomness is counter-intuitive. People seek explanations and try to impose patterns on what they observe. However, such patterns are often illusory.

Examples were given of how actions based on observation of extreme values often lead to false attributions of causality. Lack of reliability in data sources, for example economic statistics, induces inherent instability in observations which are often given spurious causal explanations.

People need to adopt an attitude of mind that accepts the fact that we live in an uncertain world. A few techniques for assessing the extent of random fluctuations in practical settings were briefly outlined.

NOTES AND REFERENCES

1. See, for example, D. H. Woods, Improving estimates that involve uncertainty, *Harvard Business Review*, 1966, **44,** 91–98, as well as R. M. Cyert and J. G. March, *A Behavioral Theory of the Firm*, Englewood Cliffs, N. J.: Prentice-Hall, 1963 (especially p. 20).
2. L. J. Savage, Elicitation of personal probabilities and expectations, *Journal of the American Statistical Association*, 1971, **66,** p. 800.
3. It is interesting to note that in asking the rhetorical question of why one should study philosophy, Bertrand Russell states 'To teach how to live without certainty, and yet without being paralysed by hesitation, is perhaps the chief thing that philosophy, in our age, can still do for those who study it.' *History of Western Philosophy*, London: George Allen & Unwin, 1961 (2nd edn.), p. 14.
4. See for example, P. H. Cootner (Ed.), *The Random Character of Stock Market Prices*, Cambridge, Mass.: The M.I.T. Press, 1964; and C.W.J. Granger and O. Morgenstern, *Predictability of Stock Market Prices*, Lexington, Mass.: D. C. Heath, 1970.
5. J. Cohen and C. E. M. Hansel, The idea of independence, *British Journal of Psychology*, 1955, **46,** 178–190. See also J. Cohen, *Psychological Probability: Or the Art of Doubt*, London: George Allen & Unwin, 1972.
6. See also the study by P. Bakan, Response tendencies in attempts to generate random binary series, *American Journal of Psychology*, 1960, **73,** 127–131.
7. See D. Kahneman and A. Tversky, Subjective probability: A judgment of representativeness, *Cognitive Psychology*, 1972, **3,** 430–54.
8. See for example H. V. Roberts, *Conversational Statistics*, Cupertino, California: Hewlett Packard, 1974, Chapter 4.
9. W. A. Wagenaar, Appreciation of conditional probabilities in binary sequences, *Acta Psychologica*, 1970, **34,** 348–356.
10. A. Tversky and D. Kahneman, The belief in the law of small numbers, *Psychological Bulletin*, 1971, **76,** 105–10.
11. H. A. Simon and R. K. Sumner, Patterns in music, In B. Kleinmuntz (Ed.) *Formal Representation of Human Judgment*, New York: Wiley, 1968, p. 220.
12. Carlo Brumat suggested this particular scenario to me. See also R. M. Hogarth, How valid is your judgement? *CEDEP Journal*, 1979, **3,** 47–56.
13. D. Kahneman and A. Tversky, On the psychology of prediction, *Psychological Review*, 1973, **80,** 237–251.
14. Y. Renard, Les incertitudes de la statistique et la baisse dite tendancielle de la rentabilité du capital, *Le Monde*, February 17, 1976, p. 17. Incidentally, a classic study

on the inherent unreliability of economic statistics is by O. Morgenstern, *On the Accuracy of Economic Observations* (2nd edn), Princeton, New Jersey: University Press, 1965.

15. A. Etzioni, 'Shortcuts' to social change? *The Public Interest*, 1968, **12**, 40–51.
16. D. T. Campbell, Reforms as experiments, *American Psychologist*, 1969, **24**, 409–429.
17. An interesting example of the 'illusion of control' in a chance situation (coin-tossing) has been provided in an experiment by E. J. Langer and J. Roth, Heads I win, tails it's chance: The illusion of control as a function of the sequence of outcomes in a purely chance task, *Journal of Personality and Social Psychology*, 1975, **32**, 951–955.
18. For example, S. Makridakis and S. C. Wheelwright, *Interactive Forecasting: Univariate and Multivariate Methods* (2nd edn), San Francisco: Holden-Day, 1978.
19. The data and graphs presented in Figures 2.4 and 2.5 were kindly supplied by S. Makridakis and B. Majani who have authorized their presentation here.

CHAPTER 3

Combining information for prediction

Predictions and evaluations are usually based on a combination of different information sources. For example, an impression of a job candidate gained from an application form can be modified during an interview. A judgement concerning the probable level of next year's sales of a company is the result of considering many factors, e.g. this year's sales, industry trends, marketing strategy, anticipated competitor reactions, etc. An evaluation of a work of art, for example a play, can be made on several dimensions: structure, style, humour, pathos and so on.

In the preceding chapter the necessity to consider the environment as probabilistic was discussed as well as several notions related to probabilistic thinking. In most examples, however, single information sources were considered, for instance the observation of a particular series of performance. In this chapter, the problems of making predictions from several information sources are discussed. Chapter 4 continues this theme but in relation to evaluative judgements and choice.

As should be expected from the discussion of the human information-processing system in Chapter 1, combination of different sources of information is particularly difficult. Consider what needs to be done. Information from both the environment and the individual's memory needs to be selected. Meaning is given to the information and, indeed, such meaning may even guide the search process in the first instance. The various sources of information selected then have to be weighted and combined to form a final judgement. It is clear that people do not have the mental capacity to do these operations in the manner of a computer. They consequently employ strategies to simplify demands of judgemental tasks involving several information sources. Some of these strategies and their consequences are explored in this chapter.

Statistical theory embodies several commonsense principles for combining information for prediction. These are also discussed in this chapter together with indications of the extent to which intuitive judgement can and does follow such principles. Specifically, the following issues are considered: (1) combining information sources that are or are not statistically independent; (2) adjusting data sources for their reliability and inherent predictive ability; (3) the combination of 'base-rate' and specific information (these notions will be explained below); and (4) effects due to the structure of the task, for example the order in which information is presented, the manner in which responses can be made, etc..

29

Finally, the chapter concludes with a discussion of mechanical aids for predictions based on several information sources.

INDEPENDENT VERSUS DEPENDENT DATA SOURCES

In the discussion of sampling in Chapter 2, it was noted that confidence in judgement should be related to the amount of information sampled. However, this was under the restriction that each item of information sampled was independent of the others. Consider, therefore, what should happen when information sources are not independent. At the limit, if when forming an opinion you observe the same information twice, you should clearly not treat it as two independent items of information. However, the more common situation is that of multiple sources of information with varying degrees of dependence on each other. For example, imagine that you are predicting a person's job potential on the basis of biographical details and an interview. Much of the information you receive will be redundant in the sense that knowledge of part of the information is related, albeit imperfectly, to other parts. For instance, assume that you are trying to assess the person's intelligence. This can be gauged from several sources: scholastic record, type of past employment, comments and answers made in the interview, etc. Whereas all these data sources are not identical, they are related, and in the prediction of intelligence, part of the information is redundant when you know the rest. For example, intelligence is often related to academic success. Although the redundancy principle may seem quite straightforward, evidence indicates that people have considerable difficulty in its application.

A case in point is the employment interview. Research indicates that in a half-hour interview situation, the interviewer typically forms a hypothesis about the candidate (e.g. favourable or unfavourable) and then spends the rest of the interview period seeking information consistent with the hypothesis.[1] Apart from the fact that this does not represent a good strategy for learning about the candidate (see Chapter 5), it is clear that in most situations a lot of the information gleaned will be redundant in the sense described above. It is, of course, true that much of the information gained in this way will also be consistent (indeed, if it is redundant it is almost bound to be consistent). However, consistency of data sources which are not independent adds little to predictive validity. Consequently, consistency of dependent data sources is not a good criterion for determining confidence in judgement.

When a person receives a lot of information it is difficult to assess whether or not much is redundant. Well-documented cases with little inconsistency are clearly cues people use for prediction. An instructive example of this is a study by Oskamp where the judgements of clinical psychologists were studied as a function of amount of information presented to them.[2] The psychologists were required to make predictions on the basis of a case study. In addition they were asked to state their degree of confidence in their judgements under different conditions of amount of information. Results indicated that as the amount of information about the case increased, so did the psychologists' confidence in their judgements. However, there was no corresponding increase in predictive accuracy.

Strategies people use for making predictive judgments appear to be dependent on consistency, and related concepts such as the degree of similarity between the features of an object and the class to which it is supposed to belong.[3] For example, a job candidate may be judged by the extent to which his characteristics match one's image of successful managers. Such 'stereotyping' was also noted in Chapter 2, when the problems of assessing random sequences of coin tosses were considered. A further example is the following exercise.

Consider this description of Tom W. which was written by a psychologist when Tom was in his senior year at high school:

> Tom W. is of high intelligence, although lacking in true creativity. He has a need for order and clarity and for neat and tidy systems in which every detail finds its appropriate place. His writing is rather dull and mechanical, occasionally enlivened by somewhat corny puns and by flashes of imagination of the sci-fi type. He has a strong drive for competence. He seems to have little feel and little sympathy for other people and does not enjoy interacting with others. Self-centered, he nonetheless has a deep moral sense.[4]
> (Reproduced by permission of the American Psychological Association)

Now, imagine that you are told that Tom W. is currently a graduate student. Rank the following nine topics as to the likelihood that they are the area of Tom's graduate specialization:

business administration
computer science
engineering
humanities and education
law
library science
medicine
physical and life sciences
social science and social work.

If you are like Kahneman and Tversky's subjects then you would rank computer science and engineering as most likely and humanities and education and social science and social work as least likely. Indeed, the consistency of the information in the personality sketch seems compelling. However, as will be explained later in this chapter, such a judgement would be erroneous.

The mental strategy of stereotyping by degree of similarity has been named 'representativeness' by Tversky and Kahneman.[3] They and others have shown that it plays a pervasive role in judgement. Unfortunately, it is valid only to the extent that data sources are not redundant or that it does not induce you to ignore other information (a point that will be explored in depth below).

Further evidence concerning the importance of consistency of data sources is related to how people make predictions on the basis of cues which are inconsistent. One strategy is to downplay or ignore the inconsistent information. This issue was specifically investigated in a study by Slovic concerning the assessment of intelligence on the basis of consistent and inconsistent profiles.[5] Slovic presented subjects with profiles of individuals based on nine cues— represented by scores on each of the nine dimensions. Previous work had indicated that 2 of the cues, high-school grade rating and English effectiveness, accounted for most of the differences in judgements. Consequently, these cues were manipulated to create a series of consistent and inconsistent profiles. Results indicated that judgements were dependent upon the two main cues when they were consistent; however, when the cues had contradictory implications, subjects relied on only one cue and excluded the other from consideration. Other investigators have reported similar results.[6]

Consistency, similarity and representativeness seem to be entirely reasonable strategies to use in making judgements. And indeed, in cases where information sources are not redundant and other relevant information is not ignored, the strategies will be quite effective. Problems occur in determining whether or not information sources are redundant and in handling apparently inconsistent information. It is clear that for many judgemental tasks such assessments exceed intuitive information-processing capacity and, as will be explored at the end of this chapter, are better handled by mechanical means.

Finally, at an anecdotal level, it is worth nothing that the principle of consistency of information in judgement seems to be well appreciated by 'con-men'. Successful con-men succeed in creating such consistent behaviour patterns that their victims never think of seeking other, independent evidence to check on them.

RELIABILITY AND PREDICTIVE ABILITY OF DATA SOURCES

When using information for predictive purposes two important concepts are (1) the reliability of the source and (2) its predictive ability. It is important to keep these related concepts distinct in one's mind. Reliability refers to the extent to which an information source actually reports what has happened; for example, trade statistics are reliable to the extent that they are accurate. A person is reliable to the extent that he or she is truthful. Whereas reliability is an inherent characteristic of the information source, predictive ability can only be defined in relation to some uncertain event. For example, trade statistics have a given level of reliability but are differentially predictive of, say, certain stock-market prices or the level of unemployment.

The predictive ability of an information source relative to something else therefore refers to the extent to which the information source can be used for predicting that uncertain event. Whereas reliability and predictive ability are distinct concepts, it should be clear that they are related in the sense that a totally unreliable information source can have no predictive ability. Furthermore, lack of reliability of an information source must clearly reduce its potential predictive ability.

The effects of unreliable data sources were briefly discussed in Chapter 2. There it was noted that lack of reliability will cause an information source to exhibit more variability than would otherwise be the case. Recall the example of the economist's interpretation of industrial investment and inflation statistics reported by INSEE in France. An empirical 'relationship', which was in fact the result of statistical errors, was attributed elaborate and erroneous causal explanations. Had there been more awareness of the unreliable nature of economic statistics, the false attribution might not have been made.

An important point to note, therefore, is that unreliable data sources exhibit more variability than they would if they were reliable. Furthermore, the assessment of a cue's predictive ability should be moderated by considerations of reliability. The importance of these two remarks are, incidentally, emphasized when it is realized that at least one study has shown that salient cues for prediction are accorded greater weight to the extent that they show more variability.[7]

Evidence indicates, however, that people are not sensitive to the reliability of data sources. They seem to treat data sources as though they were perfectly reliable.

The regression phenomenon

One phenomenon is the so-called 'regression fallacy' which was briefly discussed in Chapter 2, although in a different guise. Consider that you are using a cue such as a test score to predict a job candidate's possible future performance. Furthermore, imagine that extensive experience of the test exists and that the relationship between test score and job performance can be described by the graph illustrated in Figure 3.1.

The ellipse in Figure 3.1 indicates the extent to which the test is predictive, the narrower the ellipse, the more predictive the test and vice-versa. A test with perfect predictability is, of course, one where the relationship between test scores and subsequent job performance is represented by a straight line (the dotted line in Figure 3.1). The so-called regression phenomenon simply reflects the inability of information sources with imperfect predictive ability to predict perfectly. This can be illustrated by comparing the predictions based on sources having imperfect and perfect predictive ability. Consider the test score X' indicated on Figure 3.1 and ask yourself:

(1) What performance level is someone with a score of X' or higher on the imperfect test likely to achieve? and
(2) If the test had perfect predictive ability, how could your answer differ?

Figure 3.2 illustrates what would happen. For a test with perfect predictive ability performance corresponding to a test score of X' is indicated by the point

34

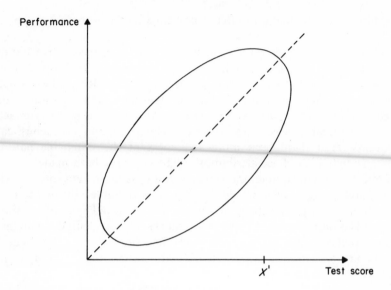

Figure 3.1 Relationship between an imperfect test and performance

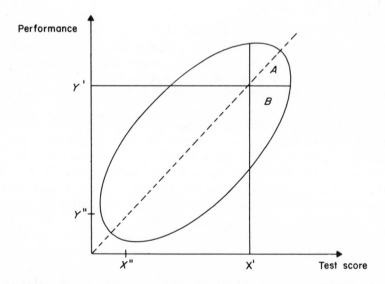

Figure 3.2 Illustration of the regression phenomenon. Note that a person scoring X' or higher on the test has a greater probability of showing performance below Y'. (The area B exceeds the area A.) By drawing the analogous lines, the reader can also confirm that someone scoring X'' or less stands a greater chance of performing above rather than below Y''

Y'. For each larger value of the test score, there will also be an associated, and unique value of performance. However, with an imperfect test, there is a range of possible levels of performance associated with test scores of X' or more. This is represented by the area of the ellipse to the right of X'. Contrast the straight dotted line (for the perfect test) with the area just defined (for the imperfect test). Furthermore, note that the area of the ellipse to the right of X' can be split into two parts at the level of performance Y'. One of these parts A, denotes cases with test scores above X' that are associated with performance above Y'; the other, B, denotes test scores above X' but performance below Y'. The key point to note, however, is that the area B exceeds the area A. In other words, a person scoring X' or more on the test has a greater probability of showing performance *below* rather than above Y'. There is regression toward the mean.

The reader will find it instructive to draw lines associated with X'' and Y'' at the bottom left of the ellipse. It should be noticed that for low test scores regression toward the mean still applies. There is a greater probability (with an imperfect test) that a person with a test score of X'' or less performs at a level *exceeding* rather than below Y''.

The implication of the regression phenomenon is that when prediction is based on sources with imperfect predictive ability, predictions should be less extreme than the information generated by the sources. The term 'regression phenomenon' simply means that in the presence of imperfect predictive sources, predictions should be 'regressed' toward the mean, e.g., in this case toward average performance which, with a totally unreliable test, would be the best prediction.

The above discussion of the regression phenomenon has been couched in terms of predictive ability of data sources and has hardly made reference to reliability per se. However, it should be recalled that lack of reliability of data sources reduces their predictive ability and therefore contributes to the regression phenomenon. Failure to recognize lack of reliability in data sources therefore leads to predictions which are more extreme than they should be.

Evidence indicates that people are strongly influenced when a predictive cue exhibits an extreme value.[7] This is salient for them and they believe it implies a correspondingly high value of the uncertain outcome. Furthermore, and as discussed above, since unreliable information sources show more variability than reliable sources, such judgemental errors will be compounded in that, other things being equal, unreliable data sources will tend to exhibit more extreme values.

Incidentally, the term 'regression phenomenon' has also been referred to in the literature to cases where unreliability of observed information has caused people to draw false inferences, for example by erroneously attributing changes observed to certain causes as discussed in Chapter 2. However, it is felt here that the term 'regression phenomenon' is more naturally reserved for instances where prediction of one event is made on the basis of the observation of another. In both cases, a failure to understand the nature of chance fluctuations leads to judgemental errors.

The illusion of validity

This and the preceding section of this chapter illustrate an apparent paradox in judgement. Two features of evidence, consistency of data sources and extreme values of predictive cues, lead to increased confidence in judgement. However, as illustrated above, these features are often inversely related to the predictive accuracy of the information sources. This has led to what Kahneman and Tversky have termed the 'illusion of validity':

> . . . factors which enhance confidence, for example, consistency and extremity, are often negatively related with predictive accuracy. Thus people are prone to experience much confidence in highly fallible judgments, a phenomenon that may be termed the *illusion of validity*. Like other perceptual and judgmental errors, the illusion of validity often persists even when its illusory character is recognized. When interviewing a candidate, for example, many of us have experienced great confidence in our prediction of his future performance, despite our knowledge that interviews are notoriously fallible.[4]
>
> (Reproduced by permission of the American Psychological Association)

More on unreliable data sources

The issue of reliability of data sources can enter judgemental problems in many subtle ways. For example, consider situations where you have to make a prediction based on a report which might itself be uncertain. An instance of this could be the following:[8] Imagine that you are a businessman facing a highly competitive marketing situation. In fact you are aware that the next move by you or your competitor could well be crucial in determining who establishes the larger market share. One of the possible weapons open to both of you is price reduction. However, given rates of profitability in the present market, this is something that you would be loath to do unless forced by competition. Nonetheless, you feel there is a fair chance (say evens) that your main competitor will reduce prices within the next week. You receive a message from one of your field sales force that your competitor has just booked large amounts of advertising space to go out in the next few days. What do you do?

First, note that there are several sources of uncertainty involved in this situation concerning: (1) whether your competitor will drop prices; (2) whether his booking of advertising space is related to a reduction in prices; and (3) whether your salesman's report is reliable (he may not, of course, be deliberately untruthful, merely misinformed). Note therefore that if these three sources of uncertainty are dichotomized, i.e. will or will not drop prices, advertising space is or is not related to the announcement of a price reduction, and the salesman's report is or is not reliable, then you should be considering the relative probabilities of 6 different scenarios as illustrated in the tree diagram of Figure 3.3. However, for most people such a situation requires the manipulation of far too much information and one is unlikely to handle it effectively without some mechanical means, be they merely pencil and paper. Experimental evidence indicates that in these kinds of situations people tend to eliminate subjectively

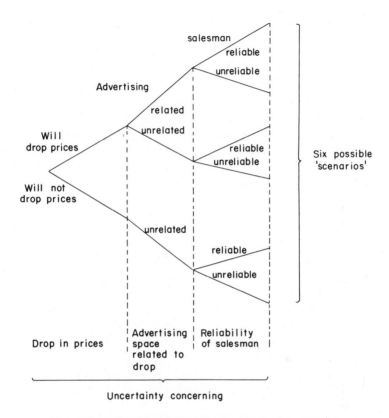

Figure 3.3   Combination of three sources of uncertainty

some of the uncertainties and focus attention on what they consider to be the most likely of different combinations of outcomes.[9] This strategy, known as the 'best guess' strategy, is clearly a result of limited information-processing capacity. In many cases, one of the uncertainties suppressed involves the issue of data source reliability.

To conclude this section, the obvious is emphasized, namely: sources of information should be weighted in predictive activity relative to their predictive ability. However, sources are usually never perfectly predictive, although they are often treated as such. There are at least two reasons for this. First, people's experience of predictors is frequently insufficient for assessing their true predictive accuracy. This issue is explored in some depth in Chapter 5. Second, lack of reliability of data sources leads to degradation of predictive ability. However, people have a tendency to treat data as through they were more reliable than is, in fact, the case.

BASE-RATE AND SPECIFIC INFORMATION

Consider the following two problems:

(1) You are going for a medical check-up which will include an X-ray for tuberculosis. Before you attend the medical, you think carefully about your state of health. Your introspection leads you to conclude that there is only a very small chance of your having TB. You estimate that chance as being about 1 in 200. You are aware that X-rays are not 100% reliable. Consequently, when attending the medical you enquire about the chances that the X-ray will give a false reading. You are informed that the X-ray is 95% reliable and are also told that this means two things; one, if you do not have TB, the X-ray will give you a clean bill of health 95 times out of 100; on the other hand, if you do have TB, the X-ray will report illness 95 times out of 100.*[10]

A couple of days after the check-up, you receive the result of the X-ray. The X-ray result indicates that you have TB. After receiving this result, how do you assess the chances of your having TB?

(2) A cab was involved in a hit-and-run accident at night.[11] Two cab companies, the Green and the Blue, operate in the city. You are given the following data:

    (i) 85% of the cabs in the city are Green and 15% are Blue.

    (ii) A witness identified the cab as a Blue cab. The court tested his ability to identify cabs under the appropriate visibility conditions. When presented with a sample of cabs (half of which were Blue and half of which were Green), the witness made correct identifications in 80% of the cases and erred in 20% of the cases.

Question: What is the probability that the cab involved in the accident was Blue rather than Green?

If you are like the typical subjects who have answered these questions, then your responses are liable to be: (1) about a 90% chance of having TB; and (2) the chance of the cab being Blue is about 80%. However, these answers are quite wrong, the correct answers being 87 chances out of 1000 (i.e. 0.087) for the first question, and 41 out of 100 for the second.

Most people are surprised when faced with these answers since they do not seem intuitively plausible. The source of the difficulty in the problems is the failure to realize that each question involves two kinds of information, one of which is ignored or at least receives less attention than the other. First, there is what is called *a priori* or *base-rate* information. For instance, in the X-ray problem there is information about your general state of health—the 1 in 200 chance of being ill. In the cab problem, it is known that 85% of cabs in the city are Green. Second, there is information concerning the case at hand, namely the accuracy of the X-ray procedure and the ability of the particular witness to

---

* Note that these rates of 95 out of 100 do not have to be the same in both cases. In practice, they frequently are not.

distinguish Blue from Green cabs. The first kind of information is called 'base-rate' in the sense that it provides the background to the judgemental situations; the second kind of information may be referred to as *specific* or *case* data. A general finding, albeit with exceptions to be discussed below, is that when people are faced with both base-rate and case data, they ignore the former and predict almost entirely on the basis of the latter. In fact, probability theory argues that one should modify base-rate data by case data and therefore that the ensuing judgement should reflect both. (The technical details of how such calculations are done are contained in Appendix A.) People's intuitions, however, do not correspond to the laws of probability in this instance. Indeed, considerable evidence has been documented of the failure to consider base-rate data.[12]

The above examples indicate that base-rate data are ignored even if they are available. However, frequently base-rate data are most important for prediction even though they may not be present in the definition of a problem. A case in point is the exercise presented earlier in this chapter concerning Tom W. Recall that you were asked to estimate, on the basis of a personality sketch, the relative likelihoods of different areas of Tom W's graduate specialization. Most people respond to that particular stimulus by suggesting computer science or engineering as most likely and humanities and education and social sciences and social work as least likely. However, such judgements ignore the relative numbers of people, or base-rates, of students in the different areas of specialization. If these are taken into account, your answer should be quite different. An additional and interesting point here is that in a series of experiments using the Tom W. example, Kahneman and Tversky[4] found that (1) even if people were aware of the inherent lack of reliability of such personality sketches this did not affect their judgements (see previous sub-section), and (2) the subjects whom they tested on the problem were quite aware of the fact that different numbers of students were involved in the different areas of graduate specialization. However, this knowledge was not used when judgements were made.

There is often emotional resistance to the inclusion of base-rate data in the kinds of problems discussed above; consequently some intuitive explanation for the rationale of probability theory is in order. Probability theory makes the following kind of argument: Assume first that the only information you have in, for example, the cab question (problem 2) is the base-rate data. That is, all you know is that 85 % of the cabs are Green, and that 15 % are Blue. If you were told that one cab had been involved in an accident, what are the chances that it was a Blue cab? Most people would say 15 % (assuming, of course, that there is no reason to believe that drivers of Blue cabs are no more or less reckless than drivers of Green cabs, etc.). Now assume that you are given additional information, which is not perfectly reliable, concerning the colour of the cab. Surely this information should modify your prior (or base-rate) estimation by a factor related to its inherent reliability. For instance, if specific or case information came from a totally unreliable source, it should be ignored; if it came from a 100 % reliable source it should dominate the base-rate information. Intermediate levels of reliability will combine with the base-rate to form the normative judgement in accord with the rules of probability.

Ignoring base-rates can clearly lead to rather substantial judgemental errors, not least of which are certain forms of self-delusion. For example, imagine that you wish to determine how good your judgement is. This could be done in several contexts, for example: personnel decisions, stock purchases, decisions concerning sales outlets, medical prognosis if you are a physician, etc. If you assess your judgemental ability simply on the basis of observed success rates this could be misleading. For instance, when checking your predictions, the relevant question to be asked is not how many predictions are successful, but how many would have been successful anyway? Your judgemental ability can only be assessed relative to a base-rate. For instance, if in a job selection situation 70 % of candidates would have turned out to be successful whether or not you selected them, a success rate of, say, 80 % is not very impressive. Unfortunately, and as will be explored in Chapter 5, determining the base-rate is not easy in judgemental situations since the requisite information is not always available. Consequently, it is often ignored, with unfortunate consequences. However, it is necessary to keep the base-rate concept firmly in mind. Perhaps one way to remember it is to recall the comment attributed to the humourist Thurber. When asked what his wife 'was like', he replied 'Compared to what?'.

No, no, no: "How's your wife?" "Compared to what?"

When are base-rates considered?

It might be thought from the above discussion that people always ignore base-rates. However, this is not true.[13] In some instances they use base-rates and in others they do not. What distinguishes the situations? First, people use base-rate information in the absence of specific or case data. For example, if as a manager you knew that on average 1 out of 5 salesmen usually succeeds in beating the target sales figure in his district, you would, in the absence of other information, predict a 1 in 5 success rate for any particular salesman. Second, recent evidence points to the use of base-rate data in instances where they have *causal* meaning for the individual. For example, recall the X-ray problem at the outset of this sub-section. Many people resist the normative answer to this problem (which includes the prior or base-rate information about your health), on the grounds that the prior information is irrelevant to the outcome of the X-ray. 'You cannot combine these two kinds of information' is a reaction I have frequently encountered when presenting this example. If people see no link between the base-rate and case data they will not combine them. The human mind is sensitive to the meaning of data and the extent to which they are consistent with existing ideas and preconceptions.

This effect can be demonstrated by a reformulation of the cab problem:

A cab was involved in a hit-and-run accident at night. Two cab companies, the Green and the Blue, operate in the city. You are given the following data:
(i) Although the two companies are roughly equal in size, 85 % of cab accidents in the city involve Green cabs, and 15 % involve Blue cabs.

(ii) A witness identified the cab as a Blue cab. The court tested his ability to identify cabs under appropriate visibility conditions. When presented with a sample of cabs (half of which were Blue and half of which were Green) the witness made correct identifications in 80 % of the cases and erred in 20 % of the cases.

Question: What is the probability that the cab involved in the accident was Blue rather than Green?[4]

This problem is the same as the previous cab problem with the exception of (i). Here it is simply stated that 85 % of accidents involve Green cabs. However, the problem is identical in terms of the numerical inputs that should be calculated by probability theory. How do people react to this problem compared to the previous version?

Although answers to the second version of the problem reflect greater variability than answers to the first, more people do make use of both the base-rate and specific data, the average response being 55 % (compared to the correct figure of 41 % and the average response to the previous formulation of 80 %). It appears that when the problem is put in the second form, people see a causal link between the overall accident rate (i.e. the base-rate) and the probability that the cab was actually Blue. This link, however, was not seen in the original form of the problem.

Ajzen has argued that people's intuitive notions of causality play an important role in their judgemental strategies. He states:

> Judgment by causality can be described as follows. When asked to make a prediction, people look for factors that would cause the behavior or event under consideration. Information that provides evidence concerning the presence or absence of such causal factors is therefore likely to influence predictions. Other items of information, even though important by the normative principles of statistical prediction, will tend to be neglected if they have no apparent causal significance. Statistical information is used mainly when no causal information is available.[14]

An example given by Ajzen is the following: subjects were given a brief description of a student (i.e. specific information) and asked to assess the probability that he had passed a particular examination. Two different forms of base-rate information were given to subjects in two different groups:

(1) Two years ago, a final exam was given in a course at Yale University. About 75 % of the students passed the exam.
(2) Two years ago, a final exam was given in a course at Yale University. An educational psychologist interested in scholastic achievement interviewed a large number of students who had taken the course. Since he was primarily concerned with reactions to success, he selected mostly students who had passed the exam. Specifically, about 75 % of the students in his sample had passed the exam.[14]

Ajzen hypothesized that form (1) contained 'causal base-rate' information in that 'Although the percentage of students who pass an exam does not have a causal effect on any given student's performance, it permits the respondent to infer the exam's difficulty level—a factor that *does* have a causal effect on a given student's success or failure.'[14] On the other hand, form (2) does not have any such causal implications. When put to the test, Ajzen's hypothesis was supported.

Differences between intuitive and statistical reasoning

The ideas presented so far in this section can be summarized as follows. People give meaning to clues for prediction that are either physically available to them or could be recalled from memory. This meaning is derived from their intuitive understanding of how events are related. Recall the model of the person's mind illustrated in Brunswik's 'lens model' in Chapter 1. From a normative, statistical viewpoint, many prediction problems involve combining base-rate data with specific information (or if one prefers, adjusting specific information by base-rate considerations. Recall the examples in this chapter). Evidence indicates that available base-rate data will be incorporated in judgement if they are causally linked with (or 'make sense' in relation to) specific data. Otherwise base-rate data are ignored. Furthermore, people have a tendency not to use pertinent base-rate data that are available to them in memory. Ignoring base-rate data can both lead to erroneous predictions and illusions concerning one's predictive skills.

From the above it should be clear that whereas people give meaning to information, the laws of probability do not. The laws are simply a set of rules that allow one to infer the relationships between probabilities of events or hypotheses depending upon a number of assumptions. Another example is the following.

Imagine that you are a juror in a courtroom and consider how you would judge the defendant's innocence or guilt given the evidence presented in the case. For concreteness, consider that the defendant is being tried for receiving stolen goods and one particular piece of evidence consists of the fact that he was found to be in possession of something which was known to have been stolen. Concentrate on the hypothesis that the defendant is guilty and ask yourself how the evidence that a stolen object has been found in his possession relates to the hypothesis. There are a number of ways.[15] First you might consider a *causal* relationship, i.e. the defendant is guilty *because* he was found to have stolen goods in his possession. Second, you could consider the evidence as *diagnostic* or *indicative* of guilt, i.e. presence of stolen goods increases the probability of guilt. And third, you might consider the evidence as *incidental*, that is neither as a cause nor even possible cause (i.e. indicative) of guilt. The crucial difference between probability theory and intuitive processes in these instances is the following: whereas people might distinguish whether data are causal, indicative or incidental, probability theory does not. Data are judged strictly on their *informativeness*. However, experiments have shown that people give more weight to data that they consider *causally* related to a target object than data perceived to be *indicative* or *diagnostic*. Furthermore, they give little weight or ignore data which are seen by them to be *incidental*. In other words, despite the fact that it is normatively incorrect, people do not weight information according to its informativeness, they weight information according to the 'level of meaning' they attach to it.

'Conservatism' in information processing

Although the relative weighting of base-rate and specific information is moderated by the meaning people attach to these sources, evidence also exists that people have difficulty in adjusting base-rate probabilities by specific information in cases where differential meaning is not an issue.[16]

Specifically, people in these instances have been found to be 'conservative' information processors in that they fail to allow the specific information to adjust the base-rate or prior information sufficiently. If you had been a subject in some of the original experiments that demonstrated this effect, the experimenter would have presented you with the following task which involves assessing which of two bookbags certain poker chips have been drawn from. Imagine that the experimenter is standing in front of you and holding one of two bookbags.

> This bookbag contains 1000 poker chips. I started out with two such bags, one containing 700 red and 300 blue chips, the other containing 300 red and 700 blue. I flipped a fair coin to determine which one to use. Thus, if your opinions are like mine, your probability at the moment that this is the predominantly red bookbag is 0.5. Now, you sample, randomly, with replacement after each chip. In 12 samples, you get 8 reds and 4 blues. Now, on the basis of everything you know, what is the probability that this is the predominantly red bag?[16]

If your answer is like that of the typical subject, it would lie in the range of 0.7 to 0.8. In fact, the appropriate statistical answer yields 0.97. That is, you should be 97 % sure that the bag contains 700 red and 300 blue chips (as opposed to 300 red and 700 blue). Whereas the above example is rather artificial, the 'conservatism' effect has been reproduced in a variety of settings including applications of military intelligence systems and medicine. Arguments have been rife as to how or why people are conservative in the sense described here.[7, 16] However, the fact remains that they are. My own explanation is that apart from their obvious lack of ability to make the appropriate mental calculations, people are not accustomed to reasoning in such clear-cut situations; data sources are usually not given but have to be sought. Furthermore, although it was argued above that people do not know how to handle redundant data adequately, they are used to dealing with a certain level of redundancy in the environment. Treating data as though they were partially redundant would account for the 'conservatism' findings. However, these remarks should be considered speculative.

TASK EFFECTS

Since a central theme of this book is that judgements are the result of interaction between the structure of tasks and the nature of the human information-processing system, it may seem strange to have a section of this chapter specifically entitled 'task effects'. The purpose, however, is to present further examples of how task structures interact with the capabilities of the mind in the course of predictive judgement.

Context

The context within which judgements are made is of course important. This particularly affects intuitive estimates of variability, a concept which, as discussed earlier, is usually not well appreciated, although it is most important for understanding the nature of uncertainty.[17] An example will illustrate the point.

Consider the following two series of numbers:

A:	6,	18,	4,	5,	17
B:	1110,	1122,	1108,	1109,	1121

Which series exhibits the more variability?

Most people answer Series A. However the statistical measure of *variance*—which indicates the amount of irregular variations from the mean of a series of numbers—is *the same* for both series. Series B is simply Series A plus a constant of 1104. However, intuitive judgements of variability are usually influenced by the size or context of the series or objects. That is, subjectively relative variability is more salient than variability per se. The following intuitive explanation of this phenomenon has been offered:

> Think of the top of a forest. The tree tops seem to form a fairly smooth surface, considering that the trees may be 60 or 70 feet tall. Now, look at your desk top. In all probability it is littered with many objects and if a cloth were thrown over it the surface would seem very bumpy and variable. The forest top is far more variable than the surface of your desk, but not relative to the sizes of the objects being considered.[18]

As has been argued both in this and the preceding chapter, when drawing inferences it is important to understand the nature and amount of variability. Thus if perceptions of variability are distorted by contextual effects, the necessity of using mechanical methods to estimate variability, as illustrated in Chapter 2, is emphasized.

Availability

The lens model diagram shown in Chapter 1 illustrated the point that predictive judgements are not made in a vacuum but by reference to other information sources or cues. These cues can either be seen physically at the time a judgement is made or imagined, that is reference to 'imaginary' cues is made from memory. Since cues are used for prediction, an important issue is therefore how certain information comes to be selected as a cue. A dimension which has been suggested as being important in this process is the extent to which cues are *available* to the individual.[19]

Indeed, Tversky and Kahneman argue that the 'availability' of information is an important clue that people use in making judgements. Specifically, if you can think of or see several instances of one kind of event as opposed to another, you can be led to believe that the former is more frequent than the latter. As examples, your estimate of the divorce rate in your country is probably heavily influenced by the number of people you know who have divorced. People often have the feeling that a traffic accident is more likely just after they have observed one than before. It has also been noted that the purchase of earthquake insurance increases after an earthquake but decreases subsequently as memory of it diminishes.[20]

To explore the operation of 'availability', experiments have tested people's intuitions of the relative frequencies of diseases or causes of death. Results indicate that the relative frequency of diseases or causes which are much publicized, such as homicide, cancer or tornadoes are over-estimated, whereas the relative frequencies of less newsworthy others such as asthma, emphysema and diabetes are under-estimated.[21] The point being made here is that to the extent that our environment emphasizes certain aspects, our judgement will be biased by the ease with which we recall instances and thus estimate their frequency.

A further example of availability bias which recently came to my attention was the following. Geologists were estimating the potential oil yields of some prospective sites. They did this by comparing the geological features of the sites with areas which had been exploited and where, as a consequence, the oil yields were known. The availability bias in this judgement is that no comparisons were made with other sites that had not been exploited but that also had similar features to the prospective sites.[22]

Tversky and Kahneman argue that availability of instances is often a valid rule for prediction. That is, events which occur frequently, either by themselves or in the presence of others, will usually occur frequently in the future. Thus relative 'availability' of past instances is a useful clue to the likelihood of future events.[19] For example, if you were asked to predict how often, in the next month, you would arrive home for work after a certain time, you would probably base that prediction on how often that had happened to you in the recent past (as adjusted, of course, for exceptional circumstances). Indeed, it seems difficult to imagine how one can make predictions on the basis of cues which are not available to you!

On the other hand, as indicated above, the environment and/or specific occurrences can increase the salience of certain cues and make them more available than they should be. An interesting phenomenon in this respect is the extent to which people are influenced by the number of occurrences of an event (i.e. frequency) rather than the relative number of occurrences (i.e. relative frequency). For example, imagine that you have been asked which of two groups in your work organization is smarter, for instance in a business setting accountants or market researchers. How would you answer this question? You might well try to think of the smart accountants and the smart market researchers you know and base your intuitive estimate on this comparison. However, in doing so, you would ignore an important element of the problem: the total numbers of accountants and market researchers. Your comparison should be based not on the absolute but the relative number of smart persons in both groups. Research, however, indicates that people often base estimates of proportions (or probabilities or relative frequencies) on the basis of their experience of absolute as opposed to relative frequencies.[23] In a sense, this is another instance of the failure to relate judgement to some base-line considerations.*

Effects of data presentation

The manner in which information is presented can also affect its salience and thus importance as a predictive cue. For example, the order in which information is presented can produce so-called 'primacy' or 'recency' effects. That is, when being presented with a number of items of information, sometimes the earlier items dominate the individual's final opinion (a 'primacy' effect) and sometimes the latter (a 'recency' effect). From a normative viewpoint, however, it is clear that one should finish with the same opinion at the end of a series of data irrespectively of the order of presentation. Furthermore, it appears that primacy and recency effects can be manipulated according to task characteristics.

Incidentally, a point to note here is that much evidence indicates that the middle of a series of informational inputs receives less attention than those at either the beginning or the end. Consequently, if you want to make an impression, avoid the middle of a series!

In addition to primacy and recency effects, giving too much information can reduce the consistency of a person's judgement;[24] simultaneous presentation of concrete data, e.g. figures, together with qualitative information, causes difficulty, with people tending to prefer one source to the exclusion of the other;[25] people find information presented with the use of negatives (e.g. 'not', 'no' etc.) instead of positive statements more difficult to process and understand;[26] seemingly complete presentations can blind people to the fact that important aspects of a problem have been omitted;[27] even if people do have appropriate statistical information they can be misled by the labels attached to cues;[28] etc. The list of items leading to judgmental bias seems interminable.

---

* Incidentally, I found myself falling precisely into this trap when asked which of two schools in which I had taught had the brighter students. In making my judgement, I forgot that there were twice as many students in one school compared to the other.

Adjustment and anchoring

One commonly used judgmental strategy which is highly dependent on information presented or available to a person has been named 'adjustment and anchoring'.[29] It can probably be best illustrated by an example. Imagine that as a manager you have been asked to forecast next year's sales of your company (or division). How would you do it? A common strategy is to take a cue such as this year's sales, or perhaps next year's budgeted sales, as a starting point—or 'anchor'—then to make adjustments to that figure according to changes in conditions that you foresee (for example due to differences in pricing or advertising strategy, competitive reactions, etc.). That is, you would adjust the anchor by amounts representing these factors. If one accepts the fact that in many time series the sheer inertia of human activity is such that each observation closely resembles the one that preceded it (see Chapter 1), such a strategy has probably much to recommend it. However, even in situations when you are making predictions across time, events can take sudden, sharp turns. Furthermore, not all important predictive activity is of this nature.

The dangers of the adjustment and anchoring technique lie mainly in the way the original anchor is generated. This has been dramatically demonstrated in a number of experiments where people were asked to make judgements about uncertain quantities.[29] The experimenter artificially generated an anchor point by spinning a random device (a so-called 'wheel of fortune') and asking subjects to make judgements relative to the number generated by the wheel of fortune. Results indicated quite significant effects in subjects' judgements due to the anchor.

Observations lead one to believe that many intuitive anticipations are made on an adjustment and anchoring basis; for example, sales forecasts expressed as a percentage increase (or decrease) on the preceding year, judgements about other people ('how do you rate him compared to . . .?'); there is also evidence that adjustment and anchoring techniques are used in many industries for price setting (e.g. as a percentage of cost). Indeed, the writer knows of one case where a company had serious financial difficulties precisely because of this. The anchor used as the basis for the price mark-up was totally inappropriate.

Adjustment and anchoring seems to be a judgemental strategy that is almost as necessary as availability. That is, predictions are made by reference to cues that are available, adjustments are then made concerning the particular case to be predicted relative to the available cues. Furthermore, availability and adjustment and anchoring are strategies that both depend heavily upon the initial point in the judgemental process: the information that is available and which forms the anchor.

To summarize this section, a number of features of judgemental tasks which can affect judgement have been mentioned: contextual effects, the extent to which cues are available, the order in which information is presented, whether comparative judgements involve similar or dissimilar information, qualitative and quantitative data, and other factors. In addition, two common and almost inevitably used judgemental strategies have been described, judgement by availability and adjustment and anchoring.

AIDS FOR COMBINING INFORMATION FOR PREDICTION

Above, the difficulties of combining information for prediction have been stressed and the dangers of certain judgemental strategies emphasized. What remedies exist?

First, it is necessary to delineate those judgemental tasks that humans are, or are not able to perform effectively. Second, means have to be found to remedy those deficiencies which largely concern assessing the predictive ability of different cues, and being able to combine several cues effectively in judgement. The apparent remedy to the deficiencies is the use of mechanical means to assess the predictive accuracy and reliability of cues and to weight them in some form of statistical prediction. However, it could be, and indeed it has been argued that no mechanical prediction method can possibly capture the complicated cues and patterns humans use for prediction. Flair cannot be programmed into a computer.

Or at least, this is what people used to think. After World War II, a number of investigators started to explore the extent to which statistical analysis could be used in certain judgemental situations, mainly involving predictions in the areas of clinical psychology and academic performance.[30] To quote Dawes:

> The statistical analysis was thought to provide a floor to which the judgment of the experienced clinician could be compared.
> The floor turned out to be a ceiling.[31]

Many studies have subsequently verified this finding and have done so in a wide variety of contexts including medicine and business applications such as auditing, loan granting, and production scheduling. Indeed, exceptions where people have outpredicted statistical models are hard to find.[32] Furthermore, many statistical models have been constructed to represent the judgements of people and have been found to predict uncertain events more accurately than the judgements of the people they were supposed to represent.[33]

The actual types of models used in these situations will be discussed in more detail in Chapter 8. However, it is appropriate to consider here *why* the above results are observed. First, as should be apparent from this chapter, statistical methods are able to weight different cues according to their predictive accuracy and reliability. Second, statistical methods are consistent. People are not. They can become tired, bored or attend to different cues at different times. Furthermore, studies have shown that people are often not aware of how they weight different cues. For example, in one study Slovic found that stockbrokers showed considerable unawareness of their judgemental rules and this was particularly the case for the more experienced brokers.[34] Similar observations have been made with respect to insurance underwriters.[35] People tend to believe that they pay attention to many cues, although models based on only a few cues can reproduce their judgements to a high degree of accuracy. A possible explanation of this paradox has been suggested by Shepard,

Possibly our feeling that we can take into account a host of different factors comes about because, although we remember that at some time or other we have attended to each of the different factors, we fail to notice that it is seldom more than one or two that we consider at any one time.[36]

Statistical models: objections and advantages

It is therefore suggested that formal, statistical models should be used for prediction. However, two objections can be raised to such a suggestion. First, such models only work on the basis of quantitative data; and second, to be able to derive a statistical rule one needs sufficient numbers of past instances. Furthermore, it must be assumed that 'rules' that applied in the past will apply in the future.

These objections are understandable, although far from invalidating the suggestions. First, qualitative information can be scaled and represented in numerical form. It is, of course, true that such operations transform the character of the data and certainly misrepresent them to some extent. However, the issue to be addressed here is the degree to which such operations reduce the *predictive* power of the information. Several studies suggest that the best role for people in judgement should be that of a 'measuring instrument' for data that are to be combined subsequently by mechanical means.[37] What is lost in the transformation of data from a meaningful but loose qualitative form to a rough (but overly precise) quantitative form may well be compensated by the ability to combine them consistently with other sources of data—be they quantitative or qualitative.

It is, of course, true that to build statistical models for prediction one needs adequate data sources. However, even when data sources are not rich some means of mechanical combination of data, for example by taking averages, often leads to better predictions.[38] The basis for this perhaps surprising statement as well as other issues are examined in Chapter 8.

A third and often emotional resistance to the use of predictive rules is that they introduce a certain mechanical rigidity which is, somehow, inhuman. People feel averse to having machines predict or make decisions for them. However, the counter-argument has been made by Dawes. He states that the advantage of such rules is that to create them you have to determine a *policy*; you therefore do not treat each case on an *ad hoc* basis. According to Dawes,

Such procedures follow the categorical imperative of Immanuel Kant: Make each decision as if it were policy for everyone, or at least as if it were a policy for yourself across time.[39]

Of course, one should not become the slave to such rules. Fortunately, if good records are maintained this should be no problem since the predictive ability of information sources can be updated according to their track records. Indeed, and as will be argued frequently in this book, good record keeping—be it by formal means or just informally in memory—is probably the key to predictive accuracy.

There are, of course, many situations where statistical models cannot be built and information combination must be done intuitively. For example, many actions have to be taken on the basis of so-called 'snap judgements'. What advice can be offered here? First, it is necessary to be aware of the nature of judgement and the kinds of biases that have been described in this and the preceding chapter. It is also necessary not to be under illusions about one's judgemental ability. Some guidelines for these types of judgement are provided in Chapter 8.

Second, it is unlikely that you will make good judgements unless you have thought about the process of judgement and consciously tried to avoid some of the traps discussed in this chapter. No-one expects superlative performance from athletes who are not fit. Can good judgement be expected from people with bad judgemental habits?

SUMMARY

This chapter has been concerned with problems of combining information from several sources in order to make predictive judgements. Since this requires mental capacity which often exceeds human capabilities, people resort to the use of different strategies for information combination. These 'cognitive simplification' strategies were considered under varying circumstances: combining information sources which are partially redundant; using data with differential levels of predictive ability and reliability; combining base-rata data with specific or case information; and several task effects. These issues were discussed with respect to various cues people used in predictive activity, such as extreme values or consistency of data sources, as well as certain judgemental strategies: attributing idiosyncratic, causal meaning to data, similarity (representativeness), availability, and adjustment and anchoring. Undesirable aspects of these cues and strategies were discussed and illustrated. The major suggestion made to overcome difficulties of information combination was to use decision aids, where possible. Although touched upon here, these will be explored more fully in Chapter 8. Finally, for judgements that cannot be automated, the importance of awareness of possible biases and the development of good judgemental habits were stressed.

NOTES AND REFERENCES

1. See, for example, E. C. Webster, *Decision Making in the Employment Interview*, Montreal: Industrial Relations Centre, McGill University, 1964.
2. S. Oskamp, Overconfidence in case-study judgments, *Journal of Consulting Psychology*, 1965, **29**, 261–265. See also P. Slovic, Toward understanding and improving decisions, in W. Howell (Ed.) *Human performance and productivity*, Hillsdale, N.J.: Lawrence Erlbaum, in press.

3. D. Kahneman and A. Tversky, Subjective probability: A judgment of representativeness, *Cognitive Psychology*, 1972, **3**, 430–454.
   In the preceding chapter, it was noted that people seek out patterns for prediction. 'Good' patterns are precisely those with a high degree of redundant information which limit psychologically the number of interpretations a person is liable to make. For an example of this principle concerning perceptual patterns see W. R. Garner, Good patterns have few alternatives, *American Scientist*, 1970, **58**, 34–42.

4. D. Kahneman and A. Tversky, On the psychology of prediction, *Psychological Review*, 1973, **80**, 237–251.

5. P. Slovic, Cue consistency and cue utilization in judgment, *American Journal of Psychology*, 1966, **79**, 427–434.

6. See, for example, N. H. Anderson and A. Jacobson, Effect of stimulus inconsistency and discounting instructions in personality impression formation, *Journal of Personality and Social Psychology*, 1965, **2**, 531–539, and P. J. Hoffman, Cue-consistency and configurality in human judgment, in B. Kleinmuntz (Ed.), *Formal Representation of Human Judgment*, New York: Wiley, 1968, pp. 53–90. Several studies concerning the difficulty of using redundant information appropriately are reviewed by P. Slovic, B. Fischhoff, and S. Lichtenstein, Behavioral decision theory, *Annual Review of Psychology*, **28**, 1977, 1–39.

7. P. Slovic and S. Lichtenstein, Comparison of Bayesian and regression approaches to the study of information processing in judgment, *Organizational Behavior and Human Performance*, 1971, **6**, 649–744, reference an unpublished study to this effect by C. N. Uhl and P. J. Hoffman.

8. This scenario, albeit in a different form, was suggested by Hillel J. Einhorn.

9. C. F. Gettys, C. W. Kelly III, and C. R. Peterson, The best guess hypothesis in multistage inference, *Organizational Behavior and Human Performance*, 1973, **10**, 364–373.

10. This problem, in a slightly different form, appears in H. V. Roberts, *Statistical Inference and Decision*, Unpublished, mimeographed book, University of Chicago, 1966 and 1970. See also M. Hammerton, A case of radical probability estimation, *Journal of Experimental Psychology*, 1973, **101**, 252–254.

11. A. Tversky and D. Kahneman, Causal schemas in judgment under uncertainty, in M. Fishbein (Ed.), *Progress in Social Psychology*, Hillsdale, N.J.: Lawrence Erlbaum, 1980.

12. See, for example, Kahneman and Tversky, *Reference 4*, D. Lyon and P. Slovic, Dominance of accuracy information and neglect of base rates in probability estimation, *Acta Psychologica*, 1976, **40**, 287–298, and R. E. Nisbett and E. Borgida, Attribution and the psychology of prediction, *Journal of Personality and Social Psychology*, 1975, **32**, 932–943.

13. M. Bar-Hillel, The base-rate fallacy in probability judgments, *Acta Psychologica*, in press; and Tversky and Kahneman, *Reference 11*.

14. I. Ajzen, Intuitive theories of events and the effects of base-rate information on prediction, *Journal of Personality and Social Psychology*, 1977, **35**, 303–314.

15. The arguments here are due to Tversky and Kahneman, *Reference 11*.

16. W. Edwards, Conservatism in human information processing, in B. Kleinmuntz (Ed.), *Formal Representation of Human Judgment*, New York: Wiley, 1968, 17–52.

17. R. G. Lathrop, Perceived variability, *Journal of Experimental Psychology*, 1967, **73**, 498–502.

18. C. R. Peterson and L. R. Beach, Man as an intuitive statistician, *Psychological Bulletin*, 1967, **68**, p. 31.

19. A. Tversky and D. Kahneman, Availability: A heuristic for judging frequency and probability, *Cognitive Psychology*, 1973, **5**, 207–232.

20. This example is cited by P. Slovic, H. Kunreuther, and G. F. White, Decision

52

processes, rationality, and adjustment to natural hazards, in G. F. White (Ed.) *Natural Hazards: Local, Rational and Global*, New York: Oxford University Press, 1974, 187–205. This paper contains other good examples of availability bias in relation to natural hazards.

21. S. Lichtenstein, P. Slovic, B. Fischhoff, M. Layman, and B. Combs, Judged frequency of lethal events, *Journal of Experimental Psychology: Human Learning and Memory*, 1978, **4**, 551–578.
22. This observation was made by Gordon M. Kaufman.
23. W. K. Estes, The cognitive side of probability learning, *Psychological Review*, 1976, **83**, 37–64.
24. H. J. Einhorn, Use of nonlinear, noncompensatory models as a function of task and amount of information, *Organizational Behavior and Human Performance*, 1971, **6**, 1–27.
25. P. Slovic, From Shakespeare to Simon: speculations—and some evidence—about man's ability to process information, *Oregon Research Institute Monograph*, Vol. 12, No. 12, April 1972.
26. P. C. Wason and P. N. Johnson-Laird, *Psychology of Reasoning: Structure and Content*, London: Batsford, 1972.
27. B. Fischhoff, P. Slovic and S. Lichtenstein, Fault trees: sensitivity of estimated failure probabilities to problem representation, *Journal of Experimental Psychology: Human Perception and Performance*, 1978, **4**, 342–355.
28. P. M. Miller, Do labels mislead? A multiple cue study, within the framework of Brunswik's probabilistic functionalism, *Organizational Behavior and Human Performance*, 1971, **6**, 480–500.
29. A. Tversky and D. Kahneman, Judgment under uncertainty: Heuristics and biases, *Science*, 1974, **185**, 1124–1131.
30. The classic works in this area are P. E. Meehl, *Clinical versus Statistical Prediction: A Theoretical Analysis and Review of the Literature*, Minneapolis: University of Minnesota Press, 1954; and J. Sawyer, Measurement *and* prediction, clinical *and* statistical, *Psychological Bulletin*, 1966, **66**, 178–200.
31. R. M. Dawes, Shallow psychology, in J. S. Carroll and J. W. Payne (Eds.) *Cognition and Social Behavior*, Hillsdale, N.J.: Lawrence Erlbaum, 1976.
32. See the reviews in Slovic and Lichtenstein, *Reference 7*, as well as in Slovic, Fischhoff, and Lichtenstein, *Reference 6*. Further comments are in R. M. Dawes and B. Corrigan, Linear models in decision making, *Psychological Bulletin*, 1974, **81**, 95–106.
33. See, for example, R. M. Dawes, A case study of graduate admissions: Application of three principles of human decision making, *American Psychologist*, 1971, **26**, 180–188; R. Libby, Man versus model of man: Some conflicting evidence, *Organizational Behavior and Human Performance*, 1976, **16**, 1–12, as well as comments by L. R. Goldberg and a response by Libby in the same issue of that journal.
34. P. Slovic, D. Fleissner, and W. S. Bauman, Analyzing the use of information in investment decision making: A methodological proposal, *Journal of Business*, 1972, **45**, 283–301.
35. L. D. Phillips, personal communication.
36. R. N. Shepard, On subjectively optimum selection among multiattribute alternatives, in M. W. Shelly II, and G. L. Bryan (Eds.), *Human Judgments and Optimality*, New York: Wiley, 1964, p. 266.
37. H. J. Einhorn, Expert measurement and mechanical combination, *Organizational Behavior and Human Performance*, 1972, **7**, 86–106.
38. H. J. Einhorn and R. M. Hogarth, Unit weighting schemes for decision making, *Organizational Behavior and Human Performance*, 1975, **13**, 171–192.
39. R. M. Dawes, Predictive models as a guide to preference, *IEEE Transactions on Systems, Man and Cybernetics*, 1977, SMC-7(5), p. 357.

CHAPTER 4

Combining information for evaluation and choice

The preceding chapter explored issues in combining different information sources for prediction. However, as emphasized in Chapter 1, decisions also depend on a person's preferences. This chapter explores issues in the assessment of preference and thus choice.

Judgements of preference, like many predictions, involve the combination of several information sources. For example, imagine that you wish to purchase a car and that within your price range there are several models. How do you choose? Each car can be characterized on a number of dimensions such as style, comfort, maximum speed, power of acceleration, etc. In your choice, you implicitly consider such factors and decide which car is best across the dimensions you value. Note that this process demands much mental effort: determining the dimensions on which you will compare the cars; assessing the relative importance of the dimensions; and finally evaluating the cars. And, as one would expect on the basis of earlier chapters, many variables can affect your judgement, for example, inability to make intuitively all the kinds of comparisons you might initially deem important, order of information presentation, uncertainty about some dimensions, missing information, etc.

This chapter explores these issues and consists of two major sections. First, a number of judgemental strategies for preference judgements are outlined together with brief discussion of their advantages and disadvantages. This serves as an introduction to a more general description of choice as a process of *conflict* resolution. That is, conflict in the form of alternatives with incompatible values, or simply the advantages and disadvantages of expending mental effort in choice, is inherent in the expression of preference. A model of choice as a conflict resolution process thus helps to conceptualize these issues. Second, some apparently reasonable choice principles are outlined prior to discussion of evidence indicating when intuitive judgements violate such principles.

STRATEGIES IN JUDGMENTS OF PREFERENCE

For expository purposes, imagine a situation where you have to make a choice between four jobs which can be characterized on the following dimensions: pay,

54

location, career prospects, and job security. The alternatives are described in
Table 4.1.

Table 4.1   Four job alternatives

Dimensions	Alternatives			
	A	B	C	D
Pay per annum*	20	18	10	15
Location	Paris	Chicago	London	San Francisco
Career prospects	High	High	Low	Medium
Job security	Low	High	High	Medium

* To avoid problems of comparability of currencies, etc., imagine that pay per
annum has been reduced to a common scale.

The different strategies or 'decision rules' you could employ to make the choice
can be classified into two groups.[1] First, strategies which are *compensatory*, that
is, strategies that allow you to trade off a low value on one dimension against a
high value on another. For example, if you used a compensatory strategy, you
would be prepared to balance the low job security of alternative *A* against its high
career prospects and pay. On the other hand, strategies can be *non-compensatory*,
that is, not allow trade offs. For instance, you might decide that job security was
very important to you and that you would not consider any position that was low
on that dimension, no matter how attractive it was on other aspects. Thus you
would eliminate job *A*.

Experimental evidence indicates there are a number of factors which affect
the strategies people actually use in different circumstances: for example, the
complexity of the task as represented by the number of alternatives and the
number of dimensions per alternative; the extent to which dimensions are
commensurable; order of information presentation, for instance seeing alternatives in sequence versus simultaneous presentation of all the information;
missing information concerning dimensions on particular alternatives; familiarity with the kind of decision task; importance of the choice, etc. Combinations
of compensatory and noncompensatory strategies are also used.

In many situations it is difficult to evaluate alternatives characterized on
several dimensions. It is therefore appropriate to consider a number of models
(strategies or decision rules) and to examine them from both descriptive and
normative viewpoints. That is, two questions can be asked. How *do* people make
choices? How *should* people make choices?

An overriding feature of the use of a model by an individual in a particular
situation is the necessity to simplify the task relative to human information-
processing capacity. This is compounded by the importance of habit in choice.
That is, many choices which have been initially based on poor strategies in the
past can lead to successful outcomes (an issue that is explored further in Chapter
5). Choices are then repeated because of memory of the outcome. For example,

consider a housewife who buys a certain product on impulse. She likes the product and repeats her purchases over time, thus developing 'brand loyalty' toward the product. Had her choice process been more discerning at the outset, she might never have bought the product. Chance and habit have determined her preferences. Many of us have used similar simplification strategies concerning, for example, choice of vacation ('We liked it last year'), form of travel, and possibly even more important decisions. Habitual choice is prevalent, requires little mental effort and is easy to justify to oneself ('after all, it worked last time'). However, habitual choices are not necessarily the best and even if they were successful in the past, continued success depends upon a stable environment.

The linear model

Conceptually, the most straightforward, and in many ways most comprehensive strategy, is the so-called 'linear compensatory' model and its variants. In this model it is assumed that each dimension (e.g. pay, location, etc.) can be measured on a scale (implicitly at least!) and given a weight reflecting its relative importance. The evaluation of each alternative is then the sum of the weighted values on the dimensions, i.e.

value of alternative = sum of (relative weight × scale value) of
all dimensions.

Choice is then made by reference to the alternative having the greatest value. Under a set of not too restrictive assumptions, this is quite a good choice model. First, all the information concerning the alternatives is explicitly considered. Second, the decision maker has assigned weights to each dimension which, given the algebraic form of the model, reflect the extent to which he or she is willing to 'trade off' one dimension against another. Apart from problems of measurement (and hence commensurability), the principal issue concerning the appropriateness of this model for choice is the extent to which the dimensions are 'independent' of each other. Two forms of lack of independence are relevant:[2] first, so-called 'environmental' correlation, that is, the extent to which dimensions tend to occur together in the environment. For example, are jobs in Paris always highly paid and those in London lowly paid? If so, then adding the weighted dimensions of the linear model will involve double-counting and be inconsistent with the scheme for weighting the dimensions. Second, there may be lack of independence in the sense that a combination of dimensions is more or less valuable to the decision maker than their weighted sum. For instance, a job in London with both high career prospects and high job security could be assessed by the individual as being more valuable than the relative weighting scheme would suggest. However, the linear model described above rules out such interactions.

Two issues are implicit in this description of the linear model. First, to what extent is the linear model descriptive of individual choice behaviour; and second, to what extent should it be used in a normative fashion? At a descriptive level, the linear model has been shown to be remarkably accurate in predicting individual judgements in both laboratory and applied settings involving, for example, production-scheduling decisions, admitting students to university programmes, judgements by auditors, etc.[3] Linear models are remarkably insensitive to deviations from underlying assumptions and thus can reproduce judgements generated by other processes to a remarkable degree of accuracy.[4]

However, as a description of choice processes, the linear model is often inadequate, since it implies a process of explicit 'calculations' and the trading off of dimensions which, when there are many alternatives and dimensions, is infeasible for unaided intuitive judgement. Furthermore, even when the numbers of dimensions and alternatives are small, people still tend to avoid this process.[5]

Whether the linear model should be used explicitly to represent a person's preferences depends, of course, on the extent to which the underlying assumptions are consistent with the individual's values and particularly in respect of independence between the dimensions. However, several reasons suggest that the linear model is well-suited for preference judgements. First, when there are several alternatives, the model is able to handle all the information in a consistent manner (it is assumed here, incidentally, that use of the linear model implies that the individual has access to some mechanical aid, be it only paper and pencil). A number of studies have shown, for instance, that preferences based on holistic or intuitive judgement differ from those constructed by use of a linear model; however, the latter are more consistent in the sense that final judgements show less disagreement between different individuals than intuitive evaluations.[6] Intuitive judgement has two sources of inconsistency: in the application of weights attributed to dimensions, and in the aggregation of information across dimensions.

An additional reason favouring the linear model lies in its robustness to deviations from the underlying assumptions (see also comments above). It is unlikely that dimensions will ever be perfectly independent in the sense described above. However, provided lack of independence is not too marked, the linear model is usually adequate. Techniques do exist for complicating the linear model to account for interactions between dimensions and other nonlinearities; however, it is frequently unnecessary to make such adjustments. Care in definition of the dimensions can often resolve many difficulties. These and related issues are reconsidered in Chapter 8 and Appendix C. Finally, a considerable practical advantage of the linear model is that it is conceptually simple and easy to explain. In one sense, however, this can also cause difficulties since decision makers often like to believe that their choice processes are more complicated than the simple algebraic formulation of the linear model.

Incidentally, a model that is similar algebraically, although not conceptually, to the linear model is the so-called 'ideal point' formulation. In this it is assumed that the decision maker has an ideal representation of what the 'perfect' (i.e. ideal) alternative would be. Consider, for example, the ideal job. Alternatives are then evaluated by their distances from the ideal point on the different dimensions. Judgement, as noted in Chapter 3, often works by a process of comparisons with imaginary stereotypes or anchors, and thus this process could well reduce mental effort. For example, given that certain alternatives are close to the ideal on some dimensions, effort only needs to be expended on considering the remaining dimensions.

Other models

Four examples of non-compensatory models are the *conjunctive, disjunctive, lexicographic*, and *elimination-by-aspects* formulations. The *conjunctive* model is one in which the decision maker sets certain cut-off points on the dimensions such that any alternative that falls below a cut-off is eliminated. For instance, in a job-selection situation with, for example, three criteria being test-scores on intelligence, motivation and aptitude, the decision maker could decide not to hire any candidates who failed to meet certain levels on all criteria. That is, to be selected, a candidate would have to reach a certain level of intelligence *and* motivation *and* aptitude. Scores below the cut-off on any of these three dimensions would disqualify a candidate.

In the *disjunctive* model, on the other hand, a decision maker will permit a low score on a dimension provided there is a very high score on one of the other dimensions. In other words, in the disjunctive model, the candidate would be evaluated according to his or her best attribute regardless of the levels on the other attributes. To continue the job-selection example, a candidate could be very low on intelligence but the decision maker would be prepared to overlook that aspect provided he was very high on motivation or aptitude. In selecting a soccer team, for example, one might use a conjunctive model vis-à-vis certain skills and characteristics when selecting a 'utility' player, i.e. someone who can play in several positions, and therefore needs a minimum level of skills on all dimensions; however, outstanding players in any position are hard to find and managers might well wish to select players who are outstanding in any one skill. In this case, a disjunctive model would be appropriate.

In the *lexicographic* model, the first action of the decision maker is to consider the relative importance of the dimensions and to make an initial comparison on the basis of the most important dimension. Assume, for example, that in the job-selection situation this is aptitude. The decision rule is simple: select the candidate who shows the greatest aptitude. If two or more candidates are equally 'best' on aptitude, distinguish between them according to the second most important dimension; if that is insufficient, use the third criterion, and so on.

A further and interesting model, which is related to the lexicographic, has been suggested by Tversky; it is the so-called *elimination-by-aspects* model.[7] This model is also of a sequential type and assumes that alternatives consist of a set of aspects or characteristics. At each stage of the process, an aspect, i.e. dimension, is selected according to a probabilistic scheme (based on the presence of aspects among the remaining alternatives) and alternatives that do not include the aspect are eliminated. The process continues until only one alternative remains. For example:

> In contemplating the purchase of a new car . . . the first aspect selected may be automatic transmission: this will eliminate all cars that do not have this feature. Given the remaining alternatives, another aspect, say, a $3,000 price limit, is selected, and all cars whose price exceeds this limit are excluded. The process continues until all cars but one are eliminated.[7]

A severe limitation of strategies of the lexicographic and elimination-by-aspects type is that they can lead to an inadequate examination of the dimensions of alternatives. However, these strategies do involve a 'quasi-logic' in the sense that some ordering of the importance of dimensions is involved, and the method used seems to be intuitively justifiable. Nonetheless, they are open to severe biases. This point has been well made by Tversky in the following example of a television commercial:

> 'There are more than two dozen companies in the San Francisco area which offer training in computer programming.' The announcer puts some two dozen eggs and one walnut on the table to represent the alternatives, and continues: 'Let us examine the facts. How many of these schools have on-line computer facilities for training?' The announcer removes several eggs. 'How many of these schools have placement services that would help you find a job?' The announcer removes some more eggs. 'How many of these schools are approved for veterans' benefit?' This continues until the walnut alone remains. The announcer cracks the nutshell, which reveals the name of the company and concludes: 'This is all you need to know in a nutshell'.[7]

Note in the above example how alternatives are eliminated before consideration of their merits. For example, is a placement service really necessary in the choice of a school relative, for example, to the quality of instruction which, incidentally, is not even mentioned in the advertisement? However, the appeal of the intuitive quasi-logic of the formulation of the announcement is powerful.

The description of the above models gives some indication of the types of processes that have been investigated. However, at a descriptive level it would not be realistic to say that people actually use any one model. Processes are liable to involve mixtures of different features of the various models. For example, in a study of apartment selection, Payne has demonstrated how people faced with complex, multi-alternative decision tasks seek to eliminate some alternatives quickly in order to focus attention on those remaining.[8] This involves a mixture of mental strategies depending on the stage of the task reached.

A CONFLICT MODEL OF CHOICE[9]

What determines the mental strategies people actually use in choice situations? A satisfactory answer to this question is lacking at present although it is clear that many diverse situational and personal factors affect both mental processes and actual choices. Furthermore, whereas in the mental strategies described above choices are made from a set of given alternatives, in most real situations people have to select and define alternatives and dimensions themselves prior to making a choice.

To provide some perspective on different issues in the study of choice processes and its inherent complexity, this subsection outlines a conceptual model of choice. The scheme illustrates the point that choices do not appear in a vacuum but are the end result of a dynamic process which itself consists of a series of choices.

Central to this scheme are three notions. First, people make choices in attempts to satisfy needs. For example, you choose to eat at a certain time (as opposed to not to eat) to satisfy your hunger, and/or perhaps a social obligation. Needs are of course often expressed in the form of goals or objectives and it is these which direct choice.

Second, different forms of *conflict* are inherent in choice, where by conflict is meant incompatibility, i.e. something cannot be obtained without giving up (or expending) something else. For instance, the choice of one action usually precludes others. Consider, for example, your decision to read this book. Reading this now prevents you from doing other things. Indeed, if there were no conflict, there would be no choice.

Third, conflicts are resolved by balancing the costs and benefits of alternative actions. However, as I shall illustrate below, this is not the kind of 'balancing' implied by the linear compensatory model discussed above in the context of a well-defined choice situation (e.g. Table 4.1), although that can be part of it. Nor are the alternatives necessarily different choices, for example jobs; they can also represent the alternatives of engaging in or withdrawing from the choice conflict itself.

A schematic representation of the conflict model of choice is outlined in Figure 4.1. An individual has needs (Box 1) which become expressed in the form of goals (Box 2). For example, the need of hunger leads to the goal to eat food. In a business enterprise the sales manager's need to increase sales (perhaps to ensure his promotion), leads to forming goals to increase sales, for example the goal to find means to increase sales.

However, to satisfy needs it is necessary to engage in action. Furthermore, contrary to the kinds of situations discussed earlier in this section, alternative actions are not necessarily given. For example, if because of dissatisfaction with your present job you have a need to seek a new job, real or hypothetical alternative jobs have to be sought or created by you. Somebody does not just hand you information in the form of, for example, Table 4.1 and say 'choose'. The ability to imagine alternatives, as will be emphasized in Chapter 7, plays a crucial role in choice.

Box 3 in Figure 4.1 represents a preliminary choice point. Do you wish to engage in the mental effort of analysing your problem, which will lead to conflict (Box 5), or simply to opt out of the situation (Box 4) and thus preserve the *status quo* by choosing not to choose? (This, of course, leaves your needs unfulfilled.)

Two important aspects of Box 3 require elaboration. First, the choice to

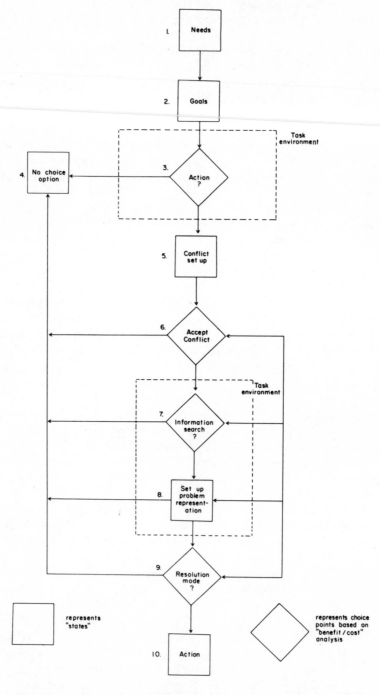

Figure 4.1   Schematic representation of a conflict model of choice

accept or reject the potential conflict in the situation takes place in a specific environment. Consequently, the way the environment is perceived at this early stage in the overall choice process can affect whether or not the individual will even attempt to make a choice. For example, if in our job selection example the person perceives the employment market as hopeless, the *no-choice* option will be selected almost immediately and any potential choice conflict avoided. Janis and Mann have documented many instances of just this type of behaviour which, as they point out, can have disastrous consequences.[10] For example, they illustrate how Admiral Kimmel and several other US military commanders and personnel refused to consider the option of preparing Pearl Harbour adequately just prior to the Japanese invasion in December 1941, and this despite the fact that warning signals could have been perceived. Their general expectations and perceptions of the environment did not make the signals sufficiently salient for them not to continue with the no-choice option. The importance of the manner in which the task is perceived by the individual is thus once again emphasized and is indicated in Figure 4.1 by the dotted box enclosing Box 3. Note that a no-choice option can be taken at a stage well before the choice situation itself is well-defined. Indeed, Box 3 can be thought of as a 'pre-decision' choice.

The second key point concerns the basis on which a person decides whether or not to face the conflict. It is argued here that this choice is made by an estimation of the benefits and costs involved in the conflictual situation. Since these benefits and costs can be involved to a greater or lesser extent at each of the choice points indicated in Figure 4.1, i.e. Boxes 3, 6, 7 and 9, they are now discussed in some detail.

The benefits and costs of thinking

What are the *benefits* of engaging in mental effort (i.e. thinking) in order to resolve the conflict inherent in choice? First, at a general level thinking helps the individual control actions and thus to have some control over the environment. Indeed, without control over one's actions, life would be intolerable. Second, thinking helps clarify goals and preferences. Although one feels needs, frequently the goals by which those needs can be expressed are not evident. For example, you may feel dissatisfied with your present job and feel the need for a change. However, your preferences concerning the type of change could be quite vague. Indeed, failure to think deeply about goals often leads people to make choices without strong preferences and it is only subsequent experience with given alternatives that determine preference. (Recall the example of the housewife given above.) This is clearly inefficient behaviour, and particularly so in a case such as job selection, where it could have important negative consequences.

Third, a further benefit of thinking lies in the creation of the habit of thinking and of effective ways of thinking, i.e. the more one engages in thinking the greater are the possibilities of developing mental strategies for handling complex tasks and in being able to face problems that would otherwise cause excessive conflict. Decision makers who do not bother to think about relatively easy problems stand little chance of being able to handle difficult ones. There are long-term benefits to be gained by thinking hard in the short term. Indeed, it is significant that the late Lord Thomson (the Canadian-born newspaper magnate), when asked the secret of his success, once replied, 'Think 'til it hurts'.

Fourth, thinking can lead to reformulating a problem and discovering alternatives that were not evident in the original perception of the task. Thinking is necessary for creativity, and as will be argued in Chapter 7, the role of imagination and creativity in choice is most important. Task variables, for example the way information is presented, also affect judgement (see Chapter 3 and the next section of this chapter). Effort expended in thinking can overcome such effects and help restructure problems.

Fifth, thinking about a problem can lead to seeking ways for finding information that will help resolve the choice conflict (see Box 7 in Figure 4.1).

The five preceding benefits of thinking are of a fairly general nature and apply across all types of consequential choice. Furthermore, implicit in each there is a short-term versus long-term trade off. Continued short-term investment in the effort of thinking has long-term benefits in the form of more control over one's actions and a greater propensity for handling choice situations adequately. A sixth major benefit of thinking, which is more situation-specific, is that it can minimize a person's *psychological* regret if the chosen alternative turns out unfavourably. The meaning of psychological regret implied here is closely linked to the responsibility inherent in choice. That is, for important issues people feel responsibility for choice, to others and/or to themselves. For example, it is hard to live with yourself if you take an important decision casually and it backfires. Consider, for instance, the purchase of a house or car. Thinking hard about a choice can, therefore, even in the event of an unfavourable outcome, minimize possible accusations of irresponsibility.

Indeed, avoiding the possible psychological regret implicit in risky alternatives could explain much so-called risk-seeking and risk-avoiding behaviour (see the next section of this chapter). That is, people are motivated to avoid outcomes that would be unacceptable either to themselves or in the eyes of other people who are important to them. Thinking cannot, of course, guarantee the avoidance of bad outcomes; but it can alleviate a sense of personal blame due to the failure to think.

What are the *costs* of thinking? First, it can highlight the uncertainties in a choice situation. For example, an advantage of thinking cited above was that it could help clarify a person's preferences. However, thinking about your preferences may in fact make you realize that you do not know what you want and the realization of this can be most uncomfortable. For instance, a traumatic experience for many middle-aged managers attending executive training programmes is the participation in exercises to determine their 'life goals'. These objectives have been implicitly determining their actions for years. However, in carrying out such exercises managers often discover that they are not too sure what those objectives really are, and furthermore, they find that they do not like several of their own objectives which are revealed through the exercises. Toda has made the point that at various points in life one makes so-called *meta-decisions* which determine behaviour for long periods of time and which are also 'cost-effective' in that they subsequently avoid the mental effort involved in raising fundamental questions.[11] Smoking is a case in point. People decide, perhaps not always too consciously, that they will smoke. Subsequently on each occasion that they smoke a particular cigarette they do not engage in mental effort to determine the advantages and disadvantages of smoking. Meta-decisions (which might also be called 'strategies') are cost-effective in terms of subsequent mental effort. However, they pre-suppose that conditions do not change as long as they are in force. For many decisions, and particularly smoking, this supposition is not well-founded (witness the number of elderly persons who regret having started to smoke when young).

A further source of uncertainty which can be accentuated by thinking concerns the structure of the choice situation itself. Careful consideration of a problem can lead you to a greater appreciation of the uncertainties. For example, imagine that you are considering a number of candidates for a job. A deep analysis of the situation can lead you to realize that there are an enormous number of uncertainties involved in the choice. For example, people can develop in ways which are not easy to predict; the nature of the job itself could also change. Furthermore, these sources of uncertainty are not necessarily independent. However, people frequently suppress such uncertainties in order to simplify the choice process.

A second cost of thinking is that it makes explicit the 'trade offs' implicit in choice. That is, even if you are aware of the uncertainties and your goals, it is uncomfortable to have to face trade offs. For example, in considering the incorporation of safety features in cars, manufacturers usually have a direct trade off to make between profits, on the one hand, and numbers of lives lost by the public at large because of mechanical failures on the other. When such trade offs are made explicit, however, people baulk at the notion.

Third, in order to think one has to process information. However, given that people have limited processing capacity, there are costs associated with the operations of acquiring, processing and outputting information. Although these costs are different from the preceding ones in the sense that they are not emotional, there may often be an interaction between emotional and processing costs. For example, in complex choice problems use of the lexicographic strategy discussed above can both be cost-effective in terms of information processing (one does not have to examine all alternatives on all dimensions), as well as reducing emotional conflicts (you do not have to make explicit trade offs between different dimensions of alternatives).

The above discussion of the benefits and costs of thinking serves to illustrate the types of consideration that are involved at each of the choice points in Figure 4.1, i.e. Boxes 3, 6, 7 and 9. In the previous discussion of that figure, the explanation had only reached Box 4 (the 'no-choice' option) and Box 5 where the individual had, after a preliminary screening (Box 3), decided to face the conflict implicit in choice (Box 5). Once the conflict has been created, the figure again allows the individual to opt out (Box 6) before searching for information (Box 7) in order to reach a representation of the choice situation (Box 8). Indeed, the figure shows that prior to choice of a conflict resolution mode (Box 9) leading to action (Box 10), the individual can cycle back and forth between Boxes 6, 7, 8 and 9 and at any point can take the 'no-choice' option (Box 4). Indeed, although the choice processes of Admiral Kimmel and his staff were described as indicating the 'no-choice' option at Box 3, this could have been taken at other boxes. The diagram is only meant to be indicative. Choice is represented as a dynamic process involving constant interactions between the person and the situation as it evolves.

Individual and situational factors

The extent to which a person is prepared to tolerate choice conflict and to work to find a 'good' alternative depends on both individual and situational factors. Furthermore, as the diagram illustrates, there is not a single conflict but a series of conflicts in which the resolution of one leads to others. Individual factors could include strength of motivation (for example, how strong are the person's needs to find a good choice solution?) as well as past choice habits, and/or experience with similar tasks. Perceived complexity of choice situations, for example, can vary from individual to individual. A task that appears difficult to a novice might be relatively easy for an experienced manager. People also differ on the extent to which they are prepared to think about problems (see above). In addition, they can react differently to time pressure. Some can be stimulated by time pressures to engage in more thought; others can use it as an 'excuse' to avoid thought and thus to 'justify' ill-considered decisions. Indeed, one can question whether people do not sometimes seek to make tasks appear complex so that they can justify to themselves strategies which essentially consist of choosing at random.[12] Knowledge about these and related issues is, however, scanty, and further speculation at this point would probably be misleading.

Situational factors are most important in choice and for this reason Boxes 7 and 8 have been drawn within a box representing what is called the task environment. In this it should be made clear that how the individual actually represents the choice situation is subjective. However, the manner in which that representation is achieved affect the processsmg strategy used and possibly the outcomes of choice (some specific examples are given in the next section). Variables that can affect the actual choice process include: the response mode (the choice alternatives may even be implied by the goals—Box 2); time pressures; the number of alternatives and relevant dimensions; type of information—qualitative, quantitative; similarities/differences between alternatives; importance of the choice to the individual; how information is presented or 'acquired'—e.g. sequentially vs. simultaneously; ambiguity of possible outcomes; etc. Whereas the effects of task variables on choice are not always predictable, evidence to be presented below suggests that they are strong. Information-processing strategies and choice are strongly affected by the *structure* of the task as perceived by the individual. Task variables contribute to such structures.

Finally, the purpose of this section has been to illuminate variables and issues in choice which is conceptualized as a dynamic series of conflicts requiring resolution. The key notion is that such conflicts may be thought of as being resolved by a corresponding series of intuitive benefit/cost comparisons.

PRINCIPLES, PARADOXES, AND PHENOMENA

The theory of rational choice under conditions of uncertainty is remarkably well-developed.[13] Three interesting practical aspects of the theory are: (1) it embodies a number of commonsense prescriptions (or principles) which are worth emphasizing and remembering; (2) it states that if a person is coherent, then his or her beliefs (i.e. predictive judgements) and preferences (i.e. evaluative judgements) can be expressed by probablities and utilities; and (3) maximizing expected utility is the sole criterion of rational choice. Consequently, it is possible to compare intuitive choices with those prescribed by the theory in order to assess people's ability to make 'rational' choices. For several reasons, such comparisons are usually only possible in well-defined choice situations (where, for example, choice alternatives are well-specified), and thus several issues raised in the preceding section are not relevant. Nonetheless, despite a certain degree of artificiality, empirical evidence of human choice even in these circumstances is most revealing.

Principles of rational choice

This theory of rational choice (or *decision theory* as it is more commonly called), can be thought to describe the behaviour of an idealized person. The theory is built upon the principles that people are capable of expressing both *consistent preferences* (evaluative judgements) and *consistent beliefs* (predictive judgements). Furthermore, preferences and beliefs should be independent of each other in the sense that you should not allow what you think is going to happen (beliefs) to affect what you would like to happen (preferences) and vice versa. In other words, *independence of preferences and beliefs* is a statement for *realism*, for warning people against engaging in 'wishful thinking' or conversely 'persecution mania.'

To say that someone has a set of *consistent preferences*, can be made operational by saying that he or she is capable of expressing a consistent order of preference over a set of outcomes. In other words, the person knows what he or she wants (which, as indicated above, is not always evident). For example, consider the four job alternatives shown in Table 4.1. Somebody who has a consistent preference order is capable of ranking the four jobs in order of their relative attraction to him or her (i.e. from most to least). This statement is not as innocuous as it might first appear since it has two important implications. First, a consistent 'preference order' implies a principle known as *transitivity*. By this is meant, for instance, that if job A is preferred to job C, and job C to job D, then job A is preferred to job D. The reader might say that this is obvious. However, experimental evidence suggests that when alternatives are represented by several dimensions (e.g. pay, location, career prospects) and people do not focus on all relevant dimensions, a process of binary comparisons (i.e. between pairs of alternatives) can lead to inconsistent choice in the form of violations of transitivity.[14] This also emphasizes the point that unless you know what your preferences are (i.e. what you want) you could be led into 'irrational' behaviour. For example, assume that you have job C (London) in Table 4.1 and that in comparing this to job D, you decide that since the pay is higher in D than C you prefer D over C and so move to San Francisco. Once in San Francisco, you compare jobs B (Chicago) and D and are attracted by the high career prospects and high job security in Chicago. You then move to Chicago. Having moved to Chicago, you decide you would really prefer to live in London rather than in Chicago and therefore try to return to C (your first job)! Clearly transitivity of preference is a most important normative principle.

The second implication that follows from a consistent preference order is known as *dominance*. This principle applies to cases with alternatives represented by several dimensions and where you are able to order your preferences on each of the dimensions. Consider, for example, the four jobs in Table 4.1 and imagine that you prefer more pay to less as well as greater amounts of both prospects and security. Furthermore, your preference for job locations (most to least) is Paris, Chicago, London and San Francisco. Assume further that although you have these preferences for the dimensions, you have not yet determined your preference order for the actual jobs. What is this?

From the information given, it is not possible to say. However, given that you are consistent it should be noted that you can immediately reject one alternative, D. Why?

Compare B and D and note that on pay, career prospects and job security B is better than D. Furthermore, your preference order over locations implies (by transitivity) that you prefer Chicago over San Francisco. Alternative B therefore *dominates* alternative D which can consequently be excluded from consideration. That is, because each dimension of B is preferred to each dimension of D, no consistent way of combining dimensions (a global preference judgement) can make you prefer D to B. *Dominance* has important practical implications. For example, it is often the case that a person can express preferences over dimensions even though determining preferences over alternatives is not so easy. Consequently, dominance (when it exists) can be used to reduce a set of alternatives and thus simplify choice. Note, however, that it is important to look for dominance between all possible pairs. For instance, although alternative C may subsequently be shown to be less preferred than D, D does not dominate C.

Dominated alternatives are, of course, easily eliminated once they have been recognized. However, in many problems the structure of the task is such that dominance is not evident. Indeed, even experienced decision theorists find when they have completed a complicated analysis that a number of alternatives were effectively dominated and could have been eliminated earlier in the analysis (and at great saving in cost and difficulty of analysis!).

The statement that people should have *consistent beliefs* can be made operational in the following manner. Predictive judgements can be formulated as probabilities and these probabilities should conform to the rules of probability theory. For instance, if you assign the probability 0.4 to a particular event (e.g. rain today), then to be consistent you should assign the probability 0.6 to its complementary event, i.e. no rain today (see Appendix A). An operational test of the consistency of your beliefs is that, when translated into probabilities on which you should be prepared to bet, no-one can make a so-called 'Dutch book' against you, i.e. create a series of bets such that you would lose whatever the outcome.

A further condition of decision theory, known as the 'sure-thing principle', also needs to be stated. An example will probably best serve to illustrate.

> A businessman contemplates buying a certain piece of property. He considers the outcomes of the next presidential election relevant to the attractiveness of the purchase. So, to clarify the matter for himself, he asks whether he would buy if he knew that the Republican candidate were going to win, and decides that he would do so. Similarly, he considers whether he would buy if he knew that the Democratic candidate were going to win, and again finds that he would do so. Seeing that he would buy in either event, he decides that he should buy, even though he does not know which event obtains, or will obtain, as we would ordinarily say.[13]

The seemingly innocuous principle implicit in the above example is the following: if a person prefers one action (e.g. invest in property) to another (do not invest), and this preference is unaffected by the manner in which a particular uncertainty is resolved (in this case whether the Republican or Democrat wins the election), then the resolution of the uncertainty (i.e. the result of the election) should not affect the choice.

Paradoxes of inconsistent choice

Two problems which involve applications of the above principles are presented in Tables 4.2 and 4.3. The reader is urged to answere these problems before continuing with this chapter.

In Problem 1 (Table 4.2), most people choose Gamble A in Situation 1 and Gamble D in Situation 2. However, it is not hard to show that these choices are inconsistent and thus violate the decision-theory principles. To show the inconsistency, let the value of £1 000 000 and £5 000 000 be written as u (£1 mil.) and u (£5 mil.) so that one can refer to the 'utility of £1 000 000' and the 'utility of £5 000 000' respectively. (This is done since for many people the subjective value of £5 000 000 is not necessarily five times £1 000 000.) With this convention it is clear that a choice of Gamble A in Situation 1 implies the condition

$$u(£1 \text{ mil.}) > 0.10u(£5 \text{ mil.}) + 0.89u(£1 \text{ mil.}),$$

where '>' means 'is greater than' and (for example) '$0.10u(£5 \text{ mil.})$' means a 10 %

chance of winning £5 000 000. Similarly, the choice of Gamble *D* in Situation 2 implies

$$0.10u(£5 \text{ mil.}) > 0.11u(£1 \text{ mil.}).$$

Table 4.2

	Probability of winning	Amount to win (£)
Situation 1		
Gamble *A*	1.00	1 000 000
Gamble *B*	0.10	5 000 000
	0.89	1 000 000
	0.01	0
Situation 2		
Gamble *C*	0.11	1 000 000
	0.89	0
Gamble *D*	0.10	5 000 000
	0.90	0

Questions: 1. Which gamble do you prefer in Situation 1? *A* or *B*?
            2. Which gamble do you prefer in Situation 2? *C* or *D*?

Problem 1   Imagine that you are required to play one of the two gambles in each of the two situations shown above.

Table 4.3

	Ticket Numbers		
	1	2–11	12–100
Situation 3			
Gamble *E*	1	1	1
Gamble *F*	0	5	1
Situation 4			
Gamble *G*	1	1	0
Gamble *H*	0	5	0

Questions: 1. Which gamble do you prefer in Situation 3? *E* or *F*?
            2. Which gamble do you prefer in Situation 4? *G* or *H*?

Problem 2   Imagine a lottery with 100 numbered tickets one of which will be drawn at random to determine the prize. There are two situations of the same type and you are required to indicate which of two gambles you would prefer in each situation. The ticket numbers and corresponding prizes (in units of £1 million) are as indicated above.

However, the above two implications of the choices are inconsistent. This can be shown by noting that the first condition (of Situation 1) can be re-expressed as

$$u(\pounds 1 \text{ mil.}) - 0.89u(\pounds 1 \text{ mil.}) > 0.10u(\pounds 5 \text{ mil.})$$

or

$$0.11u(\pounds 1 \text{ mil.}) > 0.10u(\pounds 5 \text{ mil.}),$$

which is a direct contradiction of the implication of Situation 2.

Many people object to this demonstration and still feel attached to the original choices after the inconsistencies have been indicated to them. For example, it is sometimes claimed that the situations are not comparable in that Situation 1 involves the comparison between a certain and uncertain prospect, whereas Situation 2 involves a comparison between two uncertain prospects. This is certainly true. However, if it is the case, then it implies that people are prepared to allow their degree of belief about a situation (for example, certainty versus uncertainty) to interact with their evaluations of the outcomes. This, however, contradicts the decision-theoretic principle of independence between beliefs and preferences, which states that the assessment of preference for outcomes should be made independently of beliefs about the world. (Such independent preferences and beliefs should, of course, be combined subsequently to guide choice.)

Many attempts have been made to explain why people often exhibit the inconsistent pattern of choice in Problem 1, which is known as Allais' paradox.[15] One compelling argument is a notion discussed briefly in the preceding subsection. When making choices, people often act to minimize possible regrets they might have after the decision has been taken. As discussed earlier, it is hard to face the accusations of others (and perhaps yourself) that you acted in an irresponsible manner. If this hypothesis is adopted, then it is fairly easy to empathize with the views that: (a) in Situation 1 it would be foolish to forego the chance of a certain £1 million in the hope of gaining £5 million, but with 1 chance in a 100 of ending up with nothing; and (b) that in Situation 2, since there is so little difference between 10 and 11 chances out of 100, it is not irresponsible to choose the gamble which promises the larger pay-off—and £5 million is much more than £1 million.

What was your answer to Problem 2? If you did not notice, you should be aware that Problem 2 is identical to Problem 1, the information has only been re-arranged in a slightly different manner.[16] Had you chosen A and D in Problem 1, the corresponding choices would have been E and H in Problem 2. An interesting aspect of the structure of the problem in the second formulation is that if you cover the right-hand column concerning tickets numbered 12–100, the situations are identical. Furthermore, the outcomes of the gambles in respect of tickets 12–100 *within* Situations 3 and 4 are the same. For tickets 12 to 100 Gambles E and F have the same prize in Situation 3, and Gamble G and H the same prize in Situation 4. Consequently, the 'sure-thing' principle applies and both sets of gambles should only be evaluated by reference to tickets 1–11. This being the case, consistent choice patterns are E and G or F and H in Problem 2 (Table 4.3), and A and C or B and D in Problem 1 (Table 4.2).

There has been considerable controversy about the above issues and the so-called 'sure-thing' principle in the literature. People tend to accept the sure-thing principle when it is explained to them (as in the case of the Republican and Democrat discussed above) but to resist it in certain types of choice situations.

A further choice paradox involving the sure-thing principle is provided in Problem 3. The reader will find it instructive to answer the questions posed there prior to considering the discussion in note 17.

Problem 3   An urn is known to contain 90 balls of which 30 are red and the other 60 black and yellow in unknown proportions. One ball is to be drawn at random from the urn and your 'reward' depends on the colour of the ball drawn. You must choose between the two acts described in Table 4.4, which have consequences as indicated (in £).

Table 4.4

	30 balls	60 balls	
	Red	Black	Yellow
Situation 1			
Act 1. Bet on red	100	0	0
Act 2. Bet on black	0	100	0

Now under the same general conditions, which act would you choose in this second situation?

	30 balls	60 balls	
	Red	Black	Yellow
Situation 2			
Act 3. Bet on red and yellow*	100	0	100
Act 4. Bet on black and yellow	0	100	100

* That is, you win £100 if either a red or yellow ball is drawn. The interpretation of Act 4 is similar.

Questions: 1. Which act would you take in Situation 1? 1 or 2?
2. Which act would you take in Situation 2? 3 or 4?

It has been hinted, if not explicitly shown in the preceding pages, that choice situations which have identical logical structures can nonetheless induce reversals in people's expressed preferences. Consider the following problem.

Imagine that you are standing beside a roulette wheel and you are involved in a game involving the numbers 1–36. You are shown two possible bets.

In Bet A, you will receive £4 if the ball finishes in numbers 1 through 35 (inclusive). If the number is 36, you pay £1.

In Bet *B*, you will receive £16 if the ball finishes in numbers 1 through 11 (inclusive), and lose £1.50 if the ball ends up in numbers 12 through 36 inclusive.

Now imagine you are told you have to play one of the bets. Which would you choose? *A*? *B*? Perhaps you would be indifferent between them?

Next, imagine that you have been given tickets which give you the right to play both Bet *A* and Bet *B*. Now, instead of playing the bets, you have a chance of selling them. What is the *smallest* price at which you would be prepared to sell Bet *A*? What is the *smallest* price at which you would be prepared to sell Bet *B*?

Given that you have been asked the above series of questions one after the other, there is a good chance that your answers will be consistent in the sense that the bet you would prefer to play is also the one for which you accord the higher selling price. However, had this not been the case (for example, if you had received the above problems amongst several others), it is not certain that you would have acted so consistently. Faced with a series of problems of the above nature, a majority of people who prefer Bet *A* (which emphasizes a high probability of winning a small sum), accord a higher selling price to Bet *B* (which emphasizes a larger amount to win at a lower probability). The reverse phenomenon does not, however, generally occur (i.e. prefer to play *B*, but determine a higher selling price for *A*).

The evidence here is clear. In conditions of choice under uncertainty, the structure of tasks not only causes some inconsistencies in expression of preference, but actual consistent *reversals* of preference. Furthermore, the above type of phenomenon has not only be demonstrated several times in artificial laboratory situations (involving incidentally investigations by both psychologists and economists), but also in an experiment in a Las Vegas Casino![18]

Why do people exhibit inconsistent preference judgements? One plausible hypothesis is that in making choices which involve conflicting dimensions (e.g. probability vs. amount to win), people selectively attend to one (or a limited number) of dimensions. Consequently, if the task structure, for example the required response mode, accentuates one as opposed to another dimension, the expression of preferences made across different tasks can be reversed.[19]

SUMMARY AND CONCLUSIONS

This chapter began with a discussion of different mental strategies people could use when confronted with a choice situation involving well-specified alternatives. This was then complicated by showing that the actual choice between alternatives was only part of a complex interactive process of *conflict resolution*. However, although this process is complex in the sense that it can follow many paths involving a series of sub-choices, the overall organizing principle may be quite simple, namely the comparison of costs and benefits of mental effort relative to the person's emotional state vis-à-vis the choice situation.

The subsequent section of the chapter discussed a number of normative principles of rational choice and presented several 'problems' to illustrate how people do not necessarily follow these principles. Perhaps the most striking feature of this discussion is that although people are willing to accept the principles when they are stated abstractly, they do not realize that they violate them through their actual expressions of choice.

Whereas principles and guidelines for making 'good' or 'rational' choices are not lacking, people's actual behaviour in situations involving quite consequential outcomes falls far short of these standards.

The discussion in this chapter suggests three sources of sub-optimal choice behaviour: (1) the emotional state of the individual; (2) the manner in which the choice situation is structured; and (3) human limitations in processing information. Furthermore, these three causes of sub-optimal behaviour interact in determining actual choices.

A major emotional aspect of behaviour is the individual's *psychological regret* for taking, or failing to take an action. For example, in the choice situation described in Table 4.2, it was argued that people often feel compelled to choose Gamble *A* (the certain gain of £1 000 000) on the grounds that the regret of having passed it over if they ended up with nothing from Gamble *B* would be too strong. In an interesting series of experiments, Kahneman and Tversky also show a mirror-image of 'regret' in cases where people are faced with certain losses.[20] Confronted with a choice between a certain loss, on the one hand, and a probabilistic prospect of either avoiding that loss or incurring a slightly larger one, people tend to opt for the chance of avoiding the loss. That is, when confronted with losses, the regret of failing to take an option that could possibly extract one from the situation is too strong. Further interesting phenomena have been observed in studies of insurance behaviour. People tend not to buy insurance against events which have very small probabilities of occurrence but with large possible losses (for example concerning natural hazards such as floods or earthquakes). On the other hand, they will purchase insurance for events with higher probabilities of occurrence but with lower losses (e.g. household burglary).[21] Once again, presumably in the first instance people do not feel responsible for 'acts of God', but failing to insure against burglary (which happens more frequently) can be considered imprudent. Emotional factors such as anxiety, for example fear of potential outcomes of one's actions, can also cause people to block out relevant arguments, over-emphasize different arguments in favour of preferred alternatives, fail to search for new alternatives, and even psychologically prepare themselves for negative consequences of their decisions. A recent book by Janis and Mann discusses various examples of this type of behaviour, indicating circumstances under which such information distortion is likely to occur.[9]

The preceding section gave several instances of how the structure of a choice task affects the process and thus outcomes of choice. It is clear that the key to understanding people's choice behaviour lies in understanding how they have come to represent the choice task in their minds. This means, for example, that possible alternatives for consideration as well as the relative importance of different dimensions on the alternatives can be manipulated by task variables including, for example, order of information search or presentation, and response mode (i.e. the manner in which the individual is required to indicate choice). The subjective cost of searching for information to make decisions has important implications in, for example, marketing. In an experimental study of supermarket purchasing, Russo has shown that displaying lists of unit-price information can lead to more efficient shopping since this facilitates consumers' search processes, the end result being a reduction in the average cost of consumers' purchases.[22] At the time of writing, the Post Office in the UK is pioneering a device known as 'Viewdata', which combines television, telephone, and computer in a manner such that shopping may be done at home in front of a television screen. As this mode of purchasing behaviour increases in frequency, it is clear that the effect of information displays will have great importance. The power of such displays clearly lies in the fact that they structure the choice situation for the individual.

Finally, a key aspect in choice is human incapacity to process information. We simply cannot handle all the information inherent in complex choice situations and, in particular, to make the many kinds of trade-offs implied by choices involving several conflicting dimensions. Intuitive judgement is deficient and requires 'decision aids', some examples of which will be discussed in Chapter 8.

NOTES AND REFERENCES

1. For a rather complete discussion of different rules see O. Svenson, Process descriptions of decision making. *Organizational Behavior and Human Performance*, 1979, **23**, 86–112.
2. For a fuller discussion of this issue see W. Edwards. How to use multi-attribute utility measurement for social decision making. In D. E. Bell, R. L. Keeney and H. Raiffa (Eds.), *Conflicting objectives in decisions*. Chichester: John Wiley & Sons, 1977.
3. See the review by R. Libby and B. L. Lewis, Human information processing research in accounting: The state of the art. *Accounting, Organizations and Society*, 1977, **2**, 245–268, as well as P. Slovic and S. Lichtenstein, Comparison of Bayesian and regression approaches to the study of information processing in judgment. *Organizational Behavior and Human Performance*, 1971, **6**, 649–744, and P. Slovic, B. Fischhoff, and S. Lichtenstein, Behavioral decision theory. *Annual Review of Psychology*, 1977, **28**, 1–39.
4. See R. M. Dawes and B. Corrigan, Linear models in decision making. *Psychological Bulletin*, 1974, **81**, 95–106; and H. J. Einhorn and R. M. Hogarth, Unit weighting schemes for decision making, *Organizational Behavior and Human Performance*, 1975, **13**, 171–192. For a more refined psychological analysis of the properties of linear models see H. J. Einhorn, D. N. Kleinmuntz, and B. Kleinmuntz, Linear regression and process tracing models of judgment. *Psychological Review*, 1979, **86**, 465–485.
5. See Slovic, Fischhoff, and Lichtenstein, Reference 3. However, the reader should also see Einhorn *et al.*, Reference 4, on this point.
6. See, for example, H. J. Einhorn, Expert measurement and mechanical combination. *Organizational Behavior and Human Performance*, 1972, **7**, 86–106; and K. M. Aschenbrenner and W. Kasubek, Challenging the Cushing syndrome: Multiattribute evaluation of cortisone drugs. *Organizational Behavior and Human Performance*, 1978, **22**, 216–234.

7. A. Tversky, Elimination by aspects: A theory of choice. *Psychological Review*, 1972, **79**, 281–299.

8. J. W. Payne, Task complexity and contingent processing in decision making: An information search and protocol analysis. *Organizational Behavior and Human Performance*, 1976, **16**, 366–387.

9. The conceptual scheme developed in this subsection (which can clearly make no claim to empirical verification), was developed jointly by the author and H. J. Einhorn in August 1978. Subsequent to that date, it was discovered that some similar ideas had been proposed by I. L. Janis and L. Mann, *Decision making: A Psychological analysis of conflict, choice, and commitment*. New York: The Free Press, 1977.

10. See Janis and Mann, Reference 9, An interesting analysis of 'no-choice' situations has also been made by R. M. Corbin. Decisions that might not get made. In T. S. Wallsten (Ed.), *Cognitive processes in choice and decision behavior*. Hillsdale, New Jersey: Erlbaum, 1980.

11. M. Toda, What happens at the moment of decision? Meta-decisions, emotions and volitions. In L. Sjöberg, T. Tyszka, and J. A. Wise (Eds.), *Human decision making*, *Vol. II*. Bodafors, Sweden: Doxa, 1980.

12. An interesting discussion of this point is contained in C. E. Lindblom, The science of "muddling through." *Public Administration Review*, 1959, **19**, 79–99.

13. By this theory, I mean decision theory as formulated by L. J. Savage, *The foundations of statistics*. New York: John Wiley & Sons, 1954 (Dover, 1972). See also J. Marschak and R. Radner. *Economic theory of teams*. New Haven: Yale University Press, 1972, especially Chapter 1.

14. See, for example, A. Tversky, Intransitivity of preferences. *Psychological Review*, 1969, **76**, 31–48.

15. See M. Allais, Le comportement de l'homme rationnel devant le risque: critique des postulats et axiomes de l'école américaine. *Econometrica*, 1953, **21**, 503–546, as well as P. Slovic and A. Tversky, Who accepts Savage's axiom. *Behavioral Science*, 1974, **19**, 368–373 and references cited therein.

16. The 're-arrangement' is due to Savage, Reference 13.

17. The problem presented in Table 4.4 is due to Daniel Ellsberg (Risk, ambiguity, and the Savage axioms. *Quarterly Journal of Economics*, 1961, **75**, 643–649). Most people prefer Act 1 and Act 4. However, if the right-hand column of both situations are covered, it is apparent that such a choice is inconsistent. Compare with Table 4.3.

18. References to the above types of experiment are: D. M. Grether and C. R. Plott, Economic theory of choice and the preference reversal phenomenon. *American Economic Review*; 1979, **69**, 623–638; S. Lichtenstein and P. Slovic, Reversal of preferences between bids and choices in gambling situations. *Journal of Experimental Psychology*, 1971, **89**, 46–55; and S. Lichtenstein and P. Slovic, Response-induced reversals of preferences in gambling: An extended replication in Las Vegas. *Journal of Experimental Psychology*, 1973, **101**, 16–20.

19. See P. Slovic, Choice between equally-valued alternatives. *Journal of Experimental Psychology: Human Perception and Performance*, 1975, **1**, 280–287.

20. D. Kahneman and A. Tversky, Prospect theory: An analysis of decision under risk. *Econometrica*, 1979, **47**, 263–291.

21. H. Kunreuther, Limited knowledge and insurance protection. *Public Policy*, 1976, **24**, 227–261; P. Slovic, B. Fischhoff, S. Lichtenstein, B. Corrigan, and B. Combs, Preference for insuring against probable small losses: Implications for the theory and practice of insurance. *Journal of Risk and Insurance*, 1977, **44**, 237–258.

22. J. E. Russo, The value of unit price information. *Journal of Marketing Research*, 1977, **14**, 193–201.

CHAPTER 5

On learning relationships[1]

As discussed in preceding chapters, *predictive* judgements are based on cues. That is, a prediction can be thought of as the extrapolation of an assumed relationship (or relationships) between cue(s) and a target event. For example, consider in a business setting that the difference between this and next year's sales of a company is the target event and budgeted advertising expenses is the cue. A crucial issue is whether you believe that the level of advertising expenses is related to differences in sales, and if so, what kind of relationship exists between the two variables. For example, do annual differences in sales rise or fall with the level of advertising expenditure? By how much?

The literature on judgement has documented two disturbing findings concerning people's ability to assess relationships for prediction. First, people have often been found to be over-confident in judgement.[2] That is, the degree of confidence they express in their predictions is not matched by subsequent reality. The second is the so-called 'illusory correlation' phenomenon.[3] This refers to a tendency to see relationships between variables where none exist. These findings are particularly disturbing if one believes that people learn from experience. That is, why is it that experience does not necessarily teach people to moderate the confidence they express in their judgement? Why do people continue to see predictive relationships where none exist?

An explanation that immediately springs to mind is of a motivational nature: people selectively forget instances where their judgement was incorrect. In other words, they have a 'bad memory' for their predictive failures. The second phenomenon is more problematical. It has been suggested, for instance, that illusory correlation persists in situations where people do not receive good feedback concerning their judgements and where others share the same illusions. Thus, instead of feedback concerning actual predictions, each person both reinforces and is reinforced by the illusions of the others. In many organizations, common beliefs are precisely of this nature.

Whereas so-called 'motivated forgetting' and common illusions undoubtedly play a part in maintaining people's high confidence in fallible judgement—as well as beliefs in non-existent relationships—this chapter pursues a different approach to problems of learning relationships for prediction. Instead, a detailed examination is made of one context in which predictive judgements are made. Although the presentation is consequently specific, it raises important issues involved in the learning of relationships. In particular, it illustrates the interaction between the person, judgement and the task environment in which judgement is made. The chapter concludes with a discussion of the role of experience in learning relationships and the extent to which such learning is possible.

PREDICTIVE JUDGEMENT AND DECISIONS

It is important to emphasize that predictive judgements are made for the purposes of decision.[4] For example, imagine that you are making a decision whether to employ a candidate for a particular job. The candidate is interviewed and perhaps even passes some tests. On the basis of the information collected, you judge the person to be above a certain criterion and consequently decide to hire. For expository purposes, consider that you can describe the candidate's performance on the interviews and tests by a score of some kind—to be denoted the test score.

An important issue, therefore, is the extent to which the test score—and thus by implication your judgement—is predictive of the candidate's subsequent job success.

If you were able to test and observe the results of many candidates, the relationship between scores and subsequent job success could be represented by Figure 5.1. In that figure, the predictive ability of the test can be measured by the

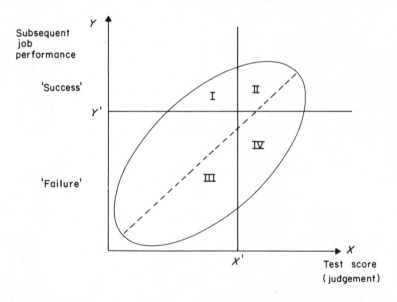

Figure 5.1 Job-selection example. (Reproduced by permission of CEDEP)

size and shape of the ellipse (cf. Chapter 3)—for a perfect test, the relationship would be a straight line (i.e. the dotted line in the figure). If there were no relationship between test and subsequent performance, the ellipse would become circular in appearance.

However, Figure 5.1 fails to represent the true situation for a simple reason. You do not hire people who fall below a certain standard on the test. To represent this, a vertical line has been drawn through the figure at the point X' on the test axis to represent a cut-off point on the judgement: candidates with scores above the cut-off are hired, candidates below the cut-off are not hired. Consequently Figure 5.1 misrepresents the true situation in that although you can observe the outcomes associated with people you hire, you do not know what happens to those you fail to hire. Furthermore, despite the fact that a particular type of decision is considered here, its features are common to many judgemental situations. You make a predictive judgement, this leads you to take an action, and because of the action taken you can only observe some of the outcomes related to your initial judgement. Consider, for example, decisions to engage someone in conversation, to buy a particular product, to allocate your time to one as opposed to another project, etc. Note too that unless you believed your judgement was valid in the first place, you probably would not base your action on your judgement. This is an important point to which we shall return below.

Reconsider Figure 5.1. In addition to the cut-off on the test-score (X'), a horizontal line has also been drawn through the line indicating the criterion of job success. There the point Y' indicates the cut-off between a candidate being a success and a failure. As can be seen, the vertical and horizontal lines divide the ellipse into four quadrants which are denoted I, II, III and IV.

Three questions are relevant to Figure 5.1: first, what information is necessary to infer the relationship between judgement and outcomes; second, what information do people actually use in assessing the relationship; and third, given that people usually have to identify and infer relationships, what is known about this process? (Cues for prediction, it should be recalled, are usually not given but have to be selected by the individual.)

To assess the relationship between test-score (X) and job success (Y), it is necessary to have information *on all four quadrants* in Figure 5.1. Quadrants I and IV represent misclassifications—respectively candidates who should have been offered jobs but were not, and candidates to whom jobs were offered but who subsequently failed. Quadrants II and III, on the other hand, represent correct classifications. (To see why one needs to have information on all four quadrants, note that if information is missing from any one of the quadrants, it is not possible to estimate the two ratios necessary to assess the relationship, namely: the number of observations in quadrant II relative to the sum of quadrants II and IV; and quadrant III relative to the sum of quadrants I and III).

A number of experiments have tested people's ability to assess relationships in situations similar to Figure 5.1.[5] Evidence indicates that even when people receive information on all four quadrants, they do not necessarily use all the information to infer the relationship. Rather, there is a marked tendency to assess the strength of relationship by the number of observations in quadrant II. This is particularly the case when, as in real life, people receive the information sequentially (i.e. over time). On the other hand, when people are presented with all the information in 'intact' displays (i.e. simultaneous presentation of the information in all four quadrants), many do use all the information. These findings are important for several reasons. First, they suggest that people have strong habits to look for certain kinds of information (i.e. quadrant II) to infer relationships from data generated across time. Second, in such circumstances other data that are necessary to infer relationships are ignored. Note, however, that the data ignored are frequently unavailable in real life, i.e. information in quadrants I and III. And third, despite the two preceding points, people are nonetheless capable of assessing relationships when all the data are made salient for them, as in intact displays. This latter point, incidentally, suggests that with intact information displays the strain of remembering outcomes in all four quadrants is obviated, an issue that is reconsidered later in the chapter.

To summarize, these studies, as well as the kinds of situation depicted in Figure 5.1, indicate both the impossibility and difficulty of learning relationships between variables in many situations: impossibility because certain information is not available, difficulty because even when it is available, it is often ignored. Note, however, this does not mean that judgements will always be followed by unsuccessful outcomes. As will be demonstrated below, the situation is more complicated.

Testing one's hypotheses

An important issue related to the above is evidence concerning how people both acquire concepts and test ideas. As an example, consider the following situation:[6]

You are told that the numbers '2, 4, 6' conform to a rule and your task is to discover what that rule is. To do so, you may generate sequences of three numbers and ask whether the sequences either conform or do not conform to the rule. That is, the person who knows the rule will simply tell you whether the sequence you generate does or does not exemplify the rule. You can continue generating numbers until such time as you believe you have inferred the rule.

There are two kinds of evidence you can seek in this kind of situation: first, evidence that is consistent with a hypothesis (e.g. you think that the rule might involve increases of +2, so you ask '8, 10, 12'); and second, evidence that disconfirms. For example, you believe that the rule might involve increases of +2 (as above) so you generate a series which does not correspond to your hypothesis, e.g. '8, 11, 12'. Both forms of information are necessary to infer the correctness of a rule: evidence that is consistent with (or confirms) the rule, and evidence that could disconfirm the rule. Indeed, the second form of information (disconfirming evidence) is often more powerful in that it allows you to eliminate hypotheses and so reduce the number of possibilities.

How do people perform in this kind of task? Most people use each trial in attempts to confirm their hypothesis. That is, few generate a sequence in order to see whether their hypothesis would be disconfirmed. Indeed, they have a strong tendency to accumulate several instances of confirming evidence, which are redundant, and in so doing to gain artificially greater confidence in their hypothesis.

The difference between this experiment and the job-selection situation described previously is that no actions are involved. Thus, it is not the fact that a person takes an action that inhibits the search for disconfirming evidence. However, in the job-selection situation, there is a direct relationship between the action to employ or not to employ and the evidence that can be observed concerning the validity of the prediction leading to the action. Indeed, if for reasons to be enumerated below, there is a high probability that people who are selected for the job turn out to be successful, then the situation becomes a self-reinforcing cycle. That is:

(1) you believe there is a relationship between the test (i.e. your judgement) and job success;
(2) you therefore select according to your judgement;
(3) most of the people you select turn out to be successful;
(4) you quite naturally conclude that your judgement is accurate.

In other words, your initial belief in the accuracy of your judgement has set in motion a sequence of events that reinforces the notion that your judgement is accurate. Your judgement might not, of course, be accurate, or at least, as accurate as you think; however, because of the structure of the task you cannot determine this. You could, of course, have tested your judgement but to do so would have involved hiring candidates you believed unsuitable for the job! Consequently, there is little motivation to test the validity of your judgement.

Incidentally, in their classic study of how people acquire concepts, Bruner, Goodnow and Austin also noted what they termed a 'thirst for confirming redundancy'.[7] This means that once people have acquired a concept, they continue to test it several times in order to really confirm it to themselves, and often redundantly. Bruner et al. also point out that people have greater difficulty in acquiring concepts defined in terms of the presence of either one, two or several traits as opposed to concepts defined by the simultaneous presence of several traits (i.e. so-called disjunctive and conjunctive concepts). Conjunctive concepts are easier because they are defined by the presence of several traits; disjunctive concepts, on the other hand, can be characterized by the absence of traits. Since concepts can be considered cues for prediction, these findings suggest that people will have differential confidence and difficulty in prediction depending on the form or kind of 'concepts' used (see also Chapter 3).

A further problem that tests your ability to seek the appropriate information to learn relationships is the following:

It is claimed that when a particular consultant says the market will rise (a so-called favourable report), the market always does rise.

You are required to check the consultant's claim and can observe any of the outcomes or predictions associated with:

(1) favourable report;
(2) unfavourable report;
(3) rise in the market;
(4) fall in the market.

What is the *minimum* evidence you would need to check the consultant's claim?

In a formal test of this problem,[1] a majority of analytically sophisticated subjects failed to make the appropriate response of both items 1 (to confirm that when the consultant makes a favourable report the market does rise) and 4 (to verify that falls in the market were not preceded by favourable reports). Note that selecting item 1 alone (a confirmatory piece of evidence) would be insufficient to uphold the consultant's claim. To test the rule, you not only need evidence confirming the claim, but you need to be able to observe possible disconfirming evidence as well.

Syllogistic slips[8]

Related to the above example are problems arising in 'syllogistic' reasoning (where people draw conclusions from premises). In this process, it is easy to make slips, a classical example being: 'All women are human; therefore, all humans are women'. Whereas most people can see the logical error in this statement, where the meaning is clear, in many inferential situations logical inconsistency is not evident. Consider the following scenario, the elements of which were first introduced in Chapter 3:

You are a businessman facing a highly competitive marketing situation. In fact, you are aware that the next move by you or your competitor could well be crucial in determining who establishes the larger market share. One of the possible weapons open to both of you is price reduction. However, given rates of profitability in the present market, this is something you would be loath to do unless forced by competition. Nonetheless, you feel that there is a fair chance (say evens) that your main competitor will reduce prices within the next week.

You receive a message from one of your field salesforce that your competitor has just booked large amounts of advertising space to go out in the next few days. If this report were true, you estimate that it is a near certainty that the advertising space has been booked to announce a reduction in prices. Therefore, you had better act fast since the first company to lower prices will gain an important competitive edge. However, before you act, you wisely stop to question the credibility of the salesman's report, since this is crucial to your decision. You clearly cannot know whether this particular report is true, so you think back on the times he has made reports to you in the recent past. His track record, it turns out, is impressive. On five occasions that you can recall within the last year, he has passed confidential information on to you. Every time he was right. You know this because just before you received each of his reports, you had also learned the same things for sure from other sources. Indeed, you were surprised that the salesman had been able to obtain the information in those cases and pleased that he had taken the initiative to approach you directly. In your view, the salesman's reports have high credibility. Consequently, you immediately order a reduction in prices. Events vindicate your action: two days after your price drop, your main competitor follows suit. However, since he followed your lead, it is you who gained the competitive edge in the 'price war'.[9]

(reproduced by permission of CEDEP)

The structure of the price-warfare scenario is fairly subtle and it is therefore helpful to decompose it. The following elements are involved:

(1) One of your field salesforce reports that the main competitor has ordered a large amount of advertising space.
(2) You estimate that if your main competitor has in fact ordered a large amount of advertising space, a price reduction is a near certainty.
(3) You question the credibility of your salesman and find it satisfactory.
(4) You order an immediate drop in prices.
(5) Your competitor follows your drop in prices, albeit with a small delay.

The crucial judgement in this chain is at (3): your questioning of your salesman's credibility. Here a logical error was made. That is, the estimation of the salesman's credibility was done by considering instances where you already knew the truth of something he reported to you, and then checking his reports against this knowledge. However, what is of concern here is estimating the salesman's credibility in cases where you do not have knowledge concerning the validity of his report. This is not the same thing. What you did was to use the information about the salesman's credibility that was readily available to you (look carefully at the wording of the scenario), and to verify the salesman's credibility using instances of the form 'given that I know the competitor has booked advertising space, how likely is my salesman to report this as going to happen?' However, the appropriate question is: 'Given that the salesman has reported that the competitor has booked advertising space, what is the probability that the competitor has indeed booked advertising space?' Note that the manner in which you questioned yourself about the salesman's credibility does not correspond to this kind of statement at all. Furthermore, to assume that both statements represent the same estimate of the salesman's credibility is to commit a logical error of the form 'All women are human; therefore, all humans are women'. In other words, whereas the salesman might be perfectly credible vis-à-vis the manner in which you posed the question, (i.e. where you knew the outcome for sure), this tells you nothing about his credibility concerning events about which you do not know the result. It is quite possible that in this 'direction' the salesman is totally unreliable.

The next judgemental error in the scenario is to assume that your competitor's decision to reduce prices is independent of yours. In this kind of situation, your competitor's price reduction is probably in retaliation to yours. The source (i.e. cause) of his reduction is your logical error concerning your salesman's credibility! Events appear to vindicate your judgement; but they are the result of errors in your judgement.

FACTORS AFFECTING FEEDBACK

The main arguments presented so far in this chapter can be summarized as follows: people learn from what they are able to observe. However, judgemental situations are often structured in a manner such that people cannot observe the information necessary to assess relationships. Furthermore, even when such information is available, people do not necessarily use it. In particular, they have a tendency to seek information that confirms existing notions rather than to seek information that could disconfirm their hypotheses.

Implicit in the preceding section is that an important element in learning relationships is the feedback one receives following judgement. Generally speaking, people will continue in actions which are positively rewarded and cease activities which lead to negative feedback. In the judgemental situation depicted by Figure 5.1, the extent of positive and negative feedback can be gauged by the relative numbers of observations falling in quadrants II and IV, which we shall simply denote as successes and failures. As stated above, people learn relationships by concentrating on the number of successes, and thus factors that affect this number are considered here.

The four factors

The relative number of successes and failures observed depends upon four factors. First, there is the 'true' relationship between judgement (i.e. test score) and outcomes. This is represented by the shape of the ellipse (covering the full range of both the test and job outcomes). As noted above, the narrower the ellipse, the greater the predictive accuracy of the test. Second, the location of the cut-off on the test also affects the relative number of successes observed. Specifically, the more stringent the cut-off on the test, the greater is the relative number of successes to failures. This can be observed in Figure 5.2, where the cut-off X'' is more stringent than that shown in Figure 5.1, i.e. it is placed further to the right. Consequently the ratio of successes to failures is greater in Figure 5.2 than in Figure 5.1, and this despite the fact that 'true' judgmental ability (as measured by the shape of the ellipse) is identical. The judgement of the position of the cut-off therefore not only precludes one from assessing the relationship between test and job outcome across the range of test scores, it also affects the relative numbers of successes and failures than can be observed.

The third factor is similar to the second: it concerns the location of the cut-off on the axis measuring the job outcomes. The lower the criterion of success, the more successes will be observed irrespective of predictive ability and the location of the cut-off on the test. This third factor, known as the base-rate of success, is

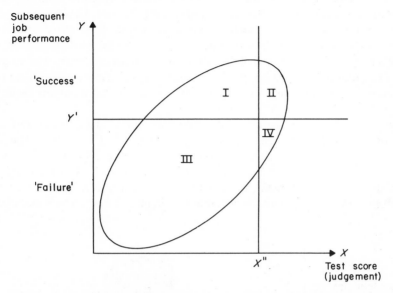

Figure 5.2   Effects of being more stringent on the test (X) relative to Figure 5.1. Note how feedback appears better. The ratio of quadrant II to IV has increased considerably. The number in quadrant I has also increased, but this is unobservable. (Reproduced by permission of CEDEP)

most important but usually unknown. For example, suppose you observe an 80 % success rate in judgement. Does this mean that your predictive ability is good? Unless you know what the base-rate is, it is impossible to make an assessment. For instance, if the base-rate is 70 % (meaning that 70 % of candidates would succeed in the job had there been no test procedure, i.e. judgement, on your part), your inherent judgemental ability does not add much. On the other hand, if the base-rate is 20 %, an observed 80 % success rate is good.

The relationships between predictive ability, cut-off on the test and base-rate are important in determining the final ratio of successes to failures observed. Furthermore, even when true predictive ability is low, so long as it has some validity, however modest, judgemental ability as indicated by the observable ratio of successes to failures can be quite high.[10]

The fourth factor is more subtle. In the model of job selection described above, there is an implicit assumption of no relationship between the judgement that someone is above the cut-off on the test-score and subsequent job performance. In other words, the act of judging that a candidate will succeed is assumed not to affect subsequent job success.

This assumption can be challenged on a number of grounds. For example, the mere fact that someone has been selected for a job can set in motion a series of events that ensures his subsequent success. The candidate may receive 'on the job' training from experienced colleagues; the person who selected him or her

84

may do things to ensure the candidate's success (intentionally or unin-
tentionally). In sport, for instance, the judgement that one player is better than
another and thus is picked for the first team instead of the reserves can mean that,
in addition to obtaining a chance denied the other, the performance of the first
player is raised by the standard of the other players in the first team. And so on. In
some situations it is almost impossible to separate the effects of judgement from
the outcome: for example, in medicine the judgement that a person needs and
receives a particular kind of therapy.

The fourth factor will be denoted a 'treatment effect' to indicate that some
form of treatment intervenes between judgement and outcome. The consequences of the treatment effect can be visualized in Figure 5.3. There, a positive
treatment effect has been assumed, so that all observations to the right of the cut-
off on the test, i.e. judgement, receive an upward impetus. Clearly such effects
disturb the feedback a person receives concerning his or her judgemental ability.

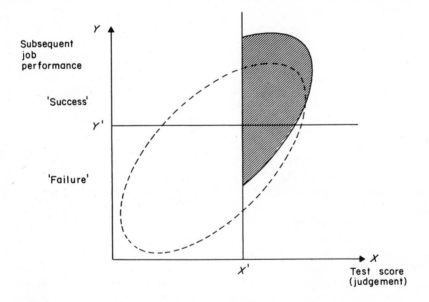

Figure 5.3 Job-selection situation when judgement leads to those selected
receiving special treatment, thus inflating apparent judgemental ability relative
to the 'true' relationship represented by the dotted ellipse. (Shaded section
reflects actual observations).Copyright (1978) by American Psychological
Association. (Reprinted by permission)

A further form of treatment effect is exhibited in Figures 5.4(a) and 5.4(b). In
Figure 5.4(a) the 'true' relationship between judgement and outcomes is
indicated. As can be seen, there is no relationship. Now assume that those
accepted receive positive treatment effects and those rejected negative effects. If it
were also possible to observe the outcomes of those rejected, the situation would

subsequently appear as in Figure 5.4(b). 'Worthless' judgement apparently shows high predictive validity. Note well, however, that treatment effects need not be biased in favour of the person making the judgement. They could have

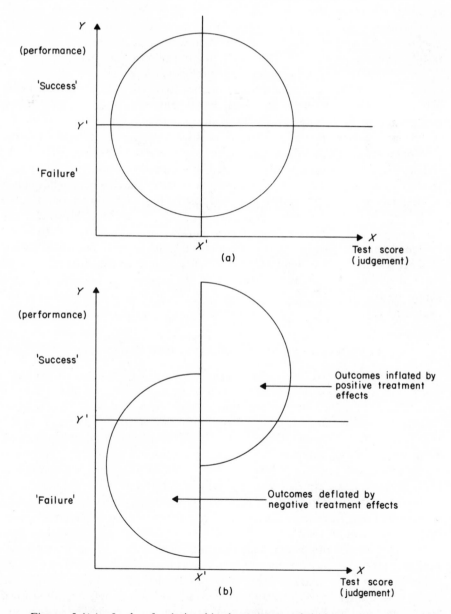

Figure 5.4(a) Lack of relationship between 'true' judgemental ability and performance; (b) observed relationship between judgement and performance. (Reproduced by permission of CEDEP)

negative or so-called 'boomerang' effects. For example, true judgemental ability could be as represented in Figure 5.4(b). With negative treatment effects, the observed situation could be that depicted in Figure 5.4(a).

The combined effects of the four factors of the model considered here are quite complex. They also illustrate that there are situations where people imagine relationships that do not exist—the so-called 'illusory correlation' phenomenon—and where good judgement does not appear to be vindicated. The results are consequently quite disturbing in terms of what they imply concerning human ability to learn relationships for predictive purposes.

The model, however, has additional implications. How does a person know whether he or she is accurate at making judgements and the level of confidence that is appropriate in judgement? The answer to this question will be affected by the extent to which the person receives positive or negative feedback from the environment and the attention that is paid to such positive or negative feedback.

These issues were specifically explored in a simulation study of the above model by Einhorn and Hogarth.[1] The results indicated that if a person has only a modest degree of judgemental ability, then positive feedback and high confidence in judgement will often be the result of predictive activity. However, the interesting aspect of the Einhorn and Hogarth analysis is the demonstration that overconfidence in judgement is not necessarily due to emotional factors, for instance so-called 'motivated forgetting' where people selectively forget instances when their judgement was incorrect. The phenomena can be accounted for simply by the structure of the judgemental task, although, as remarked at the beginning of the chapter, motivated forgetting probably also occurs.

CONDITIONS FOR LEARNING RELATIONSHIPS

Above I have indicated some difficulties of learning relationships in judgement. The model used to explain the difficulties is, of course, over-simplified in that the environment of judgement is more complex than illustrated here. For example, there is frequently a large time-lag between the moment a judgement is made and the actual observation of the outcome. There is also usually no precise cut-off point on either the criterion of job success or the test score, i.e. judgement. Furthermore, the model implies many judgements of the same type whereas real life is probably better characterized by many judgements of different types (i.e. in different situations). On the other hand, the basic model of a judgement leading to an accept/reject decision which can subsequently result in observed successes and failures is quite common.

In Chapter I, the point was made that judgemental accuracy is a function of both the task environment and the characteristics of the person. The ensuing chapters have allowed us to complicate this conceptualization by noting the dynamic and interactive aspects of judgements, actions, people and situations. Indeed, it would be more accurate to state that judgement should be understood within a framework where individual, actions and environment all affect and are affected by the other, as illustrated in Figure 5.5.[11]

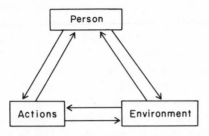

Figure 5.5 Reciprocal effects of person (judgements), actions, and environment.[11] Copyright (1978) by American Psychological Association. (Reprinted by permission)

Individuals make judgements leading to actions, actions affect the environment, the environment affects individuals who consequently form new judgements, and so on. A good example of this kind of interaction has been suggested by Bandura:

> Television-viewing behavior provides an everyday example. Personal preferences influence when and which programs, from among the available alternatives, individuals choose to watch on television. Although the potential televised environment is identical for all viewers, the actual televised environment that impinges on given individuals depends on what they select to watch. Through their viewing behavior, they partly shape the nature of the future televised environment. Because production costs and commercial requirements also determine what people are shown, the options provided in the televised environment partly shape the viewers' preferences. Here, all three factors—viewer preferences, viewing behavior, and televised offerings—reciprocally affect each other.[11]

The above is an example of judgemental behaviour at an aggregate level and which has implications for thinking about important aggregate behaviours in, for example, marketing. A more detailed individual model is provided by Figure 5.6.[1]

The main differences between Figures 5.5 and 5.6 are that in the latter the individual has been 'decomposed' (as will be explained below) and the importance of feedback has been stressed. First, note that the individual forms judgements (predictions or hypotheses) leading to actions *within* a task environment. Outcomes (box 4) are a function of boxes 1 to 3, i.e. environment, judgement and actions, and feed back into the environment (see the left-hand side of the diagram). Outcomes, however, are also observed by the individual, coded in memory (box 5) and evaluated (box 6). For example, on observing an increase in sales following an increase in advertising expenditure, a manager might attribute a causal relationship to what was observed. This would then feed back into formulation of hypotheses and judgements relating to future actions—

and so on. Observe the feedback loops on the right-hand side of the diagram. How outcomes are coded in memory is, of course, also an important issue (box 5). For example, several experiments indicate that for predictive purposes the frequency of an event is more salient in memory than relative frequency.[12] Furthermore, the relative weight given to the observation of successful outcomes exceeds that given to failures. Indeed, in the learning of relationships, some studies indicate that no weight is accorded to negative feedback.[12]

In short, an understanding of the learning of relationships used in predictive judgement necessitates an understanding of the task environment, actions, outcomes, coding of outcomes in memory, interpretation of outcomes and the different feedback loops.

Given the complexity of the above processes, what are the conditions necessary to learn predictive relationships? Estes has emphasized the need for both what he calls the 'alternative event' to occur (e.g. the outcome in the

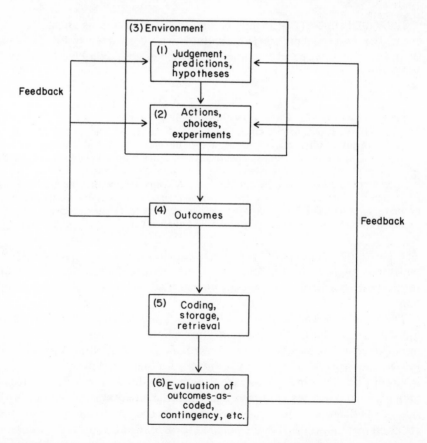

Figure 5.6 Schematic representation of judgment–action situation at the individual level. Copyright (1978) by American Psychological Association. (Reprinted by permission)

personnel model associated with the reject decision), and for people to pay attention to and encode 'all the alternative events with equal efficiency'.[12] He points out that such conditions probably apply in situations such as weather forecasting, and indeed considerable evidence indicates that weather forecasters have impressive track-records in prediction.[2] However, Estes' conditions clearly cannot apply in situations where judgements lead to actions which preclude observation of the alternative event.

In addition to the fact that many judgemental situations are precisely of this nature, two reasons suggest that people will not attempt to change situations so that they are able to observe outcomes of the so-called alternative event. First, on economic grounds people will often not wish to test their judgement. That is, taking the job-hiring situation as an example, the cost of hiring a candidate judged to be unsuitable is deemed to be greater than the benefit to be had by gauging the validity of one's judgement. Although, it should also be pointed out that not many organizations make efforts to find out what happened to candidates they rejected! In other situations, for example in medicine, ethical considerations are important. Does one withhold treatment from a patient deemed to be in need simply to observe what would happen? The second reason is that people frequently do not feel the need to test their judgement. The results of the simulation performed by Einhorn and Hogarth (see above) indicated that in many situations people do receive positive feedback in respect of their judgements and even when true predictive accuracy is low; consequently, there is little motivation to question predictive ability.

Some situations are, however, structured in such a manner that people have to consider the alternative event. For example, executives in the pop record business perceive the prediction of 'hit' records to be extremely difficult, even though the records they do select as promising are given elaborate and expensive publicity.[13] (This is, of course, an explicit 'treatment' effect—see Figure 5.3). A major reason for lack of confidence is induced by the fact that records that were initially rejected can, and do sometimes, become hits with rival companies. These mistakes are made salient publicly in the 'charts' and cannot be ignored. Thus, attention is paid to the alternative event. Note, however, that it is the structure of the environment that causes negative feedback to become salient rather than an inherent desire to test and improve predictive ability.

Based on extensive work in prediction in clinical psychology, Goldberg[14] has listed three conditions for learning predictive relationships: (1) feedback—which is necessary but not sufficient; (2) ability to re-arrange cases so that hypotheses can be verified or discounted. As Goldberg puts it, 'it does little good to formulate a rule for profile Type A, only to have to wait for another 100 profiles before an additional manifestation of Type A appears; what one must do is group together all Type A profiles in order to be able to verify one's initial preference.'[14] However, this condition is of limited practical value to decision makers faced with a range of essentially non-repetitive predictive situations; and (3) ability to keep a record of one's predictions and their outcomes. As noted earlier in the chapter, memory is important in predictive activity, and methods of bolstering this and the nature of feedback are key elements. However, as Figure 5.5 indicates, feedback has to be understood within the context in which it appears—and its interpretation is not evident. Indeed, much research indicates that feedback based on the observation of outcomes in learning situations is ineffective.[15]

What kind of feedback is likely to be effective? Some studies have shown that feedback that emphasizes the process, i.e. the structure of the judgemental task, is more effective than mere 'outcome' feedback.[16] Given what has been said above, this appears reasonable. However, the evidence on this issue is not conclusive, although it should be said that the role of memory (box 5 in Figure 5.6) has not been explicitly considered. My suggestion is that when making predictions people should be encouraged to record in writing not only their predictions (in order to compare with subsequent results) but also the bases of their predictions—i.e. the cues they used in judgement, causal assumptions etc. Such notes would be useful for two reasons: first, they would act as a means of bolstering memory; and second, taking notes would force people to consider both the basis of their judgement and the structure of the task.

Finally, what kinds of relationships do people find more or less easy to learn? Experimental evidence indicates that linear (i.e. straight line) relationships are easier to acquire than nonlinear relationships. Furthermore, positive relationships are more readily recognized than negative ones. However, consistent with evidence in Chapter 2, when learning relationships people tend to assume that such relationships are less subject to random fluctuations than is, in fact, the case.[17]

SUMMARY

This chapter has discussed problems involved in learning relationships for predictive purposes. A number of points have been stressed: first, people learn primarily on the basis of what they can observe. However, many judgemental situations are structured in such a manner that one cannot observe the data necessary to infer relationships; second, people have a tendency to seek information to confirm their ideas rather than to look for possible disconfirming evidence; third, positive feedback is weighted more heavily in memory than negative feedback; and fourth, the outcomes of judgement are the result of actions taken in specific environments. Furthermore, people are frequently unaware of the structure of the environment in which such actions take place and thus how to interpret outcomes.

In many situations it is not possible to untangle the different task and individual variables which cause the relationship between judgements and outcomes to be so complex. However, the individual can do two things over and above understanding the kinds of issues discussed in this chapter. First, an attempt can be made to bolster memory by recording both predictions and the bases of prediction. This should lead to heightened self-awareness of one's own judgement and of the nature of judgemental situations. Second, a rather special attitude of mind needs to be adopted. This is to accept the view that one does not necessarily learn from experience and, indeed, often cannot.

NOTES AND REFERENCES

1. This chapter is largely based on H. J. Einhorn and R. M. Hogarth, Confidence in judgment: Persistence of the illusion of validity. *Psychological Review*, 1978, **85**, 395–416.
2. See, for example, S. Lichtenstein, B. Fischhoff. and L. D. Phillips, Calibration of probabilities: The state of the art. In H. Jungermann and G. de Zeeuw (Eds.), *Decision making and change in human affairs.* Dordrecht-Holland: Reidel, 1977, 295–324.
3. L. J. Chapman and J. P. Chapman, Illusory correlation as an obstacle to the use of valid psychodiagnostic signs. *Journal of Abnormal Psychology*, 1969, **74**, 271–280.
4. See A. S. Elstein, Clinical judgment: Psychological research and medical practice. *Science*, 1976, **194**, 696–700; and H. J. Einhorn and S. Schacht, Decisions based on fallible clinical judgment. In M. Kaplan and S. Schwartz (Eds.), *Judgment and decision processes in applied settings.* New York: Academic Press, 1977, 125–144.
5. H. M. Jenkins and W. C. Ward, Judgment of contingency between responses and outcomes. *Psychological Monographs: General and Applied*, 1965, **79**, Whole No. 594; J. Smedslund, The concept of correlation in adults. *Scandinavian Journal of Psychology*, 1963, **4**, 165–173; J. Smedslund, Note on learning, contingency, and clinical experience. *Scandinavian Journal of Psychology*, 1966, **7**, 265–266; and W. C. Ward and H. M. Jenkins, The display of information and the judgment of contingency. *Canadian Journal of Psychology*, 1965, **19**, 231–241.
6. The example is taken from P. C. Wason, On the failure to eliminate hypotheses in a conceptual task. *Quarterly Journal of Experimental Psychology*, 1960, **12**, 129–140. This, and some other interesting and related experiments are summarized and discussed in P. C. Wason and P. N. Johnson-Laird, *Psychology of reasoning. Structure and content.* London: Batsford, 1972.
7. J. S. Bruner, J. J. Goodnow, and G. A. Austin, *A study of thinking.* New York: Wiley, 1956. Similar results have also been reported by B. Brehmer, Hypotheses about relations between scaled variables in the learning of probabilistic inference tasks. *Organizational Behavior and Human Performance*, 1974, **11**, 1–27.
8. This sub-section can be skipped without loss of continuity.
9. This scenario was suggested by Hillel J. Einhorn, albeit in a different context. See also R. M. Hogarth, How valid is your judgement? *CEDEP Journal*, 1979, **3**, 47–56.
10. This has been well known in industrial psychology for some time. See H. C. Taylor and J. J. Russell, The relationship of validity coefficients to the practical effectiveness of tests in selection: Discussion and tables. *Journal of Applied Psychology*, 1939, **23**, 565–578. For a more recent discussion see Einhorn and Schacht, Reference 4.
11. The figure is inspired by one in A. Bandura, The self system in reciprocal determinism. *American Psychologist*, 1978, **33**, 344–358.
12. W. K. Estes, The cognitive side of probability learning. *Psychological Review.* 1976, **83**, 37–64; and W. K. Estes, Some functions of memory in probability learning and choice behavior. In G. H. Bower (Ed.), *The psychology of learning and motivation* (Vol. 10). New York: Academic Press, 1976, 1–45.
13. P. Hirsch, *The structure of the popular music industry.* Ann Arbor, Michigan: Institute for Social Research, University of Michigan, 1969; and P. Hirsch, Processing fads and fashions: An organization-set analysis of cultural industry systems. *American Journal of Sociology*, 1972, **77**, 639–659.
14. L. R. Goldberg, Simple models or simple processes? Some research on clinical

judgments. *American Psychologist*, 1968, **23**, 483–496.

15. See the reviews by N. J. Castellan, Jr., Decision making with multiple probabilistic cues. In N. J. Castellan, D. B. Pisoni, and G. R. Potts, (Eds.), *Cognitive theory, Volume 2*. Hillsdale, N.J.: Lawrence Erlbaum, 1977, 117–147; and P. Slovic and S. Lichtenstein, Comparison of Bayesian and regression approaches to the study of information processing in judgment. *Organizational Behavior and Human Performance*, 1971, **6**, 649–744.

16. See, for example, K. R. Hammond, D. A. Summers, and D. H. Deane, Negative effects of outcome-feedback on multiple-cue probability learning. *Organizational Behavior and Human Performance*, 1973, **9**, 30–34.

17. See Slovic and Lichtenstein, Reference 15, as well as P. Slovic, B. Fischhoff, and S. Lichtenstein. Behavioral decision theory. *Annual Review of Psychology*, 1977, **28**, 1–39.

CHAPTER 6

The role of memory in judgement

In the seventeenth century, the French nobleman and social critic La Rochefoucauld said: 'Everybody complains about the badness of his memory, nobody about his judgement.' This statement has proved to be remarkably pertinent for at least two reasons: first, whereas judgement is still accorded a certain mystical status in our society, memory is not so revered; second, research on judgement points to the crucial role of memory in this process. Indeed, a good memory can be considered a necessary although not sufficient condition for good judgement.

Memory affects judgement in several ways: the manner in which judgemental tasks are structured; cues that are selected, either from the environment and/or from the person's memory; the 'rule' used to process the information assessed to make the judgement; and the interpretation and 'coding' of the outcome of judgement. Consider, for example, the difference between a familiar and unfamiliar judgemental task (for instance, judging the distance needed to slow down your car in traffic as against predicting the date at which oil products will no longer be necessary for motor transport). In the former case, your memory of similar situations triggers responses which, in the past, have allowed you to cope with the situation. In the second task, however, most people would have trouble in even starting to think about the problem.

Memory certainly affects the cues you use in prediction. You might remember, for example, that there is a relationship between the level of economic activity in the country as a whole and your particular industrial sector. Thus when the general economic trend is up (or down) you would make a corresponding prediction for your own sector. At a more everyday level, you learn (and remember) that there is a relationship between the external temperature and how warm or cold you feel. This leads you to predict what clothes will be suitable on a particular day, and so on.

Memory also affects the rules you use to process information. For example, when choosing between two candidates for a job you might well prefer the one whose profile reminds you most of a person who is now successful.[1] That is, you process the information concerning the candidates by comparison with some ideal. Your predictive judgement is then based on the degree of similarity between the profile you observe and the ideal profile you keep in memory. Finally, and as touched upon in the preceding chapter, memory of the outcomes of previous predictions affects expectations concerning the future.

93

This chapter consists of three main sections. We consider: (1) the effects of memory on the subjectively perceived structure of judgemental tasks; (2) the selection and processing of information in judgement; and (3) the interpretation of outcomes. In all three sections, it will be shown that limitations on human memory capacity force people to use cognitive simplification mechanisms which—although often efficient in terms of dealing with the complexity of the environment—do leave one open to biases.

PERCEPTION OF THE JUDGEMENTAL TASK

A number of points made in Chapter 1 about the nature of the human information-processing system need to be re-emphasized here. First, the capacity of the information-processing system is limited; consequences of this include the facts that: (a) perception of information is not comprehensive but *selective*. Anticipations of what we expect to see play a large part in what we do see; and (b) not only processing but *memory capacity* is *limited*. This means that ways have to be found for coding, organizing and storing information efficiently in memory. Second, the mind is not a vacuum. It not only receives information but actively seeks information which it attempts to incorporate within existing schemas and notions. Through experience, people develop an understanding of the world they live in. Furthermore, they use that understanding to select information, to interpret it (i.e. give it 'meaning') and to anticipate events.

The above points can be illustrated by considering the two series of letters and the two drawings in Figure 6.1.[2] If you look briefly at the two series of letters do you think you would be able to memorize them and repeat them perfectly without looking back at the figure? Most people can manage the first series without difficulty, but not the second. The ease of recall of the first series lies in the fact that you do not need to remember the letters at all. You can *reconstruct* the sequence if you simply recognize that the letters make up the sentence THE DOG ATE MEAT. In other words, if you manage to code the letters in a form that makes some kind of sense to you, it is possible to remember them easily

(1) THEDOGATEMEAT

(2) EMDEOAGTATTHE

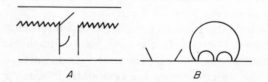

Figure 6.1 From *Method and Theory in Experimental Psychology* by Charles E. Osgood. Copyright © 1953 by Oxford University Press Inc. (Reprinted by permission)

Your memory, therefore, depends paradoxically not on your remembering the letters you were asked to recall, but on encoding a meaningful English sentence the words of which you can spell. In other words, your memory works by a process of reconstruction based on associations that have meaning for you.

What did you make of the second series of letters? This contains the same number as the first, and indeed the letters are the same, albeit in a different order. However, to remember this particular sequence you would have to work relatively hard at rehearsing the sequence unless you could develop some kind of code.[3]

What do the 'drawings' A and B mean to you? For most people these figures are at first a meaningless series of lines. However, if you are told that A represents. 'A soldier and his dog passing by a hole in a picket fence' and B 'A washerwoman cleaning the floor', both series of lines take on a meaning of their own. Indeed, once you have been told what they represent, it is difficult not to see both the soldier and his dog and the washerwoman.

These brief illustrations serve to emphasize two key points concerning memory. First, the efficiency of memory depends upon being able to encode information in such a way that it can subsequently be recalled and decoded in detail. The clue to efficient coding often depends upon associating some form of meaning with the items or units to be remembered. Indeed, it is frequently not necessary to remember things in detail. Memory can and does work by reconstructing fragments of information into a whole that makes sense to the individual. Second, meaning guides our interpretation of what we see. For example, lines such as in A and B of Figure 6.1 can be interpreted and take on a significance of their own. Furthermore, anticipations of patterns a person expects to see (i.e. based on memory) can interfere quite strongly with what he or she does see.

A striking example of this latter phenomenon was provided in an experiment by Bruner and Postman.[4] Subjects were asked to recognize and name playing cards presented to them in conditions allowing only brief exposure. Included amongst the playing cards were several incongruent cards, such as red spades or black hearts. Results of the experiment indicated that subjects both took longer to recognize and name incongruent cards and made more mistakes in doing so. For instance, on occasion 27 of the 28 subjects made what the experimenters called a 'dominance' reaction: for example red spades were reported as black or simply as hearts (dominance was of both colour and form); several subjects also sometimes reported 'compromise' colours, e.g. red spades were reported as brown; etc. In short, when perception was incongruent with expectations, distortions occurred. If you believe, a priori, that hearts are red, the perception of black hearts is difficult and can even be stressful.

The implications of this admittedly artificial situation involving incongruity between memory of what one should perceive and what is actually there are important. It has been shown, for example, that legal witnesses are often unable to report what they claim to have seen. Instead they reconstruct what they think they should have seen. Furthermore, people can be quite confident in their mistaken memory.[5] All people who work in organizations are familiar with the occurrence of misunderstandings. The same facts can be remembered quite differently and thus different parties can come to different conclusions concerning action.

To summarize, experience with the world teaches us to expect to see certain things in given situations. Such expectations can be thought of as being embedded in memory which represents a network of associations related to particular objects or situations, etc. However, memory is not a complete record of all our experience. You cannot re-access all past processing in the same way as can be done by a computer. Rather, it is fragments of experience which are remembered and the recall of total experiences takes place by reconstructing fragments in a manner that is coherent to the individual. The 'glue' used to reconstruct and make associations between fragments is the meaning people attach to fragments and their possible associations.[6]

SELECTION AND PROCESSING OF INFORMATION

An important issue in judgement centres on why people access particular pieces of information from memory; a related issue concerns why some items are weighted more heavily than others.

Availability

Tversky and Kahneman argue that the ease with which instances can be recalled from memory is an important factor in determining intuitive judgements of frequency.[7] They term this judgemental rule the 'availability' heuristic (see also Chapter 3).

For example, consider the following questions:[7]

(1) How familiar are you with the letter k? If you sample a word at random from a text in English, is it more likely that the word starts with a k or that it has k as its third letter?
(2) Are words beginning with *re* more or less frequent than words ending with *re*?
(3) If there are 10 people from whom a committee can be formed, how many different committees of size 2 can be formed? How many different committees of size 8 can be formed? How do your answers to these questions differ?

The answers to the questions are as follows: (1) k is more likely to be the third letter of a word than the first; (2) more words end with *re* than begin with *re*; and (3) the number of committees of size 2 that can be formed from 10 people is 45. This is the same as the number of committees of size 8. How did these answers compare with yours?

Most people tend to answer these questions incorrectly and it is appropriate to consider possible reasons. Tversky and Kahneman argue that in answering such questions a plausible judgemental strategy is to think of instances with the requisite characteristics, for example words with k as the first, or third letter, words beginning or ending with re, and how many 2- or 8-person committees can be formed from groups of 10 people. Words that begin with k do seem easier to recall than those with k as the third letter (consider $king$ as opposed to $acknowledge$); similarly it is easy to think of words beginning with re, such as $remember, recall, return$; but the fact that several common words end with re is not recalled so easily, viz, $there, therefore, were, are$. The committee problem is perhaps more subtle. It is somehow easier to imagine more arrangements of 2 out of 10 as opposed to 8 out of 10. However, it should be noted that for every arrangement of 2 people in the committee, there is a corresponding arrangement of 8 people outside the committee. Thus, if you realize that the definitions of being in and out of the committee can be switched, the number of possible arrangements of 2 clearly equals that of 8.[7]

The availability bias, therefore, results from assuming a correspondence between the ease with which a cue or event can be recalled or reconstructed from memory and its relative frequency.

As indicated in Chapter 3, the presence of availability bias has also been documented outside the artificial tasks considered above. Experiments have tested, for example, people's intuitive notions concerning the relative frequency of diseases or causes of death. The relative frequency of diseases or causes that receive much publicity, for example homicide, cancer or tornadoes, tend to be over-estimated, whereas other less newsworthy causes such as asthma and diabetes are underestimated.[8] Clearly the 'evidence' with which we are confronted in daily life plays a major role in determining—through memory—our anticipations of the relative frequency of events. Furthermore, such evidence is often incomplete. For example, when an aeroplane crashes or is hijacked the event is newsworthy and people are made aware of the occurrence. Furthermore, over time one can become aware of increasing trends of crashes or hijackings. However, flights that occur without incidents are not reported and thus people cannot know differences in the relative frequency of crashes or hijacks across time. If the number of flights increases across time, the rate of the relative frequency of incidents may, in fact, decrease.

Even when people are aware of non-occurrences, the availability bias in memory can distort judgements of relative frequency. This has been demonstrated in a study of assessments of mortality rates following surgery by surgeons working in different specialties.[9] Surgeons working in specialties characterized by high (2.42 %) and low (0.44 %) mortality rates were asked to assess different mortality rates. Whereas surgeons from both specialties correctly estimated that the mortality rate was higher in one group than in the other, assessments of the overall service mortality rate was biased by group membership. Specifically, surgeons in the high mortality group estimated the overall rate to be double that estimated by the low mortality surgeons.

The above result is, of course, a case of 'professional deformation'. People have a natural tendency to interpret their own experiences and corresponding anticipations as normal. This causes them to underestimate the extent to which the experiences of others lead to different sets of expectations. Since people usually interact largely with those of similar backgrounds and inclinations, such assumptions are often quite functional. However, when dealing with people (or problems) of other cultures, or even professional backgrounds, expectations based on 'inappropriate' memory can be dysfunctional.

Concrete information

In Chapter 3, comments were made about the fact that people often fail to take account of so-called 'base-rate' information in judgement.* Recall, for example, the problems involving the TB X-ray and the Green and Blue taxi cabs. It was argued in Chapter 3 that the failure to give adequate weight to base-rate information could be attributed to its relative 'causal status' in the mind of the individual. That is, if base-rate data were not seen to be causally linked to a 'target' event, they were either ignored or played down. Another, and not exclusive hypothesis, is that base-rate data are usually of an abstract, pallid and statistical nature and lack the vivid, concrete impact of specific information in memory. That is, whereas base-rate data can be comprehended, and possibly remembered, at an unemotional, cognitive level, concrete, specific case-data are frequently emotionally loaded and thus encoded and remembered on several dimensions with a correspondingly rich set of meaningful associations.[10]

And indeed, experiments on memory do show that people are more likely to remember information that has been coded on several sensory dimensions[11] (for example, information presented in the form of words and images is more easily and accurately recalled than information presented only in verbal form).

The hypothesis of the salience of concrete over abstract information dates back to at least 1927 when Bertrand Russell noted that 'popular induction depends upon the emotional interest of the instances, not upon their number'.[12] The following example serves to illustrate the point.

> Let us suppose that you wish to buy a new car and have decided on grounds of economy and longevity you want to purchase one of those solid, stalwart, middle class Swedish cars—either a Volvo or a Saab. As a prudent and sensible buyer, you go to *Consumer Reports*, which informs you that the consensus of their experts is that the Volvo is mechanically superior, and the consensus of the readership is that the Volvo has the better repair record. Armed with this information, you decide to go and strike a bargain with the Volvo dealer before the week is out. In the interim, however, you go to a cocktail party where you announce this intention to an acquaintance. He reacts with disbelief and alarm: 'A Volvo! You've got to be kidding. My brother-in-law had a Volvo. First, that fancy fuel injection computer

---

* The distinction was made in Chapter 3 between 'base-rate' and 'specific' (or case) data. In predicting a 'target' event, base-rate data should be moderated by specific data. Consider, for example, the prediction of whether someone (specific data) with a particular type of qualification (base-rate data) will be successful in a job.

thing went out. 250 bucks. Next he started having trouble with the rear end. Had to replace it. Then the transmission and the clutch. Finally sold it in three years for junk'. The logical status of this information is that the N (i.e. number)* of several hundred Volvo-owning *Consumer Reports* readers had been increased by one, and the mean frequency of repair record shifted up by an iota on three or four dimensions. However, anyone who maintains that he would reduce the encounter to such a net informational effect is either disingenuous or lacking in the most elemental self-knowledge.[13]

The effects of concrete over abstract information, such as in the above 'thought experiment', have been demonstrated in a number of experiments performed by Borgida, Nisbett and their colleagues as well as being evident iin several real-life incidents. In one experiment, Borgida and Nisbett tested the extent to which student choices of courses were affected by statistical base-rate data (statistical summaries of course appreciation forms) on the one hand, and the live comments of individual students, on the other.[14] It was found that comments of single individuals concerning their experience with courses had greater effects on choice than the more representative statistical data. Real life analogues of this experiment include: the observation that in the 1930s American farmers did not adopt early techniques of the Green Revolution after receiving pamphlets and other such information about the new procedures. However, they were converted when they observed the successful use of the new procedures by a neighbour; the dramatic increase in waiting lists at cancer detection clinics following the highly publicized mastectomies performed on Mrs Ford and Mrs Rockefeller; the discounting of results of public opinion polls by members of the press following McGovern's presidential campaign in 1972 who were used to observing McGovern being acclaimed by large, enthusiastic crowds;[13] the reluctance of small businessmen who, despite apparently full information from governmental sources, are reluctant to effect necessary relocations on planned industrial sites until they observe other businessmen moving to the site;[15] and physicians' tendencies to discount treatment reports in the medical literature if they have already had a successful experience with a particular treatment.[16]

Information that involves personal experiences or observation of incidents remains salient in memory. Indeed, this phenomenon is frequently used in different forms of propaganda. Consider, for example, the use of single examples, personal testimonials and vignettes in·advertising. Opponents and proponents in debates on social issues such as abortion, capital punishment and nuclear power will argue with incidents or statistics as it suits them.[10] For instance, if people living within a certain radius of the proposed site of a new nuclear plant are told that it is possible that the construction will involve a miniscule reduction in life expectancy for the community, no alarm will result. However, if the same information is translated into, say, the expectation of two additional cancer-induced deaths, results are likely to be quite different.[17] During a period of public

---

* Parentheses added.

debate concerning, for example, capital punishment, it is well-known that an incident involving a single person (for example, a 'lifer' who escapes and commits another crime), can have a most dramatic effect.

In one study, an article from the *New Yorker* which detailed the pathology of a single 'stereotypic' welfare case had greater effect on people's attitudes toward welfare than more appropriate data summarizing overall welfare use.[18] In another experiment, it was shown that vividness of information can have a delayed effect on judgement. Subjects in this study were required to read a brief transcript of a legal case in which the vividness of the arguments for the prosecution and defence were experimentally manipulated. After reading the case, subjects initially judged the defendant no more harshly whether the arguments for the prosecution or defence had been presented more vividly. However, a second set of judgements made 24 hours later revealed a different picture. Subjects' judgements swung to the side (i.e. prosecution or defence) for which the arguments had been presented more vividly.[19]

People remember *incidents* and these weigh heavily in judgement.

INTERPRETING THE PAST

Was World War II inevitable? Was Neville Chamberlain deluding himself about the relative possibilities of peace and war when he returned from his historic discussions with Adolf Hitler in Munich? Was the Japanese attack on Pearl Harbour predictable? Should the West have forseen the possibility of an Arab oil embargo (not to speak of its economic consequences) prior to 1973? Should the United States have realized the consequences of its initial engagement in Vietnam as early as 1964?

Hindsight bias

With the benefit of hindsight, the answer to all the above questions is a definite 'yes'. Yet how is it that people failed to make the appropriate predictions in all the above cases? Furthermore, why is it that the judgements that were made or preceded the above events were (with only a few exceptions) not called into question?

One way of thinking about the above questions is to put yourself into a situation which involves making a prediction about the future. Consider the following passage which describes a historical situation in the early nineteenth century with which most people are unfamiliar.

For some years after the arrival of Hastings as governor-general of India, the consolidation of British power involved serious war. The first of these took place on the northern frontier of Bengal where the British were faced by the plundering raids of the Gurkhas of Nepal. Attempts had been made to stop the raids by an exchange of lands, but the Gurkhas would not give up their claims to country under British control, and Hastings decided to deal with them once and for all. The campaign began in November, 1814. It was not glorious. The Gurkhas were only some 12,000 strong; but they were brave fighters, fighting in territory well suited to their raiding tactics. The older British commanders were used to war in the plains where the enemy ran away from a resolute attack. In the mountains of Nepal it was not easy to find the enemy. The troops and transport animals suffered from the extremes of heat and cold, and the officers learned caution only after sharp reverses. Major-General Sir D. Ochterlony was the one commander to escape from these minor defeats.[20]

Now would you be surprised to learn after the event that it was the Gurkhas who won the above war and who were subsequently able to negotiate a satisfactory (for them) peace treaty with the British? The terrain in which the Gurkhas were able to take the battle was, after all, better suited to their tactics and experience than to the British. A modern equivalent in differences in tactics and conditions is provided, for example, by certain aspects of the Vietnam war. Re-read the passage and think carefully about the significance of the different statements for predicting the outcome of the war.

Once you have been told the outcome of an uncertain situation, two things seem to happen. First, the outcome seems, with hindsight, to be inevitable. For example, Chamberlain should have realized that Hitler had no intention of not engaging in war. Second, one can see a direct relationship between certain other events or 'cues' and what actually happened: for instance in the Chamberlain case the growing strength of the German armed forces, the attitudes and acts of the Nazis toward Jews, etc. Indeed, after the event, we can easily interpret why things happened as they did. There seems to have been a kind of 'creeping determinism'—that is, what happens seems to flow on naturally from the preceding events.

Fischhoff and his colleagues have tested people's so-called 'hindsight' biases in a number of ways. First, Fischhoff presented subjects with unfamiliar, historical passages such as the description of the British–Gurkha war given above. He then asked them to make probabilistic predictions concerning several possible outcomes.[21] He also gave different groups different information about the actual outcome: correct information concerning the outcome of the event; false information concerning the outcome; and no information about the outcome. Subjects were also asked to indicate which items of information in the passages were particularly relevant to their judgements Results of the experiment indicated: (1) outcome 'knowledge' affected subjects' responses in that those events which were announced as actually having occurred were judged as more likely to occur (recall false as well true outcome information was given to different groups of subjects concerning the same events); and (2) the relevance attributed by subjects to particular pieces of information was related to the outcomes they had been given.

In another study (not conducted with historical scenarios), subjects were asked to make probabilistic predictions concerning current affairs.[22] This took place on the eve of President Nixon's visits to China and the USSR in 1972. The kinds of events for which subjects were asked to assess probabilities were of the form:

China: (1) The USA will establish a permanent diplomatic mission in Peking, but not grant diplomatic recognition; (2) President Nixon will meet Mao at least once; (3) President Nixon will announce that his trip was successful;

USSR: (1) A group of Soviet Jews will be arrested attempting to speak with President Nixon; (2) The USA and the USSR will agree to a joint space program. [22]

Subjects made their probabilistic predictions before Nixon's visits and, some time after the visits, were unexpectedly asked to recall what their probabilistic predictions had been. In addition, they were asked to indicate whether they thought the actual events had occurred. Results showed that subjects' recollections of the probabilities of events that had occurred were larger than the probabilities they assigned before the events did occur. There was also a tendency for the recalled probabilities of events that did not occur to be lower than the probabilities initially assigned. With hindsight, the subjects were apparently not too 'surprised' by what did and what did not happen.

The knowledge that an event has occurred seems to restructure one's memory. Our memory of the past is not a memory of the uncertainties of the past, rather it is a reconstruction of past events in terms of what actually occurred. Furthermore, that past is structured in a way that makes some kind of coherent sense to the individual, for example concerning the relationship between what actually happened and *particular* (but not all) antecedent events.

Hindsight versus foresight

What is the difference between foresight (i.e. predicting into the future) and hindsight (i.e. looking backwards)? When we look forward it is not clear what particular events or chain of events will or will not lead to the occurrence or non-occurrence of the event of interest to us. Many different paths could lead, or fail to lead, to the uncertain outcome. Furthermore, 'unexpected' events occur with an alarming frequency. Who, for example, a year before the event, would have predicted the election of a Polish Pope in 1978? However, by the 1980s it is possible that this event will seem in retrospect to have been almost inevitable given both apparent disagreements amongst Italian cardinals and the position of the Catholic Church in Eastern Europe. Prediction requires considerable powers of imagination and both the ability and willingness to entertain several hypotheses simultaneously. Keeping one's options open is not a tidy exercise and can induce considerable anxiety.

Postdiction, or hindsight, on the other hand, requires little imagination and is an invitation to impose a causal structure on a sequence of past events. Furthermore, subjectively there is less uncertainty than in prediction problems concerning the events that 'caused' what happened. One can believe any chain that seems plausible since it was seen to precede the event.

Implications of hindsight bias

The marked presence of hindsight biases in the studies by Fischhoff and his colleagues raises a number of important issues concerning: (a) judgements of the apparent failures (and successes) of others; (b) distortions in memory; (c) overcoming bias; and (d) learning from experience.

Judging others   History will undoubtedly remember Chamberlain as the person who failed to understand Hitler's true intentions in 1938. With the benefit of hindsight, we all condemn Chamberlain for his lack of foresight. Furthermore, Chamberlain-like incidents and corresponding condemnations occur with alarming frequency in most organizations. Comments are commonly heard such as 'Surely Bill must have known that our competitors were going to start a rival campaign at that time. All indications pointed to just that.'* However, it is not necessarily true that Chamberlain's judgement was any more defective than that of many other people of his day. But his judgement was made public and events proved him wrong. In the same vein, Fischhoff cites the case of what happened when a certain 'life' prisoner absconded from the Oregon State Penitentiary when released on an overnight social pass.[21] The warden of the prison promptly came under heavy fire from both the local newspaper and the Governor of the State of Oregon. It should have been known, it was said, that in the light of the particular prisoner's criminal record, there was a high probability he would abscond. However, in defence of the prison warden, it should be added that the man with the bad criminal record had also been a model prisoner. Perhaps, as Fischhoff suggests, the only way to test whether the warden should be blamed for his decision to issue a pass, would be to ask wardens of other prisons to examine the records of several prisoners (including that of the absconding prisoner presented in anonymous form), and to see what their predictions would have been. With hindsight, the decision to issue a pass seems to have been a terrible mistake. At the time the decision was taken it might have been quite reasonable, given what was known.

Distortions in memory   Memory clearly plays tricks with judgement in allowing rationalizations after the event. Above I have indicated some cases where we are quick to blame people for apparently avoidable errors. However, it must also be the case that people take the wrong decision but get away with it, and yet history—i.e. our hindsightful judgement—does not blame them. Indeed, given the above results, one can seriously question whether attributions of foresight with which many 'great' men have been credited could have been entirely fortuitous. For example, was Lord Nelson just lucky in the decisions he made in his crucial naval battles?

It is clear that hindsight bias implies distortion in memory. However, the point should also be made that in many circumstances this can be functional for the

---

* The writer recalls an incident in an organization known to him where no-one made any comment on certain predictions inherent in the annual budget. However, when it became clear that a particular source of funds would fail to materialize, many people wanted to indict the person responsible for his lack of 'judgement'.

individual. Most of our learning about the environment (see Chapter 5) is based on observing or experiencing relationships between events that occur. Furthermore, given the limited capacity of memory, it is important to store and organize events in a coherent manner that allows recall. Our environments are characterized more by the lack than the presence of useful relationships and thus it is clearly economical (in terms of memory) to concentrate and remember those that work. Similarly, forgetting relationships that you tried but that did not work is also 'cost-effective'.[23] For example, when you drive a car you learn a relationship between turning the steering wheel and your position on the road. You do not need to learn that depressing the clutch pedal in a certain way will not cause the car to move to the right. Many relationships which we use in daily life can be comprehended by observation or experience of the occurrence of two events. Indeed, it could be said that the majority of our judgements—which involve mainly short-term physical actions (e.g. judging distance when walking so as not to bump into objects or people)—are of this nature. Restructuring one's understanding of the world in terms of what is observed to happen is clearly useful, adaptive behaviour. Furthermore we are so proficient at doing this that the reaction is carried out continuously at an unconscious level.

However, and as noted in Chapter 5, learning relationships only by what is observable can lead to biases. Noting non-occurrences is often also necessary for inferring relationships. In particular, prediction problems which are difficult in the sense that outcome feedback is either not observable until some time after the judgement or is biased by the environment, require observation of non-occurrences to validate relationships (see Chapter 5). These problems usually involve more conceptual than physical relationships (for example, predicting a candidate's future success in a particular job as opposed to avoiding the tea-trolley in the corridor), and can have large consequences. As discussed briefly in Chapter 1, the nature of the human environment is changing in the sense that conceptual skills are becoming more important than physical skills. Use of higher mental processes places greater demands on memory (e.g. requiring that attention be directed to non-occurrences as well as occurrences of events as discussed in Chapter 5). Distortions in memory induced by the knowledge of outcomes, as described above, are therefore not only an important source of bias. They are becoming increasingly important as demands for conceptual skills grow.

Overcoming bias   Is it possible to 'debias' distortions in memory caused by the knowledge of outcomes? In one experiment, Fischhoff explicitly warned subjects of possible biases due to knowledge of outcomes. However, this manipulation had no effect in that the subjects warned of hindsight bias exhibited the same degree of bias as subjects who had not been warned.[24] People have a remarkable capacity for assimilating facts as being consistent with their preceding notions and thus seeming as though they 'knew it all along'. For example, how many times do people exhibit surprise when being told the result of an investigation, be it a scientific study, a market research report or a judicial enquiry? It has been said, and in the writer's experience justifiably so, that there are three stages in attitudes toward certain types of investigation. First, the investigators are told that what they propose to do is impossible.* (Imagine, for example, a study proposed to investigate the efficiency of TV advertising in a business firm.) Second, when people are told the results of the study they typically comment on how they seem evident. ('Sure, the more you advertise on TV the more you sell.') And third, when people accept the implications of findings they either say that they 'knew it all along' or that they already do it. ('Of course, that's why we advertise on TV.')

How can one overcome the bias of 'outcome' knowledge and so force people to realize the real significance of events? In the context of reporting results of scientific experiments, Slovic and Fischhoff attacked this problem by first giving their subjects false information concerning the outcomes of the experiments.[25] Once the subjects had been told and had assimilated the false outcomes they were then given the true results. This manipulation was found to be quite successful in that it overcame 'hindsight' bias. That is, it seems that when the true experimental results were made known, subjects were forced to 'undo' the mental effort they had previously expended in assimilating the false outcomes with their prior notions. That is, giving knowledge of the true outcomes following the false information provided a stimulus capable of overcoming hindsight bias.

Now, without looking back, do you recall who won the British–Gurkha war described earlier in the chapter? Why did the Gurkhas win?

In fact, it was the British who won that particular war. Look back at the passage. After the passage, I deliberately gave you false 'outcome feedback' in order to illustrate the point made above concerning means to debias the effects of outcome feedback.

Learning from experience The experiments on hindsight bias raise a number of questions concerning both people's ability to learn from experience and to make predictions. Consider, for example, the fact that outcomes fail to surprise people as much as they should. This has several implications: first, if people are not surprised this means that they apparently thought they had little to learn in the first instance. In other words, outcomes are not instructive. However, predictive 'track records' often indicate considerable inconsistencies (as documented in many chapters of this book) and the expression of excessive confidence in predictive judgement is a common human failing. Learning from experience (as also discussed in Chapter 5) is thus not evident, and memory distortions may also often be functional for the individual. It would seem that Nature has determined a trade-off between two kinds of costs: storage in memory and learning from

---

* The author has had precisely this experience when starting several research projects—an attitude expressed by both scientists and Laymen. Indeed, when people do not tell me a project is 'impossible' I now seriously question whether it is worthwhile!

experience. A real issue to be faced is whether that trade-off is appropriate in today's world.

A second implication of lack of outcome surprise concerns people's ability to construct causal explanations. There can be little doubt that the ability to construct good causal explanations is important in prediction, since accurate prediction depends on identifying key variables in the environment and their relationship to the event predicted. However, if people are unduly influenced by knowledge of outcomes in explaining the past, this means that they will accept sufficient (although not necessary) explanations too easily. For example, if increases in TV advertising appear to precede increases in the sales of the product advertised, it is easy to adopt a causal model that advertising leads to sales. However, other explanations are possible, for example corresponding availability of products at the point of sales, salesmen being told to make special efforts at the time of advertising campaigns, etc. A major problem of many post-hoc explanations is that they are not, and indeed often cannot be, put to predictive test. If people accept outcome explanations too easily, this reduces the discipline of seeking alternative explanations for phenomena observed in the past and, as a consequence, the ability to imagine and create alternative causal schemes for predicting the future. As discussed in Chapter 5, people rarely seek information that could negate their preconceptions, rather they look for possible confirming evidence. This tendency clearly interacts with the fallibility of memory discussed here in producing biased conceptions of the world.

A further important source of bias in interpreting outcomes arises from the fact that outcomes result from both actions people take and chance occurrences in the environment. As discussed in Chapter 2, people do not have good intuitions concerning the nature of randomness, and this can lead to errors in interpreting events. In particular, people are remarkably insensitive at determining whether outcomes should be attributed to their skill in a particular situation or to chance factors. Indeed, factors of chance and skill are closely intertwined in people's experience. For example, to what extent is your present job due to skill on your part or some combination of chance factors or both? This is a difficult question. However, there is disturbing evidence from psychological experiments that even in situations which people know have been governed by chance mechanisms (e.g. coin tossing), observations of success at a task are followed by attributions of skill. Furthermore, attempts to debias the supposed causes of observed phenomena fail. It seems that once memory of an outcome has been assigned a cause, it is extremely hard to erase that cause–effect relationship in the person's mind (see also above). In particular, in chance–skill situations there is a strong tendency to assign the observation of success to skill, and the observation of failure to chance.[26]

What remedies exist to correct the judgemental fallibilities noted above? I can only repeat what has been said in earlier chapters: first, an attitude of mind which is prepared both to admit the operation of chance factors and the possibility of multiple explanations; and second, to bolster memory by record-keeping. People should be encouraged to record both their predictions and the bases on which predictive judgements are made.

SUMMARY

This chapter has considered the role of memory in predictive judgement. Discussion of memory as an integral part of intuitive judgement has not, however, been restricted to this chapter, since it also affects the topics treated in other chapters.

It was emphasized at the outset that memory is not like the dump store of a computer where all past experience exists and can be referenced intact. Rather, human memory is limited and would seem to depend on two basic principles. First, information can be encoded in more or less efficient ways and this acts to increase or decrease what is recalled, i.e. memory capacity. Second, the coding process itself depends upon the meaning attached to information. This meaning both holds information and associations together in memory and permits recall of events. However, recall is based on fragments of information which the mind construes as a coherent whole according to the meaning attached to the particular fragments recalled and their associations. Perception of events, their interpretation and extrapolation to future events (i.e. prediction), thus depend crucially on a limited, fallible, incomplete system which is held together by the meaning given to events in the environment, such meaning itself being a function of previous perception and experiences. Although deficient in many respects, people's memories usually work remarkably well for a wide variety of tasks. And forgetting can often be as adaptive and functional as remembering. Indeed mnemonists (people with phenomenal memory) indicate considerable dysfunctional aspects of 'excessive' memory—inability to infer useful rules from the environment, for example, or in more familiar terms incapacity to 'see the wood from the trees'.[27] On the other hand, in a world that places increasingly greater demands on conceptual skills, certain deficiences in ordinary memory become more critical.

Why is some information more salient in memory and thus weighed more heavily in judgement than other data? The chapter explored and discussed the 'availability' heuristic, whereby the relative frequency of an event is related to the ease with which specific instances can be recalled. The fact that vivid, concrete 'case data' often outweigh more representative, but abstract and pallid statistical data was also discussed and illustrated. Incidents, which can be encoded on several sensory dimensions (e.g. sight and sound), weigh heavily in memory and thus in subsequent judgement.

The chapter also explored people's hindsight biases, that is the phenomenon of 'creeping determinism' whereby past events seem to have been inevitable. Once the outcome of an event is known, memory of events that preceded the outcome are reconstructed in a manner that distorts perceptions of the prediction task prior to having knowledge of the outcome of the event. It was pointed out that hindsight bias has important implications for how people judge others, the ability to learn from experience and to imagine, construct and entertain alternative explanatory hypotheses; the latter, it was emphasized, being particularly important in predictive activity. Finally, the necessity to bolster memory by record-keeping in order to improve predictive ability was again emphasized.

NOTES AND REFERENCES

1. This would be an example of the so-called 'representativeness' heuristic. See D. Kahneman and A. Tversky, Subjective probability: A judgment of representativeness. *Cognitive Psychology*, 1972, **3**, 430–454.
2. The examples are taken from C. E. Osgood, *Method and theory in experimental psychology*. New York: Oxford University Press, 1953, p. 214.
3. The classical reference concerning the use of coding systems in memory is G. A. Miller, The magical number seven, plus or minus two: Some limits on our capacity for processing information. *Psychological Review*, 1956, **63**, 81–96.
4. J. S. Bruner and L. J. Postman, On the perception of incongruity: A paradigm, *Journal of Personality*, 1949, **18**, 206–223.
5. See, for example, R. Buckhout, Eyewitness testimony. *Scientific American*, 1974, **231**, 23–31; and E. Loftus, The incredible eyewitness. *Psychology Today*, December 1974, 116–119.
6. It should be pointed out that the interpretation given here to how memory 'works' is personal. Memory is, in fact, a hotly disputed and actively researched area in psychology. My own views on memory have been heavily influenced by two texts: A. D. Baddeley, *The psychology of memory*. New York: Basic Books, 1976; and U. Neisser, *Cognitive psychology*. New York: Appleton–Century–Crofts, 1967.
7. A. Tversky and D. Kahneman, Availability: A heuristic for judging frequency and probability. *Cognitive Psychology*, 1973, **5**, 207–232.
8. S. Lichtenstein, P. Slovic, B. Fischhoff, M. Layman, and B. Combs. Judged frequency of lethal events. *Journal of Experimental Psychology: Human Learning and Memory*, 1978, **4**, 551–578. See also B. Combs and P. Slovic, Causes of death: Biased newspaper coverage and biased judgments, *Journalism Quarterly*, in press.
9. D. E. Detmer, D. G. Fryback, and K. Gassner. Heuristics and biases in medical decision-making, *Journal of Medical Education*, 1978, **53**, 682–683.
10. R. P. Abelson, Script processing in attitude formation and decision making. In J. S. Carroll and J. W. Payne (Eds.), *Cognition and social behavior*. Hillsdale, N.J.: Lawrence Erlbaum, 1976, 33–45.
11. A. Paivio, Mental imagery in associative learning and memory. *Psychological Review*, 1969, **76**, 241–263.
12. B. R. Russell. *Philosophy*. New York: Norton, 1927, p. 269.
13. R. E. Nisbett, E. Borgida, R. Crandall, and H. Reed, *Popular induction: Information is not necessarily informative*. In Carroll and Payne, Reference 10, p. 129.
14. E. Borgida and R. E. Nisbett, The differential impact of abstract vs. concrete information on decisions. *Journal of Applied Social Psychology*, 1977, **7**, 258–271.
15. R. M. Hogarth, C. Michaud, and J.-L. Mery, Decision behavior in urban development: A methodological approach and substantive considerations, *Acta Psychologica*, in press.
16. K. Knafl and G. Burkett, Professional socialization in a surgical speciality: Acquiring medical judgment. *Social Science of Medicine*, 1975, **9**, 397–404.
17. P. Slovic, B. Fischhoff, and S. Lichtenstein, Cognitive processes and societal risk taking. In Carroll and Payne, Reference 10, pp. 165–184.

18. R. Nisbett and L. Ross, *Human inference: Strategies and shortcomings of social judgment*. Englewood Cliffs, N.J.: Prentice-Hall, 1980, p. 57.
19. W. C. Thompson, R. M. Reyes, and G. H. Bower, Delayed effects of availability on judgment. *Journal of Personality and Social Psychology*, in press.
20. E. L. Woodward, *Age of reform*. London: Oxford University Press, 1938, pp. 383–384.
21. B. Fischhoff, Hindsight: Thinking backward? *Psychology Today*, April 1975, 71–76; and B. Fischhoff, Hindsight ≠ foresight: The effect of outcome knowledge on judgment under uncertainty. *Journal of Experimental Psychology: Human Perception and Performance*, 1975, **1**, 288–299.
22. B. Fischhoff and R. Beyth, "I knew it would happen": —Remembered probabilities of once-future things. *Organizational Behavior and Human Performance*, 1975, **13**, 1–16.
23. M. Toda, the design of a fungus-eater: A model of human behavior in an unsophisticated environment. *Behavioral Science*, 1962, **7**, 164–183.
24. B. Fischhoff, Perceived informativeness of facts. *Journal of Experimental Psychology: Human Perception and Performance*, 1977, **3**, 349–358.
25. P. Slovic and B. Fischhoff, On the psychology of experimental surprises. *Journal of Experimental Psychology: Human Perception and Performance*, 1977, **3**, 544–551.
26. See the instructive paper by E. J. Langer, The psychology of chance. *Journal for the Theory of Social Behaviour*, 1977, **7**, 185–207.
27. A. R. Luria. *The mind of a mnemonist*. New York: Basic Books, 1968.

CHAPTER 7

Creativity, imagination, and choice

Imagination and creativity play key roles in judgement and choice. For example, predictive judgement requires the ability to imagine possible outcomes, or at least to assess the relative likelihood of different outcomes. Similarly, in many choice situations alternatives are not given but must be created. Furthermore, in the act of choice the ability to imagine how one would like different alternatives is crucial (i.e. in the expression of preference). Indeed, it can be said that a person who exhibits neither creativity nor imagination is incapable of expressing 'free' judgement or choice. Such a person would have no control over his or her behaviour, which would be determined entirely by the whims of the environment.

In making choices, therefore, people use imagination. It also follows that to the extent that a person has large powers of imagination, the more rich and varied are his or her choice alternatives. This point has been implicitly illustrated in preceding chapters. It was pointed out, for example, that one cause of poor predictive performance was the failure to conceive of different possibilities in the environment. In addition, reliance on habit in choice (for example, when shopping) can both restrict the range of a person's experience and opportunities for exercising imagination through choice.

Imagination and creativity are invariably linked. People thought to be creative are imaginative, and vice versa. My own view is that imagination is a necessary but not sufficient condition for creativity, a viewpoint that is elaborated below.

However, like judgement, both creativity and imagination are subject to popular misconceptions. For example, creativity is often considered to be a gift which people either do or do not have. This is particularly the case when creativity is thought of in relation to scientific, musical, artistic, or literary genius. Einstein, Mozart, Rembrandt, and Shakespeare, for example, were clearly creative geniuses. However, and as stated above, whenever a person makes a conscious judgement or choice some degree of imagination and/or creativity is involved. What distinguishes the genius from the ordinary person, therefore, is not the act of creation or imagination itself, but the degree and scope of the act. Imagination and creativity should be thought of as varying on continua as opposed to being categoric qualities.

This chapter aims to stress the importance of imagination and creativity in judgement and choice. Indeed, the central thesis is that the quality of judgement and choice depends crucially upon these variables. The chapter begins with a discussion of the nature of creativity and characteristics of creative people. It is argued that given even a minimal level of intelligence, most people are both creative and imaginative and, furthermore, are capable of becoming even more so—although not without limit and with little probability of achieving acts of genius. The benchmark of creativity people should use to calibrate their own creative performance is not that of geniuses but rather their own habitual level. Most people *are* capable of increasing their own levels of creativity. Indeed, one clear finding that emerges from the literature is that relative creativity and imagination are a function of the amount of mental effort people are used to and willing to expend. Several devices or techniques for increasing creativity have been proposed (e.g., brainstorming, synectics, morphological analysis). These are briefly examined and discussed.

CREATIVITY AND THE CREATIVE

What is a creative act? A dictionary definition refers to the verb 'create' as the act of bringing something 'into existence'. By this definition, therefore, the use of almost all language is an example of creativity in the sense that almost all sentences are unique. However, ordinary speech is usually not considered creative in that almost everyone can speak. Furthermore, few people would characterize a nonsensical sentence as a creative act even though it might be original. Creativity, as generally understood, therefore has more meaning ascribed to it than simply bringing into existence something that did not exist previously.

Jerome Bruner argues that a creative act is one 'that produces effective surprise'.[1] He further specifies three kinds of 'effectiveness':

(1) *Predictive effectiveness.* This is exemplified by the discovery of laws in science which allow the prediction of certain phenomena. Consider, for example, the discovery of the law concerning the speed of falling bodies.
(2) *Formal effectiveness* by which Bruner means 'an ordering of elements in such a way that one sees relationships that were not evident before, groupings that were before not present, ways of putting things together not before within reach.' In this domain he cites works in mathematics, logic and, perhaps, music.
(3) *Metaphoric effectiveness* which is also 'effective by connecting domains of experience that were before apart, but with the form of connectedness that has the discipline of art.'

In fact, what Bruner—and indeed many other writers on creativity—are saying amounts roughly to the following. Creativity occurs when ideas, 'things' or associations are produced in some new combination that is either useful or appropriate for a particular problem or purpose, and/or is aesthetically pleasing. Studies show that people can agree whether certain acts or people are more or less creative, although there is less agreement about the actual definition of 'creativity'.[2] The necessity for the 'appropriateness' of a creative act is nonetheless a dimension on which most people would agree, although the extent to which a single act is appropriate under particular circumstances could be the subject of debate. Originality and appropriateness are probably the two most important aspects of creativity.

Examples of great creative acts are easy to indicate and can be used to illustrate the 'definition' given above. Einstein's theory of relativity is an example of reconstructing and seeing physical reality from a new, and more 'useful' perspective. The apocryphal story of Newton asking why the apple fell is an example of a creative question that lead to reconceptualizing many problems. The interesting aspect of the Newton story is that millions of people before Newton knew that apples fall from trees. Newton's genius was to ask 'why'. Creativity thus often involves questioning what one has always taken for granted. And indeed, the posing of a question can be a most significant creative contribution in that it allows people to see relationships in the environment from a different perspective. Keynes, for example, was a genius in that he was able to look at economic questions in a manner quite foreign to other economists of his day. Similarly, the businessman who is both imaginative and creative enough to see problems from the viewpoints of other persons in his environment (e.g. customers, suppliers, unions, etc.) is at a great advantage.

A statement was made previously that imagination was a necessary but not sufficient condition for creativity. By this I mean the following: in order to be creative, one must be able to imagine new associations between ideas, concepts or things. However, seeing novel associations does not necessarily lead to creativity. For example, one aspect of creativity that psychologists have investigated concerns the ability to produce unusual associations to given words. However, if this were adopted as a criterion for creativity, then the places with the greatest density of creative people would be mental hospitals.[2] Schizophrenics, for example, continually see relationships and associations which are novel—but dysfunctional. Imagination, therefore, is necessary to generate new solutions to problems. However, there is no guarantee that the new solutions will be better than the old. We return to this point below.

Several writers have tried to identify different stages in creative activity—and many such 'schemes' are in fact quite similar.[3] Johnson, for example, identifies three stages:[4]

(1) *Preparation*, during which the individual collects material or otherwise 'prepares' for the creative activity. This stage could include reading or thinking about the problem. Consider, for example, that you are faced with a problem concerning how to handle a contract with a new supplier. You would probably spend some time discussing issues with colleagues, considering other examples or precedents, thinking about the pecularities of the particular case, etc.

(2) *Production*—at this stage ideas relevant to the problem at hand are generated.

(3) *Judgement*, by which Johnson means evaluation of the ideas prior to selecting a 'creative' solution.

Whereas different stages have been identified, it is not necessarily the case that people follow these stages in linear fashion. For example, the judgement (more precisely evaluation) of an idea could take place before other ideas have been generated. Ideas that have been suppressed could reappear, etc.

How do people handle the above three stages of creative thinking? This question has intrigued psychologists for years and has been investigated by several methodologies.

Introspection

One interesting approach has been to examine the thoughts and recollections of eminent creators (scientists, artists, musicians, writers, philosophers) concerning their own creative efforts.[5] Although there must be doubt concerning people's ability to report on their own mental processes[6]—and particularly after the fact—the investigations have indicated some interesting insights.

One issue concerns the role of conscious and unconscious processes in creative thought. For many creators concerned with particular problems, there seems to be a feeling that solutions appear suddenly as a result of some subliminal process. For example, the mathematician Poincaré cites a case where:

> One evening, contrary to my custom, I drank black coffee and could not sleep. Ideas rose in clouds; I felt them collide until pairs interlocked, so to speak, making a stable combination. By the next morning I had established the existence of a class of Fuchsian functions, those which come from the hypergeometric series; I only had to write out the results, which took but a few hours.[5]

Most people know the feeling where, when bothered by a problem, ideas and potential solutions suddenly seem to emerge from the unconscious. Bertrand Russell has stated that he found it fruitless to try and push his creative work to completion by sheer will power. Rather, he found it necessary to wait until his subconscious had made some further development.[5]

Mozart too reported similar subliminal experiences:

> When I am, as it were, completely myself, entirely alone, and of good cheer—say, travelling in a carriage, or walking after a good meal, or during the night when I cannot sleep; it is on such occasions that my ideas flow best and most abundantly. *Whence* and *how* they come, I know not; nor can I force them. Those pleasures that please me I retain in memory, and am accustomed, as I have been told, to hum them to myself. If I continue in this way, it soon occurs to me how I may turn this or that morsel to account, so as to make a good dish of it, that is to say, agreeably to the rules of counterpoint, to the peculiarities of the various instruments, etc.[5]

The above quotations, which seem to imply that great creative acts just happen to 'great' people, could be thought to contradict the notion expressed earlier that creativity can be achieved by most people. There is, however, no contradiction. The people cited above were preoccupied by problems and had presumably concluded the 'preparation' stage of creativity. What seems to happen, if this first stage has been adequately effected, is that the mind races on subconsciously working on the problem. Furthermore, some mechanism exists, which allows the bringing into consciousness of an adequate solution—or at least, these notable creators only report the good solutions they found in the above way. Apocryphal stories exist, for example, of people preoccupied by problems waking up in the middle of the night believing they have found a solution. However, even if they commit the 'solution' to writing, they are unable to interpret it the next morning.

Campbell's model

Campbell has proposed a model whereby creative thought is but one aspect of a general process by which people acquire knowledge concerning the world.[7] He postulates—in somewhat abstract terms—three conditions / mechanisms: first, the production of 'variations' (for example, the generation and combination of different possible associations between elements of a problem); second, a consistent selection process, whereby particular combinations produced can be picked out; and third, a mechanism for preserving and reproducing the selected variations. That is, an ability to notice and replicate actions that have proven to be successful. These processes are, of course, precisely what occurs in trial-and-error learning. A concrete example would be the following. Imagine that you need to find the appropriate spanner with which to tighten a bolt. You try several spanners until one fits. You use that spanner and tighten the bolt. The next time you need to tighten that kind of bolt, you will know what spanner to take. As stated above, it is Campbell's thesis that creative thinking involves precisely the same principles as trial-and-error learning. However, in conceptual problems, instead of manipulating different spanners in order to find the one that fits the particular problem, the individual is involved in a series of 'thought trials', or imaginary experiences attempting to find a solution. That is, a problem presents itself to an individual, who then attempts several 'thought trials' until a satisfactory solution is obtained. Campbell terms this process 'blind variation and selective retention'—'blind' in the sense that attempts at solving problems are often made more or less at random. As he states:

> . . . it must be emphasized that insofar as thought achieves innovation, the internal emitting of thought trials one by one is blind, lacking prescience or foresight. The process *as a whole* of course provides 'foresight' for the overt level of behavior, once the process has blindly stumbled into a thought trial that 'fits' the selection criterion accompanied by the 'something clicked', 'Eureka', or 'aha-erlebnis' that usually marks the successful termination of the process.[7]
> (Reproduced by permission of the American Psychological Association)

This somewhat mechanical explanation of creative thought which emphasizes the role of chance both raises objections, which Campbell meets, and has many implications. Amongst possible objections are that (1) Campbell's scheme would seem to make no allowance for observations of people achieving 'insightful' solutions to problems, (2) the existence of individual differences and particularly creative geniuses, and (3) the enormous amount of thought trials that are necessary to make the creative steps inherent in increases in knowledge. Campbell counters these arguments by noting, first, that the sensation of 'insightful' solutions to problems occur *after* a problem has been solved—that is, after blind search has hit an appropriate solution. (Recall the discussion in Chapter 6 concerning how outcome knowledge seems to restructure memory and make the outcome seem inevitable after the event). Second, trial-and-error responses refer not only to actual thought trials but classes of thought trials or responses. To make an analogy, when faced with the problem of tightening a bolt, the individual does not need to try more than one screwdriver to realize that that type of instrument will not be equal to the task. The class of instrument 'spanner' can, however, be seen or remembered to fit the type of problem. People therefore learn—through trial-and-error—approaches to classes of problems.

Third, an important implication of Campbell's model is that chance plays a crucial role in creative thinking. In this he sees no problem. Indeed, Campbell warns people against attributing special 'creative powers' to particular individuals:

> Explanations in terms of special antecedents will very often be irrelevant and . . . the causal-interpretative biases of our minds make us prone to such over-interpretations, to *post-hoc-ergo-propter-hoc* interpretations, deifying the creative genius to whom we impute a capacity for direct insight instead of mental flounderings and blind-alley entrances of the kind we are aware typify our own thought processes. Ernst Mach (1896) notes our nostalgia for the directly-knowing genius: 'To our humiliation we learn that even the greatest men are born more for life than for science in the extent to which even they are indebted to accident' (p. 175)[7]
> (Reproduced by permission of the American Psychological Association)

The dangers of causal attributions to chance occurrences have, of course, been emphasized several times already in this book.

Campbell does not deny the importance of individual differences in creativity. Indeed, his model points to sources of differences. People will be more creative to the extent that: (1) they can produce a wider range and number of thought trials (hence imagination is necessary but not sufficient for creativity). In this, clearly motivation to produce thoughts and 'practice' in doing so are important. That is, individual 'investment' in thinking increases the probability of being creative; (2) a wider experience of life equips people with the capability of greater creativity (by increasing the range of possible thought trials they can produce); (3) living and working in an atmosphere with a wide tolerance for exploratory behaviour clearly liberates the mind for generating creative solutions; and (4) the ability to seize upon solutions that are appropriate. It is insufficient merely to generate possible solutions to a problem. The individual must decide *which* solution should be implemented. Such an 'editing talent' can vary considerably from individual to individual. In addition to selecting the appropriate solution to a given problem, one should also note that wide scanning of possible solutions can generate solutions to other problems. Consequently, by engaging in large numbers of thought trials, the creative individual also increases his chances of solving other problems. Indeed in science, the art of serendipity (i.e. recognizing that one has generated a solution to problem B while searching for a solution to problem A) has long been recognized—witness Fleming's 'accidental' discovery of penicillin.

Finally, Campbell's model points to the fact that to solve problems often requires what seems like a prohibitively large number of thought trials. This is indeed the case. However, Campbell points out that we only achieve satisfactory solutions to a very small number of the problems facing us. We may survive without solutions but that is, of course, a different matter. Furthermore, we are usually unaware of the extent to which many of our actions are 'sub-optimal'. In addition,

> The tremendous number of non-productive thought trials . . . must not be under-estimated. Think of what a small proportion of thought becomes conscious, and of conscious thought what a small proportion gets uttered, what a still smaller fragment gets published, and what a small proportion of what is published is used by the next intellectual generation. There is a tremendous wastefulness, slowness, and rarity of achievement.[7]
>
> (Reproduced by permission of the American Psychological Association.)

To sum up, Campbell's position is that the invention of creative solutions depends upon generating many thought experiments or combinations of factors possibly capable of leading to solutions. To this is added the notion that a mechanism must exist to select, test and retain 'successful' solutions. Many creativity techniques described later in this chapter depend precisely upon these kinds of notions.

Distinguishing the creative

What distinguishes people who are creative from those who are not so creative? As would be expected from the discussion of the Campbell model, creative people tend to work hard. That is, they engage in a greater number of thought experiments than the less creative. A series of studies has examined the characteristics of creative people and particularly scientists. Although one clearly cannot generalize from scientists, the list of characteristics of productive scientists presented in Table 7.1 is indicative.

On reviewing the list in Table 7.1, Johnson notes that what seems to emerge reads like 'a universal catalog of virtues.' However, he goes on to say that 'creative thinkers are not, as far as we know, any more agreeable, friendly, considerate, or tolerant than other people. They are seldom described as happy and well-rounded, nor are they accused, any more than others, of excessive modesty.'[4]

As stated above, the list in Table 7.1 was based on a group of scientists and thus certain traits are possibly not applicable to all types of creative people. Novelists and dramatists, for example, may well exhibit preferences for people rather than things (item 2), and they may also tend to be more interested and involved in interpersonal relations. In another study of scientists, Roe noted important differences in these respects between physical and social scientists.[9]

Table 7.1   Characteristics of productive scientists[8]
(Reproduced by permission of John Wiley & Sons Inc.)

---

(1) A high degree of autonomy, self-sufficiency, self-direction.
(2) A preference for mental manipulations involving things rather than people: a somewhat distant or detached attitude in interpersonal relations, and a preference for intellectually challenging situations rather than socially challenging ones.
(3) High ego strength and emotional stability.
(4) A liking for method, precision, exactness.
(5) A preference for such defence mechanisms as repression and isolation in dealing with affect and instinctual energies.
(6) A high degree of personal dominance but a dislike of personally toned controversy.
(7) A high degree of control of impulse, amounting almost to over-control: relatively little talkativeness, gregariousness, impulsiveness.
(8) A liking for abstract thinking, with considerable tolerance of cognitive ambiguity.
(9) Marked independence of judgement, rejection of group pressures toward conformity in thinking.
(10) Superior general intelligence.
(11) An early, very broad interest in intellectual activities.
(12) A drive toward comprehensiveness and elegance in explanation.
(13) A special interest in the kind of 'wagering' which involves pitting oneself against uncertain circumstances in which one's own effort can be the deciding factor.

Perhaps the most important traits of creative people are high autonomy (item 1) and independence of judgement (item 9). As stated above, creativity depends not only on the willingness to form new mental associations, but also judgement in selecting new combinations and the strength of character to suggest them to others, possibly at the expense of being ridiculed on occasion.[10] Independence of judgement and an ability to go against popular streams of thought are clearly important. Indeed, many important innovations are precisely of this nature. That is, once creative ideas have been suggested, it is not the case that everyone will necessarily accept them—witness, for example, the fact that many great authors and artists are not recognized until after their death, the persecution Galileo had to endure for his ideas, etc. The ideas of creative people often lead them into direct conflict with the trends of their time and they need the courage to be able to stand alone.

The above comments apply, of course, to the world of business as much as in science and the arts. As an example, consider Sir Freddie Laker, the entrepreneur who successfully introduced cut-rate trans-Atlantic air fares. Not only did Laker have brilliant ideas about the economies of flying the Atlantic, he was also willing and able to fight governments and a world-wide cartel (IATA) to bring his idea to fruition. Indeed, one could argue that his willingness and ability to fight the authorities was as, if not more, important than his ideas concerning low-cost

118

fares. Anyone who has tried to bring about a social innovation in an organization will recognize both the difficulty of the task (hence the need for a wide range of productive ideas) and the personal difficulty of implementation. In *The Prince*, Machiavelli stated this point particularly clearly:

> There is nothing more difficult to take in hand, more perilous to conduct, or more uncertain in its success, than to take the lead in the introduction of a new order of things, because the innovator has for enemies all those who have done well under the old conditions, and lukewarm defenders in those who may do well under the new.

Consider, for example, what would happen in your own organization if you were to introduce an important cost-saving innovation which would require, amongst other things, that many people alter their work habits in a way that could threaten their job security. (Such issues are, of course, the crux of the matter in many attempts to 'rationalize' certain industries or companies.)

To summarize, creativity consists of finding new combinations of ideas, concepts, or 'things' which are *appropriate*. The creative process consists of three stages: (1) preparation; (2) production; and (3) judgement (i.e. evaluation of ideas produced at stage 2). To be effective as creators, people need not only to be willing and able to invest in mental effort, but also to have *strength* of character and judgement. Creative ideas are not always immediately recognized as such and the ultimate effectiveness of creative thought depends heavily on social forces.

CONDITIONS AFFECTING CREATIVITY

Many investigations have centred on conditions affecting the production of creative ideas. These can be considered as they affect the three stages described above (i.e. preparation, production and judgement).

As might be expected, the amount of preparation a person has relative to a problem will affect the production of ideas. However, it is not true that more preparation necessarily leads to more creative ideas. Prior experience with the type of problem considered, or attempts at creative effort, can also cause blockages and limit the subsequent production of ideas. People can become stuck in 'cages of thought' which preclude the exploration of ideas.

Consider, for example, the experiment which consisted of asking personnel working in a plant manufacturing spark plugs to name as many different possible uses of a spark plug as they could imagine. The respondents generated fewer alternatives than people who did not work in the plant and thus who had less prior experience with spark plugs.[4]

The Germans have a word *betriebsblind* (company blind) which describes how a person who has worked in a particular company for some time fails to see problems in new ways. And indeed, the success of consultants depends precisely on this fact. A major advantage of consultants lies in seeing problems with a fresh eye. Psychological research supports this anecdotal type of evidence. For example, a number of experiments have shown how experience with a type of problem can lead to lack of success in solving it. On considering the problem, the individual can become trapped by the direction of his own thought.[4] When this occurs, the individual is best advised to leave the problem and return to it later when the force of the 'direction' has subsided.

It should not, however, be inferred from the above that experience related to a problem is a hindrance to finding novel solutions. On the contrary, experience with similar problems can facilitate solutions. Furthermore, for many problems, knowledge which comes through experience is necessary to be even able to generate a solution. What is important is that the individual be able to 'turn a problem on its head' before contemplating solutions.

In preceding chapters the importance of the role of 'availability' of information in the environment or memory was noted. This has also been documented in studies of problem solving. Subjects in problem-solving experiments have been found to be unusually sensitive to aspects of the experimental situation which emphasize certain features of the problem. By moderating instructions, or even handling elements of the problem, experimenters are able to indicate cues which help or hinder the subjects.[11] Indeed, it almost seems that experimenters can manipulate the probability that people will solve particular problems by the use of such cues. The practical implications of these findings are clear. When facing a problem with which they are not familiar, people will be considerably affected by 'chance' observations of aspects of the particular situation. To follow Campbell's model outlined above, 'blind variation' will be initiated at the particular 'chance point' on which people happen to focus. Consequently, if the problem is such that its basic structure is not apparent, solutions will not be easily achieved. People should therefore spend considerable time looking at problems from different 'angles' before beginning to 'emit thought trials' in attempts to find solutions (see also comments above).

Motivation and attitudes are most important in the preparatory stages of creative activity. Excessive motivation can be dysfunctional in that it tends to channelize energy into excessively narrow thought patterns. Research indicates that more relaxed postures are called for. However, motivation must be high since persistence in mental activity is so important. The effect of attitudes was nicely illustrated in a study by Hyman.[12] Two groups of engineers were asked to examine attempts to design a system for recognizing boxes in an automatic warehouse. One group was asked to study the attempts critically and to list faults; the second group was instructed to be constructive and note the useful features of the different attempts. Subsequently the individuals in the two groups were asked to propose solutions to both this problem and a similar one. The engineers who had been asked to evaluate the earlier attempts constructively were subsequently found to generate better solutions to both problems. The implications of this and similar studies are far-reaching.[4] People who tend to examine the creative attempts of others in *constructive* rather than *destructive* ways probably stand more chance of creating constructive solutions themselves.

During the actual production of ideas, two important blocks have been identified: first, the way a person conceptualizes a problem based on prior experience (see above); and second, the criteria people use to evaluate solutions before suggesting them.

As an example of the inhibiting effects of prior 'cages of thought' on the production of ideas, consider the nine dots in Figure 7.1. Can you draw four straight lines that pass through all nine dots without lifting your pencil? Try it!

Most people assume that to solve this problem you are not supposed to allow the pencil to go outside the dots. However, to solve the problem, this is precisely what you must do—as illustrated in note 13. In other words, when faced with a problem, there is a natural tendency to limit one's attempts at solution within

Figure 7.1   The nine-dot exercise: Can you draw four (and only four) straight lines that pass through all nine dots without lifting your pencil? (Reproduced by permission of Penguin Books Ltd)

self-imposed constraints. However, such constraints are arbitrary. The first task, therefore, is to free oneself of such constraints. Creative people tend, in fact, to be remarkably unconstrained—which perhaps explains why their behaviour appears to be odd to other people. However, 'odd' behaviour allows one to see the world from many different vantage points and allows a greater and richer sampling of behaviour (i.e. a scanning of a wider range of associations). It is, of course, also true that many uncreative people affect 'odd' behaviour patterns. Indeed, it is not always easy to discriminate creative and uncreative 'odd-balls'.

Constraints are not, however, only imposed internally. The conventional habits and norms of society, and industry and commerce in particular, can be a great block to the production of ideas. Furthermore, the creative person is, almost by definition, not an 'organization man'. David Ogilvy, the Scotsman who made a fortune in the advertising business on Madison Avenue, writes:

> It is sad that the majority of men who are responsible for advertising today, both the agents and the clients, are so conventional. The business community wants remarkable advertising, but turns a cold shoulder to the kind of people who can produce it . . . Albert Lasker made $50,000,000 out of advertising, partly because he could stomach the atrocious manners of his great copywriters . . .[14]

Ogilvy's comments on his own creative processes and life-style are also worth reproducing:

> The creative process requires more than reason. Most original thinking isn't even verbal. It requires 'a groping experimentation with ideas, governed by intuitive hunches and inspired by the unconscious'. The majority of businessmen are incapable of original thinking, because they are unable to escape from the tyranny of reason. Their imaginations are blocked.
>
> I am almost incapable of logical thought, but I have developed techniques for keeping open the telephone line to my unconscious, in case that disorderly repository has anything to tell me. I hear a great deal of music. I am on friendly terms with John Barleycorn. I take long hot baths. I garden. I go into retreat among the Amish. I watch birds. I go for long walks in the country. And I take frequent vacations, so that my brain can lie fallow—no golf, no cocktail parties, no tennis, no bridge, no concentration; only a bicycle.
>
> While thus employed in doing nothing, I receive a constant stream of telegrams from my unconscious, and these become the raw material for my advertisements. But more is required: hard work, an open mind, and ungovernable curiosity.[14]
>
> (Reproduced by permission of John Farquhason Ltd, Bell House, Bell Yard, London WC2)

Anyone who reads Ogilvy's book, *Confessions of an Advertising Man*, will find it hard to believe that he is 'almost incapable of logical thought'. However, what is being stressed above is the necessity not to allow the constraints of 'logic' to interfere with the generation of ideas.

As also discussed previously, willingness to invest in mental activity is a prerequisite for creativity. Indeed, a number of studies show that simply instructing people to think and produce ideas can have quite important effects. Whereas the 'quality' of ideas tends to decrease as the number increases, people are capable of generating many ideas about a variety of subjects provided, of course, that they are motivated to make the effort.[4] In producing ideas, however, people are best advised not to evaluate them too quickly, since the criteria used for evaluation can have important effects on the range and quality of ideas produced.[4]

To summarize, research shows that given the knowledge necessary either to solve problems or to be creative in a particular field, people need: (1) preparation that does not block possible channels of thought. Much time needs to be spent in reconstructing and conceptualizing problems from different viewpoints. Furthermore, motivation needs to be high to ensure persistence. However, a relaxed attitude is conducive to emitting productive 'thought trials'; (2) the production of ideas should be allowed to range as freely as possible; and (3) evaluation (or judgement) of ideas should be postponed as long as is feasible.

In the next section several techniques for stimulating creativity are considered.

CREATIVITY TECHNIQUES

As should be apparent from the preceding pages, 'effective' creativity requires free-wheeling, 'imaginative' (or even 'irrational') thought processes as well as logical structures to be able to evaluate the potential usefulness of ideas and solutions. These different types of thought processes have been described in the literature as *divergent* and *convergent*, respectively.[3] Once a problem has been perceived, convergent thinking is necessary to define it; divergent thinking is then needed to play with the problem structure, seek new and possibly unusual associations, etc.; convergent thinking is subsequently required to evaluate the appropriateness of different solutions, and so on. 'Techniques for creativity' tend to emphasize these different stages in the problem-solving process by providing means: (1) to structure problems from different possible associations; and (2) to evaluate the range of possible associations in a systematic manner.[15]

Brainstorming is probably the oldest and best-known 'creativity technique'.[16] This is a 'group' technique where several people are encouraged to work together on a problem. The group is encouraged to generate ideas, recording them, for example, on a flip-chart, under the following guidelines:

(1) All ideas are acceptable no matter how outrageous they might seem.
(2) Criticism or judgement of ideas is not permitted until all ideas have been generated.
(3) The greatest number of ideas is encouraged.
(4) The group members should use the ideas of others to spark off or cue ideas of their own. In this way it is hoped the process will induce a 'chain reaction'.

Brainstorming is now used a great deal and there can be little doubt that with a group of people who are prepared to cooperate it can be a most useful exercise. There is, however, no evidence that brainstorming in groups is necessarily more fruitful than individual brainstorming.[3,4] Both procedures can generate many ideas. The essential aspect, as stated previously, is individual investment in mental effort. If the social pressures of a group facilitate such effort, then so much the better. My own view is that one should not expect too much of brainstorming—or indeed of most creativity techniques—but it is often a useful starting point. One possible advantage of a group technique concerns situations where the group may subsequently be responsible for implementing a solution. If group members have participated in the solution-generating process, there is a greater possibility that they will regard it as their own and be willing to implement it.[17]

Synectics is another group creativity process.[18] The word 'synectics' comes from the Greek and implies the joining together of elements that were apparently unconnected. Stages in the process of the synectics method are:

(1) A common definition of the problem by different members of the group. People in a group will often have different viewpoints on a problem and a simple, but systematic exploration of the different definitions and viewpoints is frequently most revealing. The result of this stage is to define and select one viewpoint which is to be developed further.
(2) At this stage synectics differs from other methods in that the method

deliberately involves taking a 'vacation' from the problem by a free discussion on a subject unconnected with the original problem. The purpose of the discussion (which, incidentally, to be effective, requires considerable skill on the part of the discussion leader), is to help the group find analogies that could be useful in solving the problem.

Gordon, the originator of synectics, sees analogy as a powerful means of problem solving and a stimulus to creativity. Three kinds of analogy are advocated: (a) Analogy with *biology* (i.e. nature). Natural evolution has developed fantastic 'solutions' to many problems which can also inspire human solutions. For example, the organization of colonies of ants or bees has shown what and how coordination amongst parts of a society can achieve; similarly one can admire and be inspired by the beaver's ability to build dams or the intricacies of the spider's web. Nature is full of elegant solutions to difficult problems; (b) *Personal* analogy can be most revealing. In this mode, members of a synectics group are asked to imagine that they are something, for example a certain type of bridge over a river or some kind of container. In 'role playing' the object the individual can often achieve insights which were not otherwise apparent; and (c) *Symbolic* analogy, whereby individuals are asked to symbolize the problems faced by the group by a single word or phrase. For example, the member of a group faced with a problem of transporting goods across the Atlantic might symbolize the problem as a need for a 'bridge'. In symbolic analogy, it is hoped that the evocation of a symbol can help restructure the problem in a way that triggers more creative solutions and further ideas. Other analogies, for example, social or historical, can also be useful.

(3) The third stage of a synectics discussion consists of applying to the problem ideas gained during the previous divergent 'vacation', evaluating the ideas, etc. In other words, the third stage is convergent. The whole process can, of course, also be restarted from this point.

As with the brainstorming method, synectics is highly dependent upon group process, and skilled intervention in this is necessary for most groups. Some writers have suggested certain ground rules to avoid negative criticisms from spoiling the internal dynamics, for example 'before a member criticizes the idea of another, he or she must state three aspects of it which are good.'[19] Another specialist suggests that the group should be composed of people with different levels of involvement and expertise in the problem. Such heterogeneous groupings, it is claimed, are more likely to hit on unusual and probably appropriate solutions.[20] Clearly there is a great deal of artificiality in these kinds of rules and discussions. However, before all such methods are dismissed out of hand, the reader should consider the alternatives. In many cases, the alternatives consist of haphazard attempts by individuals or, what is even worse, they just do not exist.

The K–J method An intriguing methodology for structuring problems has been suggested by a leading Japanese cultural anthropologist, Kawakita Jiro.[21] It is a method for grouping and synthesizing observations and concretizing and facilitating the generation and use of 'thought trials'. Its aim is to be able to produce a useful structure from a series of seemingly unrelated observations, and it is thus based on the notion that the appropriate structure yields the appropriate solution. There are several phases.

(1) Observations concerning the problem or phenomenon of interest are recorded on separate pieces of paper. Consider, for example, observations concerning different aspects of, say, aviation technology, or of a consumer product in a particular market. The observations could be in the form of single words, phrases or short sentences. From the separate pieces of paper, full sentences are written to be entered on punched cards (which can subsequently be coded and sorted by dimensions). The problem area is thus represented by a series of such cards.

(2) The data on the cards are then shuffled so that their ordering is random. The cards are then examined by the person (or people) concerned to see if there are associations linking observations. This iterative process continues until the total set of observations has been classified into groups within which items are linked in some way. For instance, observations in the consumer-product example could be linked within one group by the fact that they all relate to the habits of a certain type of consumer. The groups of items found at the first stage are then given names or appropriate phrases.

(3) The next stage consists of trying to arrange the different groups of observations into some meaningful patterns. Many patterns are, of course, possible, and the investigators have to play with different possibilities at this stage. The patterns of groups can also be hierarchical in nature and in a really successful application a 'meta-concept' can be found from which the other classifications can be derived.

Proponents of the K–J method see its use in creativity as a step beyond brainstorming. Brainstorming generates data in the form of items that can be entered on cards. The K–J method then permits the raw data to be structured in a pattern. In other words, the K–J method is a classification procedure which uses a deliberate random mechanism to induce blind variation (cf. Campbell's model above) into the forming of associations between elements. The K–J method has, apparently, been used with some success in Japanese industry.

Morphological analysis is also based on the notion that systematic blind variation has great creative potential. The method was invented by the Swiss astronomer and aero-engine specialist, Zwicky. It 'concerns itself with the development and practical application of basic methods that will allow us to discover and analyze the structural or morphological interrelationships among objects, phenomena and concepts and to explore the results obtained for the construction of a sound world.'[22] Basically, Zwicky advocates:

(1) An explicit formulation and problem definition. Consider, for example,

attempts to think about or create new forms of human transportation.[23]

(2) Identification of the fundamental dimensions or parameters of the problem. To continue the transportation example, there are (a) the type of carrier, (b) the medium of support for the carrier, and (c) the source of power for the carrier. In addition, within each dimension there are various possibilities, for example: for (a) cart, chair, bed, etc., for (b) water, ground, air, oil, rails, wheels, and for (c) human power, steam, jet engine, electricity, oil, and so on.

(3) A so-called 'morphological box' is constructed from the parameters and dimensions identified at Stage 2. This 'box' is a multi-dimensional matrix which results from all possible combinations of parameters and dimensions. For example, if a problem were to have 6 parameters, each characterized by, say, 3 dimensions, the matrix would contain $3^6 = 729$ different combinations or 'possible solutions'.

(4) All possible solutions in the morphological box need to be scrutinized to see how they meet the specifications of the problem posed. In several instances, of course, the combinations in the box are infeasible a priori; however, this can be an aid in the sense that as the number of parameters and dimensions increase, so do the number of the possibilities. Consequently, in practice heuristic methods have to be employed to reduce the number of possibilities examined to reasonable proportions.

(5) Analyses of the best solutions selected at the preceding steps relative to their feasibility given existing resources.

Zwicky has successfully used the technique described above in several stages of the development of jet engines and he has also developed a considerable number of patents on this basis.

The 'morphological' approach is clearly a check-list system in that it systematically structures all possible combinations of parameters. The notion of a check-list is, in fact, basic to quite a number of techniques. For example, the industrial technique of 'value analysis' consists of taking a product, e.g. a screwdriver, and asking what functions it can or should perform. The different attributes of the screwdriver can then be evaluated against such a check-list and an assessment made as to whether the features of the particular screwdriver being examined do not need to be modified in light of the evaluations.[20]

Cross-impact matrices are a further 'creativity tool' based on systematic combinatorial methods.[24] They apply to problems of forecasting and thus are particularly germane to issues treated in this book. Consider, for example, that you wish to assess the probability that oil products will no longer be necessary for motor transportation by the year 1990. This development will clearly depend upon a series of other events, for example, the development of alternative sources of energy, changes in needs for transportation (for example, people working more at home and relying to a greater extent on telecommunications), etc. Each of these events can clearly have impacts on the others and thus an assessment of the target event depends on evaluating each of the other events and their interactions. A cross-impact matrix is simply a means of arranging the events in some systematic order, enumerating the different possible combinations, and subsequently assessing the possible effects of interrelationships. As pointed out in earlier chapters, human intuition is often incapable of assessing the extent of different possible combinations of future events. Cross-impact matrices can thus be a useful judgemental aid.

SUMMARY AND IMPLICATIONS

The purpose of this chapter has been threefold: first, to emphasize the point that imagination and creativity play a crucial role in judgement and choice; second, to discuss the nature of creative processes and to show that most people have the ability to be more creative than they might themselves believe; and third to illustrate the rationale behind several structured 'creativity techniques'.

'Imagination,' Napoleon is reputed to have said, 'rules the world.' Imagination affects both the predictive and evaluative aspects of judgement: the ability to conceptualize different possibilities and how one might appreciate different outcomes. Without imagination, 'free' choice is impossible. This point is so fundamental that it has to be stated both simply and frequently.

Creativity has been shown in this chapter to be linked to imagination. More specifically, creativity has been defined as the discovery of novel associations or reconstructions of ideas, concepts or 'things' that are *appropriate* to a given situation. The notion of appropriateness is important since novelty per se is not necessarily useful. For example, you could make a novel association between the words 'tree' and 'potato'. However, unless this association could be turned into something 'fruitful' the association is hardly creative. For example, could potatoes be grown on trees in a way that would facilitate harvesting them? Everybody forms novel associations in, for example, everyday speech. Thus everyone has the capacity to be creative.

Campbell's model of creative thought was discussed in some detail. This is based on the notion of 'blind variation' of possible associations and 'selective retention' of certain 'thought trials'. The model emphasizes the role of chance factors in hitting upon creative solutions, but points out that the probability of reaching good solutions can be increased by (1) the sheer number of thought trials emitted, and (2) experiencing a wide range of environmental conditions which augment the possibility of setting off productive thought trials. Campbell's model emphasizes that creative people will almost necessarily be involved in behaviour that seems different from others—since they 'must' sample a wider range of experience. Furthermore, working atmospheres that demand strict adherence to social norms do not foster creative habits.

In addition to a willingness to invest mental effort in imagination, as well as developing habits of imagination, to be creative, people need to exercise considerable independence of character and judgement. Creative ideas are not always well received, particularly in the social domain. To bring creative ideas to

Table 7.2 Aids/barriers at different stages of problem solving and creativity

Stages	Required	Aids	Barriers
(1) Preparation	Sufficient 'technical' expertise to define problem; analytical skills	Experience; several definitions; reconsidering problems from many angles; motivation; tolerance for ambiguity; questioning the obvious, what is given and assumptions (why? what for?)	Perceptual sets; defining problem too quickly
(2) Production	'Free', unconstrained thinking; generation of associations	Luck (!); generation of sheer number of possible solutions; persistence; ability to withhold judgement; constructive framework of mind; relaxed attitude but high motivation; use of analogies; lack of experience with problem area can help; sampling of many opinions from different viewpoints; willingness to entertain 'impossible' ideas; independence of mind	Self-imposed constraints; constraints imposed by others; fear of failure; fear of ridicule; critical frame of mind; conformity; conservatism; norms of group/organizational setting ('groupthink')
(3) Evaluation	Analytical ability to evaluate feasibility of alternatives	Systematic means of examining solutions; willingness to push analysis far and also to return to Stage 2; good taste; imagination; high motivation and persistence; independence of mind	Evaluation done too quickly; 'satisficing'; unwillingness to invest in mental effort; acceptance of social norms and standards
(4) Implementation	Belief in one's ideas	Independence of character and judgement ('guts'); ability to withstand ridicule; motivation; persistence; ability to continue after failure; supportive organizational climate	Fear of failure; social and organizational norms and pressures

128

fruition often requires considerable tenacity of purpose and an ability to withstand social pressures.

Creativity can be considered to consist of three stages: (1) preparation; (2) production; and (3) judgement. These stages require both *convergent* and *divergent* ways of thinking: convergent to define problems and evaluate possible solutions, divergent to produce associations, reformulate problems and generate possible solutions. Creativity techniques are largely designed to prevent creative blocks and to foster the generation of large numbers of possible solutions (i.e. making blind variation systematic). For example, techniques are supposed to help people restructure problems (to escape common 'cages of thought'), generate possible associations and solutions, and to suspend judgement of solutions until many have been discovered. Whereas creativity techniques are no panacea, their utility should be compared with the status quo. This can often be characterized by haphazard attempts which stop at the first apparently satisfactory solution or, even worse, virtually nothing. Table 7.2 provides a brief overview of aids/barriers at the different stages of problem solving and creative processes. It also adds a fourth stage to the three discussed above, that of implementation.

Finally, whereas the level of imagination and creativity that yields acts of genius is rare, the ability to increase one's own level is available to all. The prime necessities are, as with most judgemental skills, an attitude of mind that believes in the feasibility of increased imagination, and a willingness to invest the mental effort necessary to achieve it, or as David Ogilvy would put it, 'hard work'.

NOTES AND REFERENCES

1. J. S. Bruner, *On knowing: Essays for the left hand*. Cambridge, Mass.: The Belknap Press of Harvard University Press, 1962.
2. F. Barron, The psychology of creativity. In T. M. Newcomb (Ed.), *New directions in psychology*, Vol. 2. New York: Holt, Rinehart & Winston, Inc., 1965, 1–134.
3. J. P. Guilford, *The nature of human intelligence*. New York: McGraw-Hill, 1967, Ch. 14.
4. D. M. Johnson, *A systematic introduction to the psychology of thinking*. New York: Harper & Row, 1972.
5. See the fascinating collection of personal testimonials in B. Ghiselin (Ed.), *The creative process*. Berkeley, California: University of California Press, 1952. (Reprinted by Mentor Books, New York).
6. R. E. Nisbett and T. D. Wilson, Telling more than we can know: Verbal reports on mental processes. *Psychological Review*, 1977, **84**, 231–259.
7. D. T. Campbell, Blind variation and selective retention in creative thought as in other knowledge processes. *Psychological Review*, 1960, **67**, 380–400. The general model of trial-and-error learning espoused by Campbell is, in fact, no more than part of Darwin's explanation of the process of evolution.
8. C. W. Taylor and F. Barron (Eds.), *Scientific creativity: Its recognition and development*. New York: Wiley, 1963, 385–386.
9. A. Roe, A psychologist examines sixty-four eminent scientists. *Scientific American*, 1952, **187**, 21–25.
10. See, for example, some of the stories of industrial innovation contained in P. R.

Whitfield, *Creativity in industry*. Penguin: Harmondsworth, Middlesex, England, 1975.
11. R. J. Burke, N. R. F. Maier, and L. R. Hoffman, Functions of hints in individual problem-solving. *American Journal of Psychology*, 1966, **79**, 389–399.
12. R. Hyman, On prior information and creativity. *Psychological Reports*, 1961, **9**, 151–161.
13. This problem is taken from Whitfield, Reference 10, p. 36. The solution is as shown in Fig. 7.2. The trick is to allow the pencil to go beyond the limits of the dots.

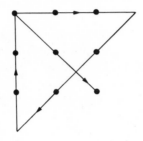

Figure 7.2   Solution to the nine-dot exercise

14. D. Ogilvy. *Confessions of an advertising man*. New York: Atheneum, 1963.
15. A short, useful, and readable overview of 'techniques' has been provided by W. E. Souder and R. W. Ziegler, A review of creativity and problem solving techniques. *Research Management*, 1977 (July), 34–42.
16. A. F. Osborn, *Applied imagination*. New York: Scribner, 1953.
17. N. R. F. Maier, *Problem solving and creativity in individuals and groups*. Belmont, California: Wadsworth, 1970.
18. W. J. J. Gordon, *Synectics*. New York: Harper & Row, 1961.
19. G. M. Prince, How to be a better chairman. *Harvard Business Review*, 1969 (Jan.–Feb.), 98–108.
20. J. P. Sol, *Techniques et méthodes de créativité appliquée*. Paris: Editions Universitaires, 1974.
21. T. Hoshino and J. H. McPherson, *The K. J. Method of creative problem solving*. Menlo Park, California: Stanford Research Institute.
22. F. Zwicky, Morphology of propulsive power. *Monographs on morphological research* No. 1, Pasadena, California: Society for Morphological Research, 1962, p. 275.
23. Example quoted by Guilford, Reference 3, p. 399.
24. See, for example, S. Makridakis and S. C. Wheelwright, *Forecasting: Methods and applications*. New York: Wiley, 1978, Ch. 14.

CHAPTER 8

Problem structuring and decision aids

The preceding chapters of this book have indicated a large variety of judgemental deficiencies. Indeed, they give considerable cause for concern when one considers the wide range of problems, both trivial and important, to which intuitive judgement is necessarily applied. Recent decades have, however, seen the development and growth of several 'decision aids' which range in complexity from highly sophisticated computer-based models to simple rules of thumb. The purpose of this chapter is to discuss such decision aids and how they can help counteract human fallibilities. It should be pointed out, however, that the use of decision aids has met with mixed enthusiasm. Comments will therefore also be addressed to this issue.

The most comprehensive approach to structuring decision problems is the method of *decision analysis*. Consequently, the chapter begins by outlining the steps involved in the decision analysis approach. It is not, however, intended to provide a detailed presentation of decision analysis, familiarity with which can be better gained by consulting specialized references.[1] Rather, the aim is to provide a framework within which (1) the questions that need to be asked in decision situations can be posed, and (2) procedures and aids that have been suggested for answering those questions discussed and illustrated. In many decision situations, there is insufficient time to make a thorough analysis. It is therefore hoped that this discussion of relevant questions can aid in the process of suggesting where available analytic effort should be spent.

A DECISION ANALYSIS FRAMEWORK

Decision analysis recognizes that all decisions depend on the answer to two questions:[2]

(1) What are the consequences of alternative actions? That is, what is 'at stake'?
(2) What are the uncertainties in the environment relevant to the decision?

As the reader will recognize, these questions relate to the *evaluative* and *predictive* dimensions of judgement, i.e., how much you 'like' consequences of different alternatives, and what you expect to happen.

The steps involved in decision analysis, which are essentially an elaboration of these two questions, are outlined in flow-chart form in Figure 8.1. These steps and their interrelationships are now briefly considered. To provide focus, consider a situation where you are hiring a candidate for your organization. Whereas this is a single example of a type of decision, it does illustrate many general points.

1. Structuring the problem

The key questions at this stage are:

Who is (are) the decision maker(s)?
What are the alternatives?
On what dimensions should the alternatives be evaluated?
What are the key uncertainties?
At what level of detail does the problem need to be structured? (To this there is also a subsidiary question: To what level of detail can the problem be structured?).

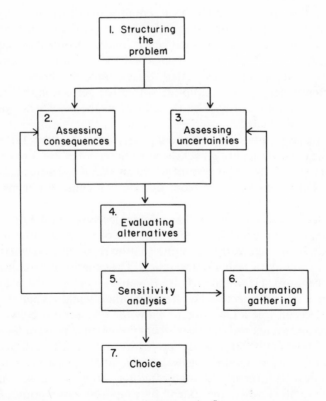

Figure 8.1 Simplified flow-chart of the decision analysis approach

Determining the identity of the decision maker(s) is a necessary but not always evident step. In the job-hiring situation, for example, lack of clarity concerning the decision maker's identity can exist with respect to whether the person is being hired for a particular department or for the firm as a whole. If this issue is not resolved, disagreements and difficulties can arise. More generally, the question of determining *the* decision maker is an important issue in instances where several people are party to a decision. Consider, for example, a corporation. The members of the board of directors may be *the* decision maker; furthermore, there may be differences between these individuals concerning particular decisions which would need to be reconciled. As further examples, consider issues involving relationships between head-office and branches or subsidiaries. What is optimal for one party may not be the best for the other, and vice versa.

A decision situation is clearly defined by the existence of alternatives. That is, with no alternatives, there is no choice. However, alternatives are not necessarily given but must also be sought and/or created. Furthermore, as illustrated in Chapter 7, imagination in the creation of alternatives greatly increases the scope for choice. In short, alternatives—in the job situation candidates—must be identified.

It is rare that an alternative, be it an investment opportunity or a job candidate, can be evaluated on a single dimension, e.g. discounted cashflow over five years in the first case, or intelligence in the second. Consequently, an important aspect of structuring problems is the specification of dimensions on which alternatives are to be evaluated; for example, intelligence, motivation, prior experience, personal compatibility with other persons in the organization, etc. These dimensions can also be thought of as the *objectives* against which alternatives are evaluated.

'Assessing uncertainties' is given as a separate step in Figure 8.1. However, it is crucial at the outset to identify *what* the key uncertainties are. For example, is it certain that a specific candidate would accept an offer if one were made? Is there a possibility that hiring someone from outside will cause problems within the organization?

Finally, decisions can be analysed at different levels of detail. For example, one may wish to analyse the job situation in the form of a 'decision tree' as illustrated in Figure 8.2. In that figure, the decision situation represented is whether to make an offer *now* to one of two candidates, A or B. The situation is complicated by two levels of uncertainty: (1) whether A and B would accept an offer made *now*; and (2) whether if A or B rejected the offer, the other would accept an offer made *later*. The decision tree allows one to show the connections between different possible acts and events and can clearly be represented in more or less detail.[1] An advantage of formally structuring problems is that one can see both the complexity of decision situations as well as the simplifying assumptions one has to make to deal with them (although often the latter can cause some salutary personal discomfort when the extent of simplistic assumptions inherent in intuitive judgement is realized). The level of detail at which one chooses to analyse a decision is an important consideration. Decisions usually become more

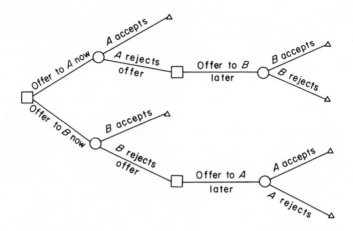

Figure 8.2 Illustrative decision tree: The decision here is whether one should make an offer first to candidate *A* or to candidate *B* in a situation where only one post is available. (The possibility of making an offer to both and hoping that one declines is excluded.) If, for example, *B* rejects an offer made *now*, then the delay in making an offer to *A* reduces the probability that he will accept *later*—the same applies to *B* if *A* rejects the initial offer. The possible decision points are represented by square boxes, □, uncertainties by circles o

complex as one starts to analyse different possibilities; thus the best general advice is to start somewhat simplistically since complications will soon become apparent. In any event, the guiding principle should be an assessment of the costs and benefits of different levels of detail of analysis.

2. Assessing consequences

The major issues at this stage are:

How adequate are the measures of the dimensions on which the alternatives are to be evaluated?
How should the different dimensions be weighted?

The first of these issues subsumes two questions: (1) How well do the dimensions chosen represent the alternatives? In the job selection example, do the dimensions (i.e. selection criteria) cover all relevant domains? Has an important dimension, e.g., 'character', been omitted? (2) Where and how can measures on the dimensions be obtained? That is, how do you judge a person's motivation or intelligence? In many instances it is necessary to obtain 'expert' opinion. However, which experts should you consult? What should you do if experts disagree?

The importance of identifying the decision maker(s) is emphasized by the second question. Different parties to a decision are liable to attach different 'weights' to different dimensions (or, in other words, they can have different objectives). For example, one decision maker could believe relevant prior experience to be the most important dimension in job selection. Another might de-emphasize this criterion in favour of intelligence or motivation. In situations where several decision makers are involved, the weights attached to different evaluative dimensions are the primary source of disagreement. The relative weights decision makers attach to different dimensions translate how they value the alternatives. Value, it is emphasized, therefore depends on who is making the evaluation and the purpose for which it is made. This issue is explored further below.

3. Assessing uncertainties

Assuming that the uncertainties have been identified (see Section 1 above), one needs to ask:

What information is relevant to the uncertainties?

As will be explained below, uncertainties should ideally be quantified in the form of probabilities. For example, one could attach, say, a 75 % probability to the event that a certain candidate accepts a job under specific conditions. Sources of information, i.e. data and/or people, clearly need to be identified to make the necessary probabilistic judgements. As with assessing consequences, there are similar issues involved in consulting 'experts'.

4. Evaluating alternatives

The issues here can be summarized by a single question:

What criterion (i.e. decision rule) do you wish to use?

Decision theory prescribes choosing the alternative, i.e. job candidate, for whom *expected utility* is greatest.[3] That is one should weight the assessed consequences (i.e. utilities) by the assessed uncertainties (i.e. probabilities) and choose the alternative for which the weighted sum is largest. For example, consider Figure 8.2. If one assigns utilities to the different outcomes (i.e. *A* accepts, *B* accepts, *B* accepts after *A* rejects, *A* accepts after *B* rejects, neither *A* nor *B* accepts), and probabilities have been assessed for the events (*A* and *B* accepting now or later), it is possible, by multiplying (i.e. weighting) the utilities of outcomes by the probabilities of the events upon which they depend, to assess the relative expected utilities of the strategies of offering jobs *now* to *A* and *B*. The decision is then made by choosing the action that has the larger expected utility. (Assessment of utilities is discussed further in this chapter and in Appendix C.)

This method of evaluating alternatives emphasizes the importance of separating Steps 2 and 3 (i.e. assessing consequences and uncertainties, respectively). In evaluating alternatives, it is crucial that one should not allow the assessment of consequences (i.e. *evaluative* judgements) to affect the assessment of uncertainties (i.e. *predictive* judgements). That is, although the relative values of actions should be calculated by combining 'preferences' and 'beliefs', to avoid the pitfalls of 'wishful thinking' the assessment of preferences should be done independently of the assessment of beliefs, and vice versa.

5. Sensitivity analysis

Decision analysis aims to provide an explicit quantitative representation of a problem and the expected benefits of different courses of action. However, it is wise to adopt the maxim that whatever figures are used to model a situation *they must be wrong*. This therefore leads to the question:

How wrong are the estimated consequences and uncertainties?

This question is resolved by the technique of *sensitivity analysis*. What degree of variation in the inputs of assessed consequences and uncertainties would change the decision indicated at Step 4 above? That is, it is possible to vary both the estimated values of alternatives (e.g. by using different weighting schemes for the dimensions), and the probabilities of events, and to observe the extent to which the decision is *sensitive* to such changes.

This technique can be of great importance for two reasons. First, many inputs to a decision are necessarily 'subjective'. If it can be shown that the choice between alternatives, e.g. job candidates, is relatively insensitive to a range of such inputs this provides some answer to the question concerning *how* wrong estimated consequences and uncertainties can be, and yet not affect the decision. Second, when people disagree concerning inputs to the decision it is not necessarily the case that this implies different actions. Thus one can, through sensitivity analysis, test the extent to which actions (e.g. make an offer to candidate *A now*), are compatible with a range of opinions and values (i.e. weights accorded to dimensions of consequences).

6. Information gathering

An important output of the preceding step can be the revelation that the decision is sensitive to lack of knowledge concerning certain variables. There is a need for more information. However, this leads to the question:

What are the costs and benefits of securing additional information?

For example, in a job-selection situation one may wish, before offering a job, to obtain more information about a candidate. However, the delay incurred in obtaining the information may be more costly than the value of the information (the candidate might, for instance, accept a job from a competitor in the interim). There is often a tendency to defer taking decisions on the grounds that there is insufficient information available. However, the costs of deferral and the fact that 'perfect' information is usually an unattainable goal are also frequently ignored.[4]

Information gathering is shown in Figure 8.1 after 'sensitivity analysis' to emphasize the point that the need for additional information should be undertaken only once the key aspects of the decision have been isolated. It would clearly be wasteful to collect additional information about a factor which had little effect on the decision. The information-gathering step has also been shown to relate to the assessment of uncertainties since the effect of information is to reduce uncertainty. Conceptually, 'information' could, of course, also be collected to refine inputs concerning the assessment of consequences, for example by reassessing the decision maker's preferences (i.e. the relative weights attached to the dimensions used to evaluate alternatives). However, this aspect is assumed here to be covered under the heading of sensitivity analysis.

7. Choice

The questions posed here are simple:

Has there been sufficient analysis of the problem?

The absolute answer to this question is invariably 'no'. However, the sufficiency of the analysis should be judged relative to the costs, benefits and constraints of the situation. If the answer is positive, one then asks:

Which alternative has the greatest expected utility?

The decision rule is simple: Choose the alternative with the greatest expected utility.

The above presentation of the decision analysis approach is clearly simplistic. Prior to the more detailed discussion of different aspects below, the following points are emphasized. First, although the presentation has been made in a step-by-step fashion, in practice there is considerable recycling between steps. Indeed, the process of analysis often indicates new alternatives or dimensions of evaluation and the problem structure may go through several iterations after the first passes through Steps 4 and 5. Although the aim of the analysis is an explicit quantitative problem formulation, use of Step 5 (sensitivity analysis) enables one to see 'how quantitative' the formulation needs to be. Given that most inputs to problems are necessarily subjective, this is a particularly important consideration. Third, although the theory of decision analysis strictly applies to a single decision maker, if the analysis is nonetheless effected simultaneously for several persons or groups, this can highlight the real extent of agreements and their relative importance. Fourth, by decomposing problems in the manner illustrated here, it is possible to synthesize the opinions of experts in different subject areas to the extent that their expertise relates to different aspects of the problem.

Table 8.1 summarizes the steps and the questions.

Table 8.1. Summary of questions by steps in decision analysis

Step 1: Structuring the problem
Who is (are) the decision maker(s)?
What are the alternatives?
On what dimensions should the alternatives be evaluated?
What are the key uncertainties?
At what level of detail does the problem need to be structured?

Step 2: Assessing consequences
How adequate are the measures of the dimensions on which the alternatives are to be evaluated?
How should the different dimensions be weighted?

Step 3: Assessing uncertainties
What information is relevant to the uncertainties?

Step 4: Evaluating alternatives
What criterion (i.e. decision rule) do you wish to use?

Step 5: Sensitivity analysis
How wrong are the estimated consequences and uncertainties?

Step 6: Information gathering
What are the costs and benefits of securing additional information?

Step 7: Choice
Has there been sufficient analysis of the problem?
Which alternative has the greatest expected utility?

DECISION AIDS

Structuring the problem

There are no decision aids that can structure a problem 'automatically'. Rather, this crucial phase must be largely achieved through unaided human judgement. Furthermore, apart from the issue of identifying the decision maker(s), it is unlikely that a first attempt at answering the subsequent questions will yield a satisfactory representation of anything but the simplest of problems. The structure of the problem typically emerges once one has grappled with the other steps outlined in Table 8.1. Nonetheless, the questions indicated at Step 1 have to be posed at the outset in order to begin the analysis.

Assessing consequences

There has been much work involved in finding means to represent the consequences of alternatives.[5] The underlying rationale consists of decomposing the alternatives into a number of dimensions (sometimes called attributes) and then finding means to aggregate across the dimensions to find a value for each alternative.

To illustrate, consider the problems involved in evaluating alternative plans for a business organization, i.e. determining corporate strategy. Plans can only be assessed against objectives and this therefore necessitates making objectives explicit. Much clarity can be achieved by noting that objectives are often hierarchical in nature. For example, in 1972 the San Francisco-based Woodward–Clyde Consultants translated their overall *Statement of Purpose* into the 'goal hierarchy' illustrated in Figure 8.3. The *Statement of Purpose* read: 'The combined efforts of Woodward–Clyde Consultants and its affiliates are directed toward the creation and maintenance of an environment in which their employees can realize their personal, professional, and financial goals.'[6]

As can be seen in Figure 8.3, the overall objective has been broken down into two main sub-objectives, financial growth and growth in professional capabilities. These sub-objectives have also been further subdivided. When objectives are considered in this manner, what typically occurs is that a loose-sounding global objective is gradually broken down until at the base of the hierarchy it can be represented by some rather specific items. As a further example, consider Figure 8.4, which shows part of a goal hierarchy developed for considering training plans in a company. The company's overall objective was to 'Maintain and improve training practices within the company in order to foster management development.'[7] This statement was subsequently broken down into distinct 'maintain' and 'improve' objectives. As shown in the illustration, four attributes of the 'improve' sub-objective were determined and measures of the attributes identified. As can be seen, two of the four measures required consulting experts whereas the other two could be based on 'hard' data.

How does one know whether a goal hierarchy adequately characterizes the alternatives? There can clearly be no blanket answer to this question, although the following points should be considered. Edwards states that when first starting an analysis one should be careful not to include too many dimensions; specifically, 'As a rule of thumb, eight dimensions is plenty, and fifteen is too many.'[2] It is probable that as an analysis evolves, and the decision maker becomes more aware of the different complexities, more rather than less dimensions will be included in the final model. Keeney and Raiffa have suggested five criteria for considering the adequacy of dimensions chosen to represent a problem:[6] (1) *completeness*, all important aspects of the problem should be covered by the dimensions; (2) *operational*, by which is meant that the attributes should be meaningful to the decision maker as well as to persons with whom he or she might communicate concerning the decision. Political considerations can play a role here. Keeney and Raiffa, for instance, cite the case of a mayor

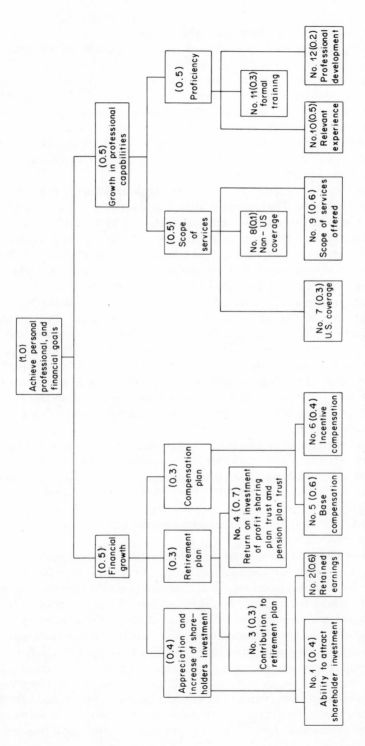

Figure 8.3   Objectives hierarchy of Woodward–Clyde Consultants in 1972.[6] The figures in parentheses represent relative importance weights within branches. (Reproduced by permission of John Wiley & Sons Inc)

considering alternatives for handling solid wastes; they state, 'It may not be possible for him, in a publicly discussed study, to include an attribute like "annual number of tons of untreated solid waste dumped into the ocean" even though this amount might be extremely important'[6]; (3) *decomposable*. Given the complexity of most decision problems, attributes need to be decomposed into simpler parts in order to be handled intelligibly; (4) *nonredundancy*. The final set of attributes should not contain redundancies in the form of conceptualizing/measuring the same thing by different means. Otherwise, unintentional double-counting can occur; and (5) *minimal*. The number of dimensions should be kept as small as possible.

Keeney and Raiffa point out that the actual attributes chosen for a particular problem are not unique. The search for attributes should therefore cease when it is felt that a satisfactory set has been found relevant to the problem at hand. When considering the addition of an attribute to a set, an important question to ask is how the relative attractiveness of the alternatives considered would change if the new attribute were included. If the new attribute does not induce significant changes, it should clearly be omitted from the set of attributes.

A complication frequently arises in that it is not possible to find attributes that actually measure the dimensions of concern to the problem. For example, consider Figure 8.4. It would be difficult to maintain the argument that the 'incremental cost per course participant' *is* the attribute 'facilities' under the 'improve' branch. However, the incremental cost can be taken to represent the improvement in facilities. Clearly a judgement has to be made as to the adequacy of the measure. Fortunately, sensitivity analysis can often help in this respect. That is, one can test the degree to which variations in this imperfectly measured attribute would have significant effects on the decision.

Having identified the set of attributes/dimensions, the next issue concerns how alternatives can be characterized by a single figure across all the dimensions. Two problems are involved here. First, what 'weights' should be attached to the different dimensions; and second, what kind of mathematical form should be used to aggregate across dimensions? For example, should the index of attractiveness of an alternative be based on a weighted sum of the dimensions? Or perhaps their product?

There are technical issues involved here which are discussed in greater detail in Appendix C. For conceptual clarification, therefore, concentrate on the situation where the overall index is based on a weighted sum of the dimensions. The issue thus centres on how the weights should be assessed. However, prior to this it should be noted that the units in which the measures of the dimensions are recorded will also affect relative weighting. Thus it is essential to transform the measures to common scales (a procedure is explained in Appendix C). A second problem, which also becomes evident at this stage, is the potential violation of an assumption implicit in the model: this is, that dimensions may not be what is known as *value independent*. Value independence means that preferences for any dimension of a particular alternative should be unaffected by its measurements on the other dimensions. For example, given that an alternative has certain

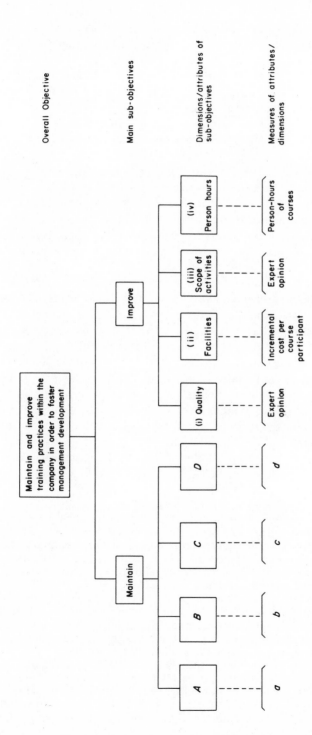

Figure 8.4 Illustration of a hierarchical structure of evaluation objectives for assessing company training plans. [7] (Reproduced by permission of John Wiley & Sons Ltd.)

positions on dimensions A, B, and C, evaluation of the alternative's position on D should be independent of its position on A, B, and C. In other words, there are no strong 'interactions' between dimensions in terms of the decision maker's preferences. This kind of consideration must be examined, and if found to exist, corrected. The correction can often be achieved by redefining the attributes in such a way that the interactions no longer exist. Whereas this point is clearly of a technical nature, it illustrates the fact that decision models can rarely be structured in their final form at the outset; rather, they seem to grow out of the total process.

The actual weights assigned to attributes represent the decision maker's values. For example, the weights in Figure 8.3 which are assigned to the various objectives and sub-objectives of Woodward–Clyde Consultants indicate the relative importance attached to the different objectives by the company. How should one actually set about assessing such relative weights? This is clearly a subjective matter. One procedure, which is based on first ranking the attributes in importance, is outlined in Appendix C.

As stated above, it is in respect of the assessment of relative weights given to the attributes that different decision makers are most likely to disagree. If agreement between parties to a decision is a crucial issue, a useful procedure is to calculate relative preferences for alternatives under different possible weighting schemes and to see how this affects the ranking of alternatives. Sensitivity analysis carried out at even this early stage can be most instructive. For example, if it is clear that the same action can accommodate differences in objectives this is worth knowing *before* different parties allow themselves to become involved in dispute. Experience with these types of models shows that the crux of the matter usually centres on determining the appropriate variables, i.e. attributes, rather than how they are weighted.

In this respect, extracts from a letter written by Benjamin Franklin to the British scientist Joseph Priestley in 1772 are most revealing. Franklin wrote:

In the affair of so much importance to you, wherein you ask my advice, I cannot, for want of sufficient premises, advise you what to determine, but if you please I will tell you how. When these difficult cases occur, they are difficult, chiefly because while we have them under consideration, all the reasons pro and con are not present to the mind at the same time; but sometimes one set present themselves, and at other times another, the first being out of sight. Hence the various purposes or inclinations that alternatively prevail, and the uncertainty that perplexes us. To get over this, my way is to divide half a sheet of paper by a line into two columns; writing over the one Pro, and over the other Con. Then, during three or four days consideration, I put down under the different heads short hints of the different motives, that at different times occur to me, for or against the measure. When I have thus got them all together in one view, I endeavor to estimate their respective weights; and where I find two, one on each side, that seem equal, I strike them both out. If I find a reason pro equal to some two reasons con, I strike out the three. If I judge some two reasons con, equal to some three reasons pro, I strike out the five; and thus proceeding I find at length where the balance lies; and if, after a day or two of further consideration, nothing new that is of importance occurs on either side, I come to a determination accordingly. And, though the weight of reasons cannot be taken with the precision of algebraic quantities, yet when each is thus considered, separately and comparatively, and the whole lies before me, I think I can judge better, and am less liable to make a rash step, and in fact I have found great advantage from this kind of equation, in what may be called moral or prudential algebra.[8]

Although simplistic, Benjamin Franklin's method has much to recommend it. Indeed, it is the forerunner of many more complicated schemes that have been advocated in recent years. It concentrates on identifying key attributes and their relative weights.

In summary, the stages involved in assessing consequences are, first, determining a set of attributes (which may often be organized in hierarchical fashion); second, finding measures of the attributes which are subsequently transformed to a common scale; and third, assigning weights to the attributes which reflect their relative importance. As indicated in the quotation from Franklin's letter to Priestley, it is not the precise figures placed on dimensions (arguments 'pro' or 'con') that are important. What is important is a procedure for bringing all important dimensions of a problem to bear on the decision. In this respect systematic methods, although clearly imperfect, are far superior to intuition.

Assessing uncertainties

Most decision situations are subject to uncertainty. It is therefore important to identify uncertainties and quantify them. Consider, for example, the decision situation modelled in Figure 8.2. Whether a job is offered *now* to *A* or *B* clearly depends upon the assessment of the relative likelihoods of *A* and *B* accepting offers *now* and *later*. In this section, it is assumed that uncertainties in the decision situation have been identified. The focus is on the expression of uncertainty or, more accurately, *partial knowledge*.

What does it mean when someone says something is 'likely', 'possible' or 'probable'? If you were told that a price rise by one of your competitors was expected within the next 48 hours, should you take this to mean that it was certainly going to happen? Would you be prepared to bet on it? And if so, how much?

Words describing uncertainty are used frequently, although their precise meaning is often unclear. For example, groups of managers attending some executive training programmes were asked to rank by decreasing order of certainty ten expressions used to describe forecasts made in the consumer durable field—see Table 8.2.[9] Results indicated considerable inconsistency between respondents as measured by the range of ranks observed and the fact that when a group was asked to repeat the exercise after the lapse of a month, they were unable to reproduce their original rankings. Although results of these experiments did show less inconsistency in meaning ascribed to the expressions by managers working within the same organizations, it is clear that the translation and communication of states of uncertainty by words is subject to ambiguity.

Uncertainty is best communicated through the medium of probability theory, that is by saying that an event has, say, a 30% chance of occurring. The quantitative form is precise and readily interpretable.

Table 8.2 Ranking of uncertainty expressions.[9]
(Reproduced by permission of the Royal Statistical Society.)

Expression	Average rank	Range of ranks
Quite certain	1.10	1–3
Expected	2.95	1–4
Likely	3.85	2–7
Probable	4.25	2–9
Not unreasonable that	4.65	3–7
Possible	6.10	3–9
Hoped	7.15	3–10
Not certain	7.80	3–10
Doubtful	8.60	7–10
Unlikely	8.75	3–10

Results observed when 40 managers were asked to rank ten expressions by decreasing order of certainty. The above table indicates the average ranks assigned to the expressions as well as the range of ranks accorded to each expression. As can be seen from the column on the right, the ranges are often quite wide and indicate considerable disagreement concerning the relative degrees of uncertainty implied by the different expressions. The results of this group of 40 managers represent a typical outcome from experiences with some 250 managers.

An objection that is frequently raised to the use of probability as just illustrated is that for many events the probabilities are unknown. For example, whereas most people would readily agree that the probability of observing a 6 on the throw of a fair die is 1/6, it is more problematical in 1979 to determine the probability that President Giscard of France will be re-elected in 1981. The difficulty stems from the fact that whereas the first event can be considered 'repetitive', the second is unique. That is, even if one did not know that the die was fair, it would be possible to throw it several times and observe the relative frequency of the outcome '6'. (Knowledge that the die is fair obviates the need to make such an experiment.) On the other hand, we cannot replicate the 1981 election in order to assess President Giscard's probability of success. For unique events, therefore, a probability simply translates our subjective opinion into a number and so measures our 'degree of belief'. (This is in fact also true of repetitive events—see Appendices A and B.) One cannot therefore say whether a probability or opinion is wrong in any absolute sense unless a person is found to be mistaken when he or she had previously expressed total certainty or uncertainty. On the other hand, if over a series of events a person consistently over- or underestimates probabilities, for example by assessing probabilities of about 30% to events that occur 90% of the time, one can seriously question his or her sense of realism. The objection that the probabilities of specific events are unknown is clearly unrealistic. Probability is an expression of one's degree of knowledge about an event. Thus probabilities per se are not unknown. Rather people have difficulty in expressing their degree of knowledge.

Probability theory serves two purposes as a decision aid. First, and as discussed above, it is a common language for expressing states of uncertainty. Second, the rules for manipulating the probabilities of several events, the so-called 'probability calculus', provide a mechanism for determining the logical interrelationships between uncertain events. Numerous studies have shown fallibilities in intuitive attempts to guess probabilistic relationships from given facts. However, there is no reason that people should be constrained to guess the probabilistic relationships between events. Arithmetic, to make an analogy, is not done by guesswork and few businessmen balance their books on this basis.

Expression of uncertainty in probabilistic form is not easily achieved. We are simply not used to making statements in such a precise form. Furthermore, and as emphasized in Chapter 2, our cultural backgrounds do not train us to distinguish consistently between situations involving certainty and belief. Sometimes we act and speak as though we were certain when, in fact, we are not too sure. On other occasions, we do not give enough weight to our opinions.[10]

In Appendix A, the rules of probability theory are briefly outlined and Appendix B offers guidelines concerning the assessment of probabilities.

There is, however, one aspect of probability-assessment techniques which deserves mention at this point. An event about which a probability, or indeed any non-quantified opinion, is expressed should be unambiguously defined. One way to think about this is to apply the so-called 'clairvoyant' test.[11] Could a clairvoyant—assuming one existed—tell you unambiguously whether the event would or would not occur? Alternatively, if a bet were placed contingent on the outcome, the event would have to be defined in such a way that the subsequent loser of the wager could not escape from his or her obligation.[12] A characteristic of much predictive activity is that we have loosely held opinions about loosely defined events. In probabilistic prediction, however, one has to be precise.

A distinction was made above concerning events that are unique and repetitive. For the latter a number of decision aids have been developed and tested.

Repetitive predictions

There are many decision situations where predictive judgements have to be made on a repetitive basis. Consider personnel selection problems, medical prognosis, vetting loan applications, predicting expected returns of companies quoted on the stock market, production-scheduling decisions, short-term sales forecasts, etc. The predictive activity in such situations can often be described by the relationship between the outcomes (e.g. sales, job success, stock market returns, etc.) and a number of indicators or cues on which judgement is based. For example, in determining whether a loan should be granted to a company, a bank lending officer could consider, amongst other evidence, various financial ratios in the balance sheet of the company requesting the loan. Consequently, for such decisions, information on which judgement is based can be coded, either as hard data in the form of, say, a financial ratio, or by an opinion expressed on a scale— concerning, for example, the bank's assessment of the managerial competence of the company requesting the loan.

In situations of repetitive prediction such as described here, how should one proceed? The evidence overwhelmingly suggests that statistical methods should be used instead of intuitive judgement. That is, more accurate predictions can be achieved by using statistical rules to predict outcomes as opposed to relying on intuitive judgement.[13] Indeed, some studies have gone even further than this. Statistical models have been built of the individual's judgements (i.e. linking the person's responses to cues or indicators in the environment), and these models have then been found to outpredict the people on whom they are based. This procedure, known as 'bootstrapping', has been found to hold in situations as diverse as admissions to graduate school, loan-granting and predicting returns on stocks.[14]

The counter-intuitive aspect of these findings is that one could suppose that through intuitive judgement people are able to capture important information which escapes codification and is thus not amenable to statistical analysis. Intuitive judgement does indeed capture much information; however, it is inconsistent. That inconsistency necessarily attenuates human predictive validity. In other words, although humans may on occasion exhibit high accuracy in judgement, inability to apply judgemental rules consistently across a series of cases means that *on average* models outpredict people.

One may ask why the question has been posed in a manner whereby either a person or a model is better. Surely a combination of person and model should be preferred to either alone? And indeed, some work has been pursued along these lines in respect of repetitive predictions[15] (see also below). Perhaps the reason that this approach has not been investigated more fully to date is that human pride has taken (and is still taking) some time to appreciate the notion that intuitive judgement can be improved by simple statistical models. Once this is fully realized, use of combination models can be expected to follow.

As noted above, inconsistency is a major source of human judgemental fallibility. One way to reduce inconsistency amongst a series of observations, e.g. judgements, is to take averages (see Chapter 2). This can be done in two ways. Either one can average a person's past judgements to predict the future, or the judgements of several persons can be averaged. Although the first suggestion might initially seem counter-intuitive, it has much to recommend it in situations where the system of which the outcomes are being predicted is not subject to important changes. Bowman did in fact test this notion in settings involving production–scheduling decisions, and found that managers' past average decisions were in fact superior to their actual decisions. He explained his findings in the following way:

It seems useful to attempt an explanation of why decision rules derived from management's own average behavior might yield better results than the aggregate behavior itself. Man seems to respond to selective cues in his environment— particular things seem to catch his attention at times (the last telephone call), while at other times it is a different set of stimuli. Not only is this selective cueing the case, but a threshold concept seems to apply. He may respond not at all up to some point and then over-respond beyond that. It is this type of behavior which helps explain the variance in the organization's (or its management's) behavior.

Departures of the decision making behavior of management from the preferred results, in this sense then can be divided or factored into two components, one which in the manner of a grand average departing from some preferred figure, we call bias . . ., and one which representing individual occurrences of experience departing from the grand average, we call variance . . . It is the latter and more important component which seems to offer the tempting possibility of elimination through the use of decision rules incorporating coefficients derived from management's own recurrent behavior.[16]

(Reprinted by permission from E. H. Bowman, Consistency and optimality in managerial decision making, *Management Science*, 9(2), Jan. 1963. Copyright 1963 The Institute of Management Sciences)

To paraphrase Bowman, there are two kinds of error: *bias*, which represents systematic error, and *variance* which results from inconsistency. Averaging acts to reduce the variance and bias is usually only of secondary importance. Furthermore, as has been pointed out subsequently to Bowman, it is relatively easy to remove bias from judgement by a statistical adjustment.

The use of an average of the judgements of several persons raises the whole issue of how to combine several judgements for prediction.[17] Consider, for example, economic forecasters. The empirical evidence indicates that averages have remarkably good predictive performance. However, two remarks should be made. First, although the average stabilizes the variability in individual judgements, one has to be aware of the fact that judgements between individuals are likely to be correlated. Thus one is often averaging redundant information with the result that beyond a certain point gains in adding experts to a group are small. Indeed, it has been estimated that in most predictive situations involving the use of experts there is little point in averaging more than about ten persons and that six or seven will often be sufficient.[18] Second, there is something to be gained by weighting experts in a prediction group differentially, e.g. proportionally to their expertise. However, if this is done the penalty for assessing relative expertise incorrectly is high. Given that people are inconsistent in judgement, the use of averages is therefore often to be preferred even when one suspects differential expertise amongst members of a group.[19]

Delphi and other methods

A method for aggregating group opinion which has attracted much attention in recent years is the so-called Delphi procedure.[20] This method, which is usually employed for predicting unique as opposed to repetitive events, relies on the fact that statistical aggregates of opinion must, by definition, be more accurate than a large proportion of the opinions aggregated. Another tenet is that interaction between people in groups is often dysfunctional. Consequently in the Delphi procedure face-to-face interaction between group members is avoided with communication being handled by anonymous statistical summary measures of the opinions of others administered by a third party. There have been some interesting Delphi applications. However, the reader should be warned that merely aggregating opinion through a Delphi-like procedure implies no guarantee of predictive validity.

Other aids have also been suggested for the prediction of unique events. One such system named PIP—an acronym for probabilistic information processing—decomposes the probabilistic prediction task in a way that allows humans to give inputs to a model that can then be aggregated mechanically.[21] This system has been experimentally tested in laboratory simulations with a view to potential military applications, but has not, to my knowledge, been applied in actual business situations. On the other hand, similar models for evaluating probabilities in underwriting (i.e. in the insurance business) are currently under development and there have been several applications in medicine.[22]

In many situations assessing uncertainties is extraordinarily difficult since there are many different sources of uncertainty and it is therefore unclear what combinations of contingencies might prevail. Such situations can often be usefully explored by *simulation* techniques. This involves modelling the decision by a series of equations in a computer and then observing what happens under a range of different possibilites. Furthermore, since inputs to such models are uncertain, the model can be run many times to assess the effects of the uncertainties empirically by observing the simulated distribution of outcomes. Clearly the output of such models is conditioned by the quality of the input and the assumptions underlying the design of the model. However, they do provide powerful means to extend intuition and explore the implications of one's assumptions.

Rules-of-thumb

The decision aids mentioned above usually require a certain degree of technical sophistication to be constructed for a particular situation. Furthermore, decision makers need to have sufficient knowledge of their structure in order to use them for decisions of any real consequence. What is lacking are simple rules of thumb which can be applied with confidence under specified circumstances.

Perhaps the only rule that meets this specification is that of using average judgements as described above. On the other hand, Kahneman and Tversky have recently proposed a five-step procedure for intuitive prediction which focuses on aspects of prediction which are often overlooked.[23] In particular, they point out that the major error in predictive judgement is to treat each case as *unique*. Although, every future event is, by definition, unique (i.e. it has never occurred before), it should be recognized that most events can be considered to belong to a 'reference class' about which quite a lot is known. For example, consider estimating sales of a new book by a new author. Clearly the book is unique.

However, facts about new authors publishing books of a similar type are known. Furthermore, even if no similar books exist, other book analogies exist with which the new author's work can be categorized. In Kahneman and Tversky's procedure, it is suggested that information about the particular book (so-called 'singular' data) used for prediction by modified by 'distributional data' (i.e. information concerning the reference class). In this manner, Kahneman and Tversky suggest that intuitive prediction will not ignore relevant 'base-rate' data when predicting a 'target' event. Kahneman and Tversky also suggest a procedure for moderating intuitive predictions to allow for 'regression' effects (see Chapter 3).

In earlier chapters, several deficiencies in probabilistic thinking were noted. However, since probability theory itself is difficult to learn and apply, Table 8.3 outlines eight key points. These are provided as a guideline to avoid probabilistic traps and review many of the points made earlier in the book.

Table 8.3   Eight key points for probabilistic thinking/prediction

---

(1) Think in terms of variation around the arithmetic average. The amount of variation depends upon (a) the 'true' variation of the phenomena and (b) lack of reliability/measurement error (see also point (5) below).
(2) Averages of data show less variation than the data averaged. Furthermore, variation of averages is reduced as the number of observations averaged increases. (Variation of averages is affected both by the amount of variability in the data averaged—*upwards*—and by the number of items of data averaged—*downwards*.)
(3) What is the *base-rate*? (Recall Thurber's: 'Compared to what?')
(4) What is the validity of the information source? How does it relate to the predictive target?
(5) What is the *reliability* of the information source? Recall that imperfect reliability implies lowered predictive validity, e.g. measurement error in economic statistics. Assess the 'signal/noise' ratio (margin of error). Avoid extreme predictions based on extreme observations from data sources that are not perfectly reliable (the 'regression' fallacy).
(6) When predicting from several items of information, distinguish between:
(a) redundancy(extent to which different sources overlap/can be predicted from each other); and
(b) validity of different data sources *vis-à-vis* the target.
Remember, consistency between data sources is only a valid cue to confidence in prediction to the extent that sources are not redundant/overlapping.
(7) To what extent could a 'random hypothesis' account for your data?
(8) Is it possible to test your predictions?

In summary, I have argued that the most appropriate way to express uncertainties is through the language of probability, both because of its numerical precision, which obviates the ambiguity of ordinary language, and because it provides a logic for structuring the relationships between uncertain events. Second, I have discussed problems of prediction for repetitive and unique events. For the former, a number of decision aids have been developed which show great promise, although unjustified human reluctance to entrust predictive activity to mechanical aids does not favour the widespread adoption they merit. Some devices also exist for structuring intuitive prediction of unique events; however, these are not easily accessible to most decision makers. Nonetheless, the widespread introduction and growing use of mini-computers may well bring about the adoption of many such decision aids in the near future.

Aids for other steps

Structuring a problem and assessing consequences and uncertainties are the major aspects of decision analysis. The other steps indicated in Figure 8.1 and Table 8.1 are simply refinements of the former. Indeed, it is often the case that once a decision problem has been structured, many of the other steps become superfluous. However, as pointed out above, the actual structure will frequently only emerge once detailed work has been attempted on other phases. In most problems, several starts and blind alleys are inevitable.

CONCLUDING REMARKS

In this chapter an attempt has been made to outline some of the principles and problems of applying aids for structuring decisions. The approach given here was based on outlining the so-called decision analysis methodology, although other valuable methods also exist. Decision makers understandably ask for concrete examples when decision methodology is discussed. Many can now be given and cover a wide range of applications in science, medicine, the public sector and industry. Note 24 provides references to a cross-section of such applications.

Several decision makers reading this book will have had some, even minimal, contact with decision aids derived from disciplines with such esoteric names as 'operations research', 'management science' or even 'decision analysis'. Furthermore, many decision makers have opinions concerning the practical usefulness of these disciplines, such opinions often being of a sceptical nature. To place this chapter in perspective, it is therefore necessary to clarify several issues.[25]

First, when evaluating decision aids it is crucial to specify a basis of comparison. The base-line is usually unaided, intuitive judgement. However, as illustrated in this book, intuitive judgement does not have an impressive track-record, although for several reasons most decision makers are loath to accept this fact. One way to think through this issue is to consider the following analogy: 'When driving at night with your headlights on you do not necessarily see too well. However, turning your headlights off will not improve the situation'. Decision aids do not guarantee perfect decisions, but when *appropriately* used they will yield better decisions *on average* than intuition. The choice of a decision aid or procedure is itself a decision. Therefore one should not necessarily expect perfection, but rather strive to find the best available procedure.

Second, the decision aids discussed in this chapter all involve the translation of a problem into a mathematical model, which is subsequently manipulated to produce a 'decision'. There are a number of resistances to such quantification. The first concerns the ability to translate the problem situation into mathematical terms. The issue that should be addressed here is that a trade-off is involved between, on the one hand, having the problem loosely but perhaps veridically represented in its complexity in the decision maker's mind*, and on the other representing it simplistically, over-precisely and probably somewhat inaccurately in a form that is open to scrutiny. In the former case, one leaves oneself open to the deficiencies as well as the capabilities of the human information-processing system. And in many cases, it is none too clear that capabilities dominate deficiencies. In the latter, the defects of the mode of analysis are exposed. For example, assumptions which may be hidden in intuitive reasoning are made explicit and thus questioned. The "public" nature of decision aids is clearly one of their great strengths. You know what you are doing with them. However, this strength can also reveal weaknesses which lead to their rejection in favour of the hidden weaknesses of intuitive processes. A further problem with quantification is lack of understanding of mathematical manipulations. People naturally resist the analysis of a problem in a 'language' they do not fully comprehend. Furthermore, this attitude can be aggravated by the failure of the mathematically inclined to empathize sufficiently with those lacking their skills. Common sense dictates that a decision maker would certainly be ill-advised to delegate his responsibilities to a model he does not understand.

Third, there seems to be a belief that the use of models somehow diminishes the role of the decision maker who ends up relinquishing control to an 'algorithm' which, as noted above, he may not fully understand and is therefore unable to trust. However, decision aids are not to be 'believed', but used. Furthermore, the person using a decision aid has no lesser role to play. On the contrary, the decision maker must recognize and structure the problem as well as provide many of the subjective inputs necessary for the analysis. In this sense, decision aids should be considered a mental 'crutch' that allow operations which are often lost in intuitive processes to be made explicit. This does not, of course, mean that no part of the analysis will be intuitive; much will inevitably remain so. However, it does mean that certain intuitive processes which the human mind performs ineffectively (e.g. aggregating across data sources), can be avoided. Furthermore, it implies that the decision maker probably has to think a lot harder about many of the issues involved. It is my view that many decision makers avoid using decision aids precisely because they imply greater investment in mental effort as well as the necessity to face squarely the inadequate means we have to deal with complex problems.

Fourth, a real problem arises in many applied settings where the decision maker is under pressure and has no time to use a formal decision aid. What can be done in such circumstances? Clearly intuitive judgement is the only resort. However, I would submit that if intuitive judgement has been trained in the use of formal aids, there is a greater probability that, under pressure, more appropriate

---

* Although intuitive capacity to do this must be doubted for problems of any complexity.

questions will be asked. Structuring and taking decisions is highly dependent upon formulating questions pertinent to the situation. Indeed, this is probably one of the most important aspects of decision making. Therefore, if the use of aids does enhance this aspect of intuitive judgement, it should lead to improved decision performance in situations where aids cannot be formally applied. For example, simply posing the questions in Tables 8.1 and 8.3 might clarify several issues in a decision taken under pressure.

There are costs and benefits associated with using decision aids. Furthermore, they are no panacea; nor, however, is unaided intuition. Writing several centuries ago, it is Francis Bacon who has best encapsulated my own view: 'Neither hand nor mind alone, left to themselves, amounts to much; instruments and aids are the means to perfection.'

NOTES AND REFERENCES

1. See, for example, R. V. Brown, A. S. Kahr, and C. R. Peterson, *Decision analysis for the manager*. New York: Holt, Rinehart & Winston, 1974; R. L. Keeney and H. Raiffa, *Decisions with multiple objectives: Preferences and value tradeoffs*. New York: Wiley, 1976; P. G. Moore and H. Thomas. *The anatomy of decisions*. Harmondsworth, England: Penguin, 1976; D. V. Lindley, *Making decisions*. Chichester, England: Wiley, 1971; and H. Raiffa, *Decision analysis*. Reading, Mass.: Addison-Wesley, 1968.
2. W. Edwards, Use of multiattribute utility measurement for social decision making. In D. E. Bell, R. L. Keeney, and H. Raiffa (Eds.), *Conflicting objectives in decisions*. Chichester, England: Wiley, 1977, pp. 247–275.
3. Indeed, it can be shown under a set of not too restrictive assumptions that maximizing expected utility is the *only* decision criterion that should be considered by a 'rational' person. See, for example, J. Marschak and R. Radner, *Economic theory of teams*. New Haven: Yale University Press, 1972, Chapter 1.
4. For an analysis of the personnel decision situation along the lines indicated here, see R. M. Hogarth and H. J. Einhorn, Optimal strategies for personnel selection when candidates can reject offers. *Journal of Business*, 1976, **49**, 478–495.
5. See, for example, Keeney and Raiffa, and Bell, Keeney, and Raiffa, References 1 and 2.
6. Keeney and Raiffa, Reference 1.
7. This example is taken from R. M. Hogarth, *Evaluating management education*. Chichester, England: Wiley, 1979, Chapter 12.
8. J. Bigelow (Ed.), *The complete works of Benjamin Franklin*. Vol. 4. New York: Putnam, 1887, p. 522. My attention to this reference was drawn by R. M. Dawes and B. Corrigan, Linear models in decision making. *Psychological Bulletin*, 1974, **81**, 95–106.
9. P. G. Moore, The manager struggles with uncertainty. *Journal of the Royal Statistical Society, Series A (General)*, 1977, **140**, 129–148.
10. L. J. Savage, Elicitation of personal probabilities and expectations. *Journal of the American Statistical Association*, 1971, **66**, p. 800.
11. C. S. Spetzler and C.-A. S. Staël von Holstein, Probability encoding in decision analysis. *Management Science*, 1975, **22**, 340–358.
12. This point has been made many times by B. de Finetti.
13. See the considerable evidence reviewed by P. E. Meehl, *Clinical versus statistical prediction: A theoretical analysis and review of the literature*. Minneappolis: University

of Minnesota Press, 1954; P. Slovic and S. Lichtenstein, Comparison of Bayesian and regression approaches to the study of information processing in judgment. *Organizational Behavior and Human Performance*, 1971, **6**, 649–744; and J. Sawyer, Measurement *and* prediction, clinical *and* statistical. *Psychological Bulletin*, 1966, **66**, 178–200.

14. R. M. Dawes, A case study of graduate admissions: Application of three principles of human decision making. *American Psychologist*, 1971, **26**, 180–188; L. R. Goldberg, Man versus model of man: Just how conflicting is that evidence? *Organizational Behavior and Human Performance*, 1976, **16**, 13–22; and R. J. Ebert and T. E. Kruse, Bootstrapping the security analyst. *Journal of Applied Psychology*, 1978, **63**, 110–119.

15. H. J. Einhorn, Cue definition and residual judgment. *Organizational Behavior and Human Performance*, 1974, **12**, 30–49; and L. D. Pankoff and H. V. Roberts, Bayesian synthesis of clinical and statistical prediction. *Psychological Bulletin*, 1968, **70**, 762–773.

16. E. H. Bowman, Consistency and optimality in managerial decision making. *Management Science*, 1963, **9**, p. 316.

17. See the review by R. M. Hogarth, Methods for aggregating opinions. In H. Jungermann and G. de Zeuuw (Eds.), *Decision making and change in human affairs*. Dordrecht, Holland: Reidel, 1977, 231–255.

18. R. M. Hogarth, A note on aggregating opinions. *Organizational Behavior and Human Performance*, 1978, **21**, 40–46.

19. H. J. Einhorn and R. M. Hogarth, Unit weighting schemes for decision making. *Organizational Behavior and Human Performance*, 1975, **13**, 171–192.

20. H. A. Linstone and M. Turoff, *The Delphi method: Techniques and applications*. Reading, Mass.: Addison-Wesley, 1975.

21. See the fascinating literature on this topic in W. Edwards, Dynamic decision theory and probabilistic information processing. *Human Factors*, 1962, **4**, 59–73; W. Edwards, H. Lindman, and L. D. Phillips, Emerging technologies for making decisions. *New directions in psychology II*. New York: Holt, Rinehart & Winston, 1965; W. Edwards and L. D. Phillips, Man as transducer for probabilities in Bayesian command and control systems. In M. W. Shelly and G. L. Bryan (Eds.), *Human judgments and optimality*. New York: Wiley, 1964; and W. Edwards, L. D. Phillips, W. L. Hays, and B. C. Goodman, Probabilistic information processing systems: Design and evaluation. *IEEE Transactions on Systems Science and Cybernetics*, 1968, Vol **SSC-4**, 248–265.

22. B. H. Beach, Expert judgment about uncertainty: Bayesian decision making in realistic settings. *Organizational Behavior and Human Performance*, 1975, **14**, 10–59.

23. D. Kahneman and A. Tversky, Intuitive prediction: Biases and corrective procedures. In S. Makridakis and S. C. Wheelwright (Eds.), *TIMS Studies in Management Science*, 1979, **12**, 313–327.

24. The works cited above in note 1 as well as the book by Bell, Keeney, and Raiffa in Reference 2 indicate many empirical examples as well as discussing theoretical issues. Another useful source of decision analysis readings is R. A. Howard, J. E. Matheson, and K. E. Miller, *Readings in decision analysis*. Menlo Park, California: Stanford Research Institute, 1976. A review of medical decision making applications can be found in R. M. Hogarth, Judgement, drug monitoring and decision aids. In W. H. W. Inman (Ed.), *Monitoring for drug safety*. Lancaster, England: MTP Press, Ltd., in press. Some fascinating studies have also been done from the viewpoint of social judgement theory. See W. M. Balke, K. R. Hammond, and G. D. Meyer, An alternative approach to labor-management negotiations. *Administrative Science Quarterly*, 1973, **18**, 311–327; K. R. Hammond, T. R. Stewart, B. Brehmer, and D. O. Steinmann, Social judgment theory. In M. F. Kaplan and S. Schwartz (Eds.), *Human judgment and decision processes*. New York: Academic Press, 1975, 271–312; K. R.

154

Hammond and L. Adelman. Science, values and human judgment. *Science*, 1976, **194**, 389–396; K. R. Hammond, J. Rohrbaugh, J. Mumpower and L. Adelman, Social judgment theory: Applications in policy formation. In M. F. Kaplan and S. Schwartz (Eds.), *Human judgment and decision processes in applied settings.* New York: Academic Press, 1977; and K. R. Hammond, J. L. Mumpower, and T. H. Smith, Linking environmental models with models of human judgment: A symmetrical decision aid. *IEEE Transactions on Systems, Man and Cybernetics*, Vol **SMC-7**, 1977, 358–367.

25. Useful discussions on this issue are contained in B. Fischhoff, Cost-benefit analysis and the art of motorcycle maintenance. *Policy Sciences*, 1977, **8**, 177–202; B. Fischhoff, Decision analysis: Clinical art or clinical science? In L. Sjöberg, T. Tyszka, and J. A. Wise (Eds.), *Human decision making, Vol. I.* Bodafors, Sweden: Doxa, 1980. C. J. Grayson, Jr., Management science and business practice. *Harvard Business Review*, July–August 1973, 41–48; M. Zeleny, Managers without management science? *Interfaces*, 1975, **5**, 35–42.

CHAPTER 9

Human judgement—an overview[1]

In many ways, this book can be considered a 'catalogue' of human judgemental fallibilities. Chapter 1 set the scene by stressing the limitations of human information-processing capacity. It was pointed out that whereas human conceptual skills have served us quite well to date, they are no longer adequate to meet the needs of the 'information revolution'. Furthermore, in today's world, the consequences of judgement are more far-reaching than was ever the case in the past. Consider, for example, the complexity of judgemental issues involved in the use of atomic power or genetic engineering, the multiple contingencies that need to be monitored in running an organization of any size, and the rapidly changing nature of the environment, namely, the evolution of social and demographic trends, technological advances, etc.

Chapter 2 discussed human difficulties in dealing with uncertainty, and particularly in distinguishing systematic trends from random fluctuations. The attribution of *causes* to *random* occurrences was shown to be a common source of erroneous judgement. Recall, for instance, the so-called regression phenomenon. When observations, for example, sales or job performance, oscillate irregularly around a trend or level, extreme observations (large or small) are usually followed by less extreme observations, i.e. there is *regression* toward the mean or trend level of the series. However, people's intuitions frequently fail to realize the nature of this phenomenon.

Chapters 3 and 4 considered the combination of information sources for predictive and evaluative judgements, respectively. Here it was shown that inability to process information leads people to adopt mental 'strategies' that simplify judgemental and choice processes. These strategies are often effective but can sometimes lead to systematic biases. In Chapter 5, the difficulties of learning relationships for prediction were described. It was shown that the structure of many judgemental tasks often inhibits efficient learning. Consider, for example, judgements made in job selection. Frequently no learning can occur concerning the outcomes of candidates who either decline offers or are rejected. Judgemental relationships and their corresponding accuracy can often only be assessed on partial information. This is further compounded by the human tendency to seek information that supports one's hypotheses rather than information that could invalidate them.

Chapter 6 emphasized the role of memory in judgement recalling La Rochefoucauld's apt comment that although people tend to complain of the badness of their memory, nobody complains about their judgement. It was pointed out that memory is not a faithful reproduction of the past. Rather people reconstruct the past from fragments of items remembered, the reconstruction being heavily dependent on the meaning attached to ideas, incidents, associations, etc. The prevalence of 'hindsight' biases was also stressed. The past seems inevitable in retrospect. It holds few surprises and people have considerable facility in constructing causal explanations to account for past occurrences. However, people exhibit excessive confidence in judgement. They are quick to forget how uncertain they were in the past and they are far from proficient at inventing causal scenarios for predicting the future.

The ability to 'create' scenarios and explanatory models capable of yielding accurate predictions about the future is highly dependent upon powers of imagination and creativity, the subject of Chapter 7. Indeed, without imagination there can be no 'free' choice. In Chapter 7, creativity—defined as the reconstruction of ideas, concepts, associations, 'things' etc. in a manner that is novel and appropriate to a given situation—was shown to be dependent on a willingness to invest in mental effort (by emitting many 'thought trials') and an ability to retain and test novel associations. It was also shown that 'creativity techniques' are based on these principles; furthermore, most people are capable of being both more imaginative and creative than they are at present. Creative ideas are, however, exposed to social pressures and thus considerable independence of character and judgement are frequently necessary to implement such ideas effectively.

The fallibility of human judgement was further accentuated in Chapter 8, where various means of aiding judgement were illustrated and discussed.

The purpose of this chapter is to provide an overview of human judgement in a manner that synthesizes the various findings reported in the book. The plan of the chapter is as follows. First, a conceptual model of judgement is outlined. This shows, inter alia, that judgemental biases can be thought of as occurring at different stages of information processing. The subsequent section of the chapter reviews biases associated with these different stages. Next, a way of thinking about the conditions leading to the occurrence of judgemental bias is presented. This is followed, prior to a conclusion, by some speculative comments on the origins of judgemental bias.

On considering the synthesis presented here, it is important to emphasize that human judgemental activity is proficient in a wide range of demanding tasks. However, judgemental abilities have developed in circumstances of relatively slow evolutionary change. As increasing technological development acts to accelerate change, the deficiencies of human judgement are inevitably accentuated. Nonetheless, technology can be adapted to complement human judgement rather than expose its weaknesses. However, to accept such aids, people must first be willing to admit their own deficiencies.

In many ways this chapter presents ideas at a conceptual, and sometimes abstract level which exceeds that of other chapters. This results from the intent to provide a more general framework with which the reader will be able to consider his or her own judgemental activity, and perhaps that of others. Despite the more abstract level of the chapter, I believe it should still be accessible to those who understood the preceding chapters.

A CONCEPTUAL MODEL OF JUDGEMENT

The conceptual model presented here conceives of judgement taking place within a system composed of three elements. First, there is the person; second, the task environment within which the person makes judgements; and third, the actions that result from judgement and which can subsequently affect both the person and the task environment (cf. Chapter 5). To be specific, consider a waiter in a restaurant who believes that young people do not tip generously.[2] Consistent with his belief, he concentrates attention on older customers. The result is that younger customers receive poor service which they reflect by giving small tips. This in turn reinforces the waiter's belief.

A schematic, and more detailed, representation of this model is presented in Figure 9.1. Judgement occurs within a so-called task environment—box 1. Within the task environment is what we shall call the person's *schema*—box 2. This symbolizes the person's beliefs concerning the task environment and his or her representation of it; that is, how he or she perceives the judgemental task. For example, part of the schema of the waiter described above is the belief, 'Young people do not have the means to tip well. Thus efforts in service directed at younger customers are unlikely to be rewarded.' In any given situation,

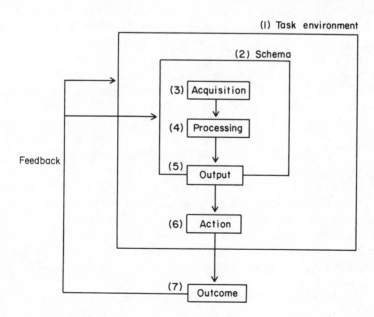

Figure 9.1 Conceptual model of judgement (refer to text as well as Table 9.1)

therefore, the schema is created both by the person's memory and characteristics of the judgemental task (e.g. the age distribution of customers in the restaurant at a particular time).

The actual processing of information, that is the operations that lead to judgement, can be decomposed into: (a)*acquisition* of information—box 3; (b)*processing* of information—box 4; and (c) *output*—box 5. To continue the example of the waiter, when deciding how much attention to give to different customers, he first accesses information both from memory (i.e. beliefs concerning tipping habits and age), and the environment (the age distribution of customers); second, this information is processed; and third, the result of processing is the waiter's judgement as to how much attention should be devoted to different customers. In this example, the 'output' is probably internal to the waiter. However, in other situations the output could be expressed externally. Consider, for instance, a salesman giving an estimate of sales in his region for the next quarter.

Output (box 5) has been drawn at the interface of the schema and the task environment to emphasize the location of its occurrence. However, frequently—and this is true of the waiter example—the output is indistinguishable to a third party from the *action* (box 6) which occurs within the task environment. (The waiter's judgement is reflected in the quality of service he actually gives to different customers.) Subsequently the action leads to an *outcome* (box 7)—in this case the tips given by the different customers. These outcomes can then feed back into the person's schema (e.g. reinforcing the notion that younger customers do not tip generously), and may even affect the environment in which the action takes place. For example, if young people receive poor service at the restaurant they may cease to frequent it and thus affect the subsequent age distribution of customers.

Bias in judgement can be thought of as intervening at the different stages of information processing outlined above. First, the acquisition of information from both the environment and memory can be biased. The crucial issue here is how certain information does or does not become *salient*. Second, the manner in which information is processed can be biased; for example, if the individual simplifies the judgemental situation by using an inappropriate mental strategy (cf. Chapter 4). Third, the manner in which the person is required to respond can induce bias. Examples of this kind of bias were given in Chapter 4, where it was noted that relative preference for gambles could be reversed when people were asked to express their choices in different ways. Finally, and as outlined in Chapters 2 and 5, outcomes of judgement can induce bias in both (1) interpretation of their significance (For example, is the outcome attributable to one's action or simply a chance fluctuation?), and (2) learning relationships for predictive activity.

Biases can, of course, also occur as a result of interactions between the different stages of information processing. For example, the requirement to make a specific type of response can direct attention to accessing a certain kind of information.

However, prior to reviewing these different sources of judgemental bias, it is appropriate to recall the relevant features of the human information-processing system.

As stated in Chapter 1, people have limited information-processing capacity. But they are adaptive. The nature of a judgemental task determines to a large extent how people can and do deal with the task. For example, if information is presented sequentially, this induces a judgemental strategy that is different from that used when all information is presented simultaneously. Consider, for instance, the difference between selecting one of several products on a supermarket shelf as opposed to being given a complete information display indicating the different attributes of the alternatives.

There are four major consequences of limited human information processing capacity (cf. Chapter 1): (1) perception of information is not comprehensive but *selective*; (2) since people cannot simultaneously integrate a great deal of information, they process information in a predominantly *sequential* manner; (3) information processing is necessarily dependent upon the use of mental operations that *simplify judgemental tasks* and *reduce intellectual effort*; and (4) people have *limited memory* capacity. It is important to add, however, that people do not submit passively to their environment. On the contrary, in order to meet their needs people require some degree of control over the environment. Behaviour is thus purposeful and characterized by people *acting on* the environment. For example, at a very basic level, to fulfil one's needs to eat it is necessary to take action to insure that one can obtain food. Furthermore, in order to survive, those actions have to be such that you have an excellent chance of actually obtaining food. Thus, as this simple example illustrates, the need to have some control over the environment is basic.

In summary, the conceptual model of human judgemental activity described here is the following: The context of judgement is that of a three-element system involved in mutual interaction. There is the person, actions that result from judgements made by the person, and the environment in which judgements, actions and their outcomes take place and are interpreted by the individual—see Figure 9.1. It is important to emphasize that each of the elements affects and is affected by the others as illustrated, for instance, in the example of the waiter given above. When one considers the information-processing capacity of the person within the three-element system, the picture is one of a selective, essentially sequential information processor with limited powers of 'computation' and memory. Although limited, people have the ability to be creative and do seek to understand, control and master their environments. Indeed, understanding and control of the environment is essential to survival. However, in this task unaided human judgement is often deficient in a number of important respects.

Table 9.1 summarizes the above and indicates the key issues involved in judgemental bias.

Table 9.1   Key issues in judgemental biases

---

(1) *Characteristics of human information processing system*
    (a) Selective perception
    (b) Sequential processing
    (c) Limited 'computational' ability
    (d) Limited memory
    (e) Dependence on task characteristics—'adaptiveness'.

(2) *Need to understand, control and master the environment*

(3) *Location of judgemental bias*

	Key questions
(a) Information acquisition	Salience of information
(b) Processing	Choice of 'decision'/processing rule
(c) Output	Response mode
(d) Feedback	'Veridicality' of outcome feedback.

SOURCES OF BIAS

Information acquisition

The issue of bias in information acquisition can be conceptualized by enquiring when and why information becomes *salient* to an individual. This question can be further broken down by noting that information can be accessed from two sources: (1) the individual's memory; and (2) the task environment. Consequently the relative salience of information can be a function of memory, features of the task environment or both. A related point is that the mind is not a vacuum. It actively seeks and selects information.

Several sources of memory bias in information acquisition were noted in earlier chapters:

(1) The ease with which information can be recalled from memory is a clue people use to predict the frequency of an event (the so-called 'availability' bias). Thus people may believe, for example, that events that are well publicized (such as tornadoes or certain causes of death), are more frequent than is in fact the case. There is also a tendency to consider one's own range of experience as 'normal' and thus to make erroneous attributions in judging the 'deviant' behaviour of others. People's jobs often induce so-called 'professional deformation', evidenced in tendencies to perceive problems in ways related to specific experience. More generally this is known as *selective perception*. The same administrative problem, for instance, can be perceived to be an 'accounting' problem by accountants, a 'personnel' problem by personnel officers and a 'marketing' problem by marketing managers.[3]

(2) The mind does not register what it does not or cannot perceive. Judgement of the likelihood of events are thus not influenced by what might have happened but did not. To clarify these apparently obscure statements, consider what

happens when a candidate is rejected for a job. A judgement has been made. However, that judgement will (usually) produce no feedback, since the rejected candidate can neither be a success nor failure in the job.

(3) Related to the preceding point is the tendency for people to judge strength of predictive ability by frequency rather than relative frequency. For example, if you have been told that company A has successfully marketed 12 innovations in the last 3 years while company B has only marketed 6, there is a tendency to believe that company A has greater success in this area. However, one should also ask how many innovations—in total—both companies have attempted!

(4) Information that is *concrete* is more salient in memory than information that is *abstract*. That is, information that is vivid, e.g. describing an experience or perhaps involving a personal incident, is more easily recalled than, for example, statistical summary data. Furthermore, this tendency can have important effects on judgement. For instance, if you are contemplating buying a car, witnessing the positive or negative experience of a neighbour with a particular model is liable to be recalled more vividly in your memory—and thus weigh more heavily in judgement—than more extensive data published about that model in a consumer or motoring magazine. Data coded in memory by images and through several associations can become disproportionately salient.

The physical structure of a judgemental task can also bias information acquisition:

(1) Order effects have been noted. Sometimes the first in a series of items dominates (a primacy effect), sometimes the latter (a recency effect).

(2) As with acquisition from memory, 'availability' bias can play an important role. In problem solving and creative thinking, for example, hints can induce a way of perceiving a problem or suggesting a solution. Consider, for instance, the 'Eureka' effect, on the one hand, or the difficulty in solving a problem when one has a negative 'set', on the other (i.e. you only see one side of a problem and this inhibits you from solving it). Other availability biases can be induced by the simple absence of some data and presence of other information. Data that are physically 'available' somehow seem more important.

(3) Information is usually not 'given' but must be sought. Consequently, when information is presented to a person in a readily accessible form this can have important consequences. Russo's study of the effects of different presentations of 'unit-price' information in supermarkets attests precisely to this point.[4] Task variables, such as manner and order of presentation, context effects, etc., contribute to how a person perceives a situation, and consequently how he or she makes judgements. Other task variables that could be mentioned here include (a) data displays that seem so logical and complete that important omissions are not noted, (b) information overload—there is so much information present that the individual is unable to discern the important variables—and (c) redundant information displays. All information presented seems so consistent that the individual is only able to come to one, possibly erroneous conclusion.

The interaction of memory (i.e. a person's schema) and features of the task environment can also bias judgement:

(1) What a person expects to see affects what a person does see. This effect was dramatically illustrated by Bruner and Postman's playing-card experiment (Chapter 6).[5] People had extraordinary difficulty recognizing *red* spades and often distorted their perceptions to concur with what they expected to see. More generally, taking expectations for reality can clearly have serious dysfunctional consequences.

(2) The meaning people attach to information can produce serious distortions in omitting to consider certain information. Several studies show that even when so-called base-rate data are available, people will ignore them in the presence of 'specific' data. When the latter are missing, however, base-rate data do become salient in judgement.

(3) A related issue concerns the biases involved when people seek information in judgemental activity. People have a strong tendency to seek information that is consistent with their hypotheses rather than information that could cause them to reject a hypothesis. Consider the employment interview. Evidence indicates that once an interviewer has formulated an impression (e.g. the person will be successful/unsuccessful in the job), the rest of the interview is spent seeking information that is consistent with this hypothesis. Little weight or thought is given to information that could be inconsistent. Some studies also show more general evidence of tendencies to ignore, or at least discount conflicting evidence.

(4) A person's causal framework or schema for thinking about a situation guides his or her interpretation of information. If the schema is biased (see below), then acquisition of particular information can also be biased.

Processing

The key question identified in Table 9.1 relating to the 'processing' stage is the individual's choice of a 'decision'/information-processing rule. That is, what is the series of mental operations the person applies to the information that has been accessed? Furthermore, from a perspective of bias, what is the relative effectiveness of different types of operations? As in information acquisition, bias in processing can be induced by both memory and task characteristics.

Memory biases in processing include the following:

(1) Recalling that a particular choice/judgement worked well in the past. Habit in judgement and choice is clearly important. However, the fact that a previous choice or choice rule was successful in the past carries no guarantee of future success.

(2) 'Availability' bias (see above) can also operate in the choice of a decision rule. That is, certain 'rules' may be more available to a person than others because of his or her type of experience. For example, a common human fallibility is to assume that because one is expert in a given area, expertise also

'generalizes' to other areas. However, processing rules that operate well in, say, financial decision making, do not necessarily carry over to problems of general management.

The bulk of processing biases noted in the literature, however, result from (1) task variables (see below), (2) unwillingness to expend mental effort, and (3) inconsistency in applying a judgemental rule:

(1) Task variables that bias processing include: amount of information, time pressures, sequential vs. intact data presentation formats, inconsistent or missing values in information. Since the biases induced by these types of task characteristics are somewhat idiosyncratic they are not elaborated here (but see Chapters 3 and 4).

(2) People adopt processing strategies to reduce mental effort and these can often lead to bias. There is a general preference to avoid direct comparisons or trade-offs amongst different information sources. Over-reliance on subsets of the information can, however, lead to choices that are inconsistent with a person's preferences, as can be the case when subsets of information are eliminated in a sequential manner. Furthermore, several strategies discussed in Chapters 3 and 4 seem to be based on a potentially misleading 'quasi-logic'. The 'representativeness heuristic' leads to underestimating the extent of variation in the environment, and in the 'adjustment and anchoring' strategy people may not make sufficient adjustments away from the anchor.

(3) The major source of processing bias, however, appears to be the lack of consistency in judgement. People do not seem capable of applying the same judgemental rule across a series of cases. Indeed, several studies show that the validity of judgement is considerably attenuated by this particular fallibility.

Output

'Output' biases appear to be triggered by the way in which people express judgement or choice (i.e. the 'response mode'—see Table 9.1). There are many examples:

(1) Estimates of probabilities have been found to differ according to the method with which people have been asked to respond as well as the scale used to measure responses.[6]

(2) As noted above, people evaluate risky prospects (and even change their preferences) according to the basis on which they are asked to evaluate them (i.e. playing a bet vs. setting a minimum selling price).

(3) As most market researchers know, responses to questions can vary under the variety of possible methods used to elicit responses (e.g. open interviews, different types of questionnaires, etc.).

(4) In choice situations, response modes can accentuate different aspects of alternatives and, in some circumstances, even lead people into making *intransitive* choices.

The ubiquity of 'response mode bias' is a problem that has and will cause problems for both social science and its users for many years.

Feedback

The importance of feedback in judgement relates to its effects on learning. If a person's judgement is not accompanied by some form of feedback, then learning simply cannot occur. Consider what happens when you make a judgement in a situation where feedback is not possible—concerning, for example, the ability of a person to do a job for which he or she was rejected. Bias in feedback, caused either because it is not 'possible' to observe outcomes associated with the total range of judgements (as in the job-selection example), or for other reasons (e.g. feedback is delayed inordinately, other events affect outcomes etc.), is one of the most important sources of difficulty in judgement. Consider the following:

(1) Misinterpretation of 'chance' and 'cause'. As noted in Chapter 2, people have great difficulty in distinguishing whether particular outcomes (for example, the result of a sales campaign), are due to a specific cause (e.g. a special advertising effort), or to chance factors (e.g. a freak combination of circumstances increasing demand). That people should confound 'chance' and 'cause' is, of course, understandable, since they both occur simultaneously in experience. Furthermore, 'chance' is an artificial concept in the sense that everything must have some causal agent, or combination of such agents. 'Chance' thus refers to a combination of unidentifiable causes, and to state that something occurs 'by chance' is no more than an admission of ignorance (to which, of course, no negative connotation need be associated). The misinterpretation of chance and cause therefore involves an *erroneous causal attribution* concerning an outcome which was in fact 'caused' by some other unidentified agents. Instances of such misinterpretation were exemplified by the *regression phenomenon*. People fail to understand that when observations vary irregularly around some average value or trend, then extreme values are likely to be followed by less extreme values. Thus when monitoring performance levels, for example, it is unclear whether corrective actions taken after observing a case of sub-standard performance provoke the subsequent improvement, or whether the improvement would have occurred anyway. More generally, in tasks involving both skill and chance, it is difficult to disentangle the relative contributions of both factors. Furthermore, there is a tendency for people to attribute 'good' outcomes to skill and 'bad' outcomes to chance. Langer has further demonstrated what she has called the 'illusion of control'.[7] Either through observing a sequence of successful outcomes or spending time analysing a situation, people can acquire the impression of having more control over outcomes than is justified by the situation. This bias clearly has important implications for decision makers when considering their track-records of past successes and failures, as well as their efforts to make plans for the future.

(2) A second bias arising from observation of chance occurrences is the so-called 'gambler's fallacy'. After seeing a sequence of successes or failures in a situation known to be of a random nature, people tend to believe that the event that has not appeared recently becomes more probable.

(3) From early childhood people learn predictive relationships by observing the joint occurrence of events, for example reducing the sensation of hunger by eating. However, even if memory were perfect, use of the observation of the joint occurrence of events as a clue to predictive relationships could lead to systematic bias. First, to infer predictive relationships, it is often necessary to have information concerning non-occurrences (consider again the missing outcome concerning the rejected job candidate). However, even when such information is available, people tend to ignore it unless it is made salient for them. Second, ideas of association based on the observation of a few joint occurrences can take on a life of their own and become resistant to disconfirming evidence.[8] Consider, for example, the case of a manager observing an increase in efficiency in a troublesome department after placing it under the control of a new supervisor. The 'joint occurrence' of (1) the increase in efficiency and (2) the appointment of the new supervisor can lead to a more general belief in the supervisor's competence which can be upheld even if negative evidence about the supervisor's competence becomes available subsequently. More generally, people are prone to believing in a priori plausible 'illusory correlations'. Furthermore, these beliefs can persist in the face of disconfirming evidence.

(4) An effect of the knowledge of an 'outcome' noted in Chapter 6 was the creation of *hindsight* bias. Cognizance of an outcome can restructure memory in a way that makes the presumed causal links leading to the observed outcome seem inevitable. Thus people have short memories concerning their prior uncertainties. This, in turn, can lead to a diminished ability to imagine alternative explanatory schemes for the past, and by extension for the future.

(5) Misplaced confidence in judgement is another possible feedback bias which was explored in some depth in Chapter 5. Because people are unaware of the characteristics of the task structure in which they make judgements, interpretation leading to misplaced confidence (usually over-confidence) is common.

In Table 9.2 the main sources of bias reported in the literature, together with brief descriptions and examples, are summarized according to the stages of information processing indicated in Figure 9.1.[9]

SITUATIONS PRONE TO JUDGEMENTAL BIAS

Above, a list of information-processing biases associated with different stages of processing has been outlined. In this section, a scheme is presented for thinking about the conditions when bias is liable to occur. Whereas the scheme cannot claim to be a 'validated' scientific model for predicting the occurrence of bias in judgement, it should facilitate identification of such situations.

Table 9.2   Biases in information processing[9]

Bias/source of bias	Description	Example
Availability	– Ease with which specific instances can be recalled from memory affects judgements of frequency.	– Frequency of well-publicized events are over-estimated (e.g. deaths due to homicide, cancer); frequency of less well-publicized events are under-estimated (e.g. deaths due to asthma and diabetes).
	– Chance 'availability' of particular 'cues' in the immediate environment affects judgement.	– Problem-solving can be hindered/facilitated by cues perceived by chance in a particular setting (hints set up cognitive 'direction').
Selective perception	– People structure problems on the basis of their own experience.	– The same problem can be seen by a marketing manager as a marketing problem, as a financial problem by a finance manager, etc.
	– Anticipations of what one expects to see bias what one does see.	– Identification of incongruent objects, e.g. playing cards with red spades, are either inaccurately reported or cause discomfort.
	– People seek information consistent with their own views/hypotheses.	– Interviewers seek information about candidates consistent with first impressions rather than information that could refute those impressions.
	– People downplay/disregard conflicting evidence.	– In forming impressions, people will under-weight information that does not yield to a consistent profile.
Frequency	– Cue used to judge strength of predictive relationships is observed frequency rather than observed relative frequency. Information on 'non-occurrences' of an event is often unavailable and frequently ignored when available.	– When considering relative performance (of, say, two persons), the absolute number of successes is given greater weight than the relative number of successes to trials, i.e., successes *and* failures (the denominator is ignored). Note, however, that the number of failures is frequently unobservable.

INFORMATION

OF ACQUISITION	Concrete information (ignoring base-rate, or prior information) – Concrete information (i.e. vivid, or based on experience/incidents) dominates abstract information (e.g. summaries, statistical base-rates, etc.).	– When purchasing a car, the positive or negative experience of a single person you know, is liable to weigh more heavily in judgement than available and more valid statistical information, e.g. in Consumer Reports.
	Illusory correlation – Belief that two variables covary when in fact they do not (Possibly related to 'Frequency' above).	– Selection of an inappropriate variable to make a prediction.
	– Order effects (primacy/recency).	– Sometimes the first items in a sequential presentation assume undue importance (primacy), sometimes the last items (recency).
	– Mode of presentation.	– Sequential vs. intact data displays can affect what people are able to access. Contrast, for example, complete unit-price shopping vs. own sequential information search.
	Data presentation – Mixture of types of information, e.g. qualitative and quantitative.	– Concentration on quantitative data, exclusion of qualitative, or vice versa.
	– Logical data displays.	– Apparently complete 'logical' data displays can blind people to critical omissions.
	– Context effects on perceived variability	– Assessments of variability, of say a series of numbers, is affected by the absolute size (e.g. mean level) of the numbers.
PROCESSING OF INFORMATION	Inconsistency – Inability to apply a consistent judgemental strategy over a repetitive set of cases.	– Judgements involving selection, e.g. personnel/graduate school admissions.
	Conservatism – Failure to revise opinion on receipt of new information to the same extent as Bayes' theorem. (Note this may be counterbalanced by the 'best-guess' strategy and produce near optimal performance in the presence of unreliable data sources).	– Opinion revision in many applied settings, e.g. military, business, medicine, law.

Table 9.2   (contd)

Bias/source of bias	Description	Example
Non-linear extrapolation	– Inability to extrapolate growth processes (e.g. exponential) and tendency to underestimate joint probabilities of several events.	– Gross underestimation of outcomes of exponentially increasing processes and overestimation of joint probabilities of several events.
'Heuristics' used to reduce mental effort:		
– Habit/'rules of thumb'	– Choosing an alternative because it has previously been satisfactory.	– Consumer shopping; 'rules of thumb' adopted in certain professions.
– Anchoring and adjustment	– Prediction made by anchoring on a clue or value and then adjusting to allow for the circumstances of the present case.	– Making a sales forecast by taking last year's sales and adding, say, 5%.
– Representativeness	– Judgements of likelihood of an event by estimating degree of *similarity* to the class of events of which it is supposed to be an exemplar.	– Stereotyping, e.g. imagining that someone is a lawyer because he exhibits characteristics typical of a lawyer.
– Law of *small* numbers	– Characteristics of small samples are deemed to be representative of the populations from which they are drawn.	– Interpretation of data, too much weight given to small sample results (which are quite likely to be atypical).
– Justifiability	– A 'processing' rule can be used if the individual finds a rationale to 'justify' it.	– When provided with an apparently rational argument, people may follow the ensuing rule even if it is inappropriate.
– Regression bias	– Extreme values of a variable are used to predict extreme values of the next observation of the variable (thus failing to allow for regression to the mean).	– Following observation of bad performance by an employee, a manager could attribute subsequent improvement to his intervention (e.g. warning to the employee). However, regression effects would imply that improvement (performance closer to the mean level), is highly likely *without* intervention.

INFORMATION

Consider the conceptual model outlined in Figure 9.1. Judgement is made against the background of a particular task environment and the person's schema for dealing with the task. Consequently the joint characteristics of schema and task affect judgement. We therefore now consider ways of thinking about how both a person's schema and task characteristics can influence bias in judgement. However, before doing so, it is important to recall, first, that judgements are usually made to determine actions, and second, actions are taken to meet goals. For example, the judgement of whether a job candidate is suitable for a particular post implies an action (hire or do not hire) which has to be evaluated relative to a goal (finding an appropriate person for the job). This point is fundamental, since it helps one think about a crucial issue in judgement, namely: Why does a person invoke a particular schema to deal with a particular task? The importance of this question is discussed below.

A person's schema relative to a particular task can be characterized as varying on three dimensions: *veridicality, stability* and *generality*. A *veridical* schema is one that accurately represents reality (e.g. 'the sun rises in the East'). A *stable* schema is one that is not subject to change; and a *general* schema is one that applies to a wide range of phenomena. Schemata, it is argued here, vary on these dimensions and different combinations of the dimensions. However, other things being equal, it can be said that schemata that are either not veridical, or not stable, or not general, are liable to induce bias in judgement. An example of a non-veridical schema is provided by the phenomenon of so-called 'illusory correlation'. People believe that there are relationships between variables (e.g. advertising and sales in a particular situation), which do not in fact exist. The nature of judgemental bias induced by a non-veridical schema is clear: people access inappropriate information when making a prediction.

The stability of a schema is important for two reasons. First, a person with a stable schema is liable to approach the same kind of problems in the same kind of way, and look for and process information in a consistent manner. Consequently, use of a stable schema should be resistant to different physical aspects of a task. Consider, for instance, the judgemental schema invoked when you start a car. Through experience, most people have acquired a stable schema which sets into motion a series of actions (e.g., looking for information by checking the rear-view mirror or across the road, etc., before deciding to place the gear-lever in a position to go forward). On the other hand, if a person's schema is not stable, bias in judgement due, for example, to the clues 'available' in the immediate environment is quite likely.

It should be pointed out, however, that stability alone is not sufficient to avoid bias in judgement. A schema could be both stable *and* non-veridical. In this case, it would clearly lead to consistent bias.

By the generality of a schema is meant the range of situations to which it can be applied. A distinction has been elaborated by Abelson between three levels of types of schema ('cognitive scripts' in his jargon) which can vary from the concrete (i.e. specific) to the abstract (i.e. general).[10] First, a schema can be *episodic*, that is, based on a single experience. Second, a schema can be *categorical*, i.e. apply to a class of experiences which are considered to be identical on several dimensions abstracted by the individual (for example, one could have a categorical schema concerning how you would expect certain types of people to perform in a particular job, based for instance on their type of prior experience). And third, Abelson distinguishes what he calls a *hypothetical* schema. This is a general abstract representation of a situation and, contrary to the other kinds, both allows and facilitates reasoning about the judgemental task. Abelson postulates that the construction of such a general schema can be achieved only if the preceding levels were established beforehand. That is, a series of *episodes* can lead to a person developing a *categoric* schema, experience with this can subsequently be combined with other categoric schemata and lead to developing a *hypothetical* schema. An example of the different levels of schema is the following. A salesman may have had an experience where omitting to emphasize a particular quality of his product seemed to lead to the failure to make a sale. The episodic schema is thus 'failure to mention quality *Y* reduces the probability of making a sale'. Subsequently, this episode could be stored in memory at a more general level, i.e. a *categoric* schema of the form, 'it is important to mention all the qualities of the product when attempting a sale.' After much experience with this and other categoric schemata, the salesman may develop a hypothetical schema involving product quality, price, mode of presentation and some other variables. Consequently, when considering a particular sales pitch he would make a judgement as to how effective a particular presentation would be by evaluating alternative presentations on a number of dimensions. Furthermore, this generalized schema could be applied to a wide range of selling tasks.

Following the above reasoning, it can be seen that to the extent that a schema is generalized, information processing is less likely to be biased (under the assumption, of course, that the schema is *veridical*). A person with a well-developed schema will be more sensitive to information needs relative to a particular task, and thus less liable to availability bias. Furthermore, the person's ability to take into account several variables in making the judgement should be superior to someone with a less well-developed schema. A schema helps a person structure a problem. A generalized schema is, by definition, abstract and thus will be capable of handling abstract and concrete information. An episodic schema, on the other hand, is concrete. It will thus be particularly prone to bias by concrete, as opposed to abstract information. In handling a particular task, of course, one must keep open the possibility that the person invokes several schemata, for example, a general schema for thinking about the problem abstractly, then a specific schema for actually determining a judgement.[11]

As noted above, judgement is the result of interaction between a schema and the task environment. Consequently, an important issue is why a person invokes a particular schema to deal with a given task. There would appear to be two sources that cause a particular schema to be used. First, as stated above, judgement is goal-oriented (i.e. it is instrumental in leading to actions to reach goals). Consequently, prior to dealing with a task a person might invoke a schema for making a judgement. For example, consider that you wish to predict sales of your company. Furthermore, prior to even considering particular values of possible 'cues' you know that estimated GNP and budgeted sales expenses are both strongly related to sales. You therefore invoke the 'sales are influenced by the level of GNP and budgeted sales expenses' schema before either looking for other information or checking the figures concerning GNP and budgeted expenses. In other words, prior to dealing with the problem you invoke a schema out of memory, and it is this that guides your search for information. Second, the actual task variables may suggest a schema to you. For instance, you may not have strong ideas as to what relates strongly to sales, and thus the information you actually see, e.g. records of past sales, budgeted and actual expenses, etc., could suggest a schema to you. Bias in judgement is thus heavily dependent upon the *veridicality* of the schema invoked by the person and/or the task. Other things being equal, one would expect that for problems where people have an available hypothetical schema, this will be invoked. However, in other situations judgement will be more dependent on the structure of the task.

As a final note to the subject of schemata, consider what happens in a situation where a person has no available schema—that is, a judgemental task that is entirely new. In this case the person will bear considerable uncertainty concerning what to do, i.e. *how* to proceed. Consequently, one would expect bias in the form of distractions due both to characteristics of the judgemental task itself and attempts to assimilate the task to a schema the person has already developed (i.e. use of a 'similar' existing schema to handle the task).

In summary, a schema for a particular task can either be imposed by the person on the situation, stimulated by the task variables, or both. A schema can furthermore be classified by the extent to which it is veridical, stable and general. Bias in information processing will clearly depend on whether the schema used is veridical; furthermore, given that a schema might be veridical, bias is more likely when it is unstable and/or specific (i.e. not general).[12]

This book has presented many examples of bias in judgement due to physical task variables, for example: response mode, form of information presentation (e.g. sequential vs. simultaneous), type of information (qualitative, quantitative), etc. In this section four characteristics of judgemental tasks are enumerated, one which reflects these physical aspects. The four characteristics considered are *task complexity*, *procedural uncertainty*, *psychological regret*, and *emotional stress*.

A judgemental task can be complex for a variety of reasons. Variations in quantity and type of information can cause difficulties both in accessing information and actually processing it. Time constraints and various distractions can further complicate these processes.[13] The manner in which a person is required to express a judgement can also induce differential degrees of complexity. For example, consider the difference between being asked which of two alternative scenarios for the future is more likely as opposed to assessing a numerical probability for each of the scenarios. In general, the more complex a judgemental task, the more susceptible people are to judgemental bias.

The second characteristic of judgemental tasks related to bias is what has been called here *procedural uncertainty*. By this is meant the extent to which a person feels uncertainty with a task in respect of knowing how to handle it. This concept links in, of course, with the notion of schema discussed above. In a situation of high procedural uncertainty, a person will not know what to do (i.e. he has no schema). This can lead to bias in the sense that the person is unduly influenced by chance occurrences in the task environment. Situations characterized by high procedural uncertainty are clearly accompanied by deficient or even non-existent schemata and thus open to the biases discussed above in this respect.

The third task characteristic, *psychological regret*, refers to the individual's feelings in the judgemental situation concerning the possibility of making a mistake. This concept was introduced in Chapter 4 where the notion was advanced that a person would engage in mental effort concerning a problem to the extent that he or she felt personally responsible for the outcome—the notion of regret being linked of course to the importance of the outcome. In situations involving little psychological regret, one can anticipate quite high susceptibility to judgemental bias. Care in judgement is not sufficiently exercised. On the other hand, when psychological regret is large, bias in judgement may or may not ensue. It may well occur if the regret forces people to concentrate exclusively on only a part of the problem. However, if people take more care in judgement, potential for bias can be reduced.

Finally, consider the effects of *emotional stress* on judgement. There can be little doubt that stress increases the potential for bias. When under stress, people have greater difficulty in assimilating information and are often unwilling to expend effort in processing the information they do receive.[14]

Table 9.3 summarizes this discussion of characteristics of schemata and tasks that affect bias in judgement. The table indicates situations when bias is likely to occur—that is, when the potential for bias is *large* or *small*. The table does not, of course, delineate the type of bias that could be expected. However, hopefully it can help the reader think through and determine situations where the occurrence of bias is more or less probable.

ORIGINS OF JUDGEMENTAL BIAS

As will become apparent, much of this section is of a speculative nature.[15] The issue is the following: Why do humans, who are capable of considerable physical and conceptual achievements, exhibit the systematic judgemental biases described in this book? How can the minds that design systems capable of placing men on the moon also commit the vast range of elementary errors documented here?

The tentative answer to this question is based on an evolutionary argument. The human mind and body have evolved over millions of years. Furthermore, it is important to realize that our skills have developed to meet the challenges and needs of the environment. That is, evolution consists of adaptation to the environment, which it should be recalled is also composed of other species adapting to the environment. The consequence of ineffective adaptation is

Table 9.3   Potential for bias in judgement (large or small) under different characteristics of schema and task environment

Characteristics of schema

	Veridicality	Stability	Generality
Low	Large	Large	Large
High	Small	Depends on veridicality	Depends on veridicality

Characteristics of tasks

	Complexity	Procedural uncertainty	Psychological regret	Stress
Low	Small	Small *but* depends upon veridicality of schema	Large	Small
High	Large	Large	Large or small (depending on other variables)	Large

extinction of the species. Thus effective adaptation is oriented toward survival.

On considering the development of human skills from this evolutionary perspective, three points should be borne in mind. First, physical skills have had to develop earlier to a greater extent than mental/conceptual skills. That is, in early human development physical skills were at a premium for survival. Second, the design of the human body that has evolved over the centuries by adaptation to environmental conditions represents a compromise between the skills necessary to perform different types of task and the coordination between such skills. For example, in some respects it would be helpful if the human race were taller. However, height can also be a disadvantage—consider the force of gravity, the need to manipulate objects on the ground, etc. Third, our human systems have not evolved in a manner that necessarily implies some 'optimal' design; rather the human species began its existence in a decidedly sub-optimal form. Since then, it has been evolving and developing through natural selection. Furthermore, it is still developing.

Below, a number of judgemental biases are considered in light of the above comments. In doing so, one point will be continually emphasized. Judgemental bias can often be considered the result of a 'trade-off' between different types of error in the design of the human system. This point has been nicely stated by Toda:

To win a survival game, the subject need not be always correct, always precise, nor always very rapid in performing his individual functions, but the co-ordination of these functions should be well balanced and efficiently organized.[16]

Failure to appreciate randomness

It has been pointed out frequently in this book that failure to distinguish random from non-random occurrences, or to confuse chance with cause, can lead to dysfunctional behaviour. People are inept at making predictions involving known random sequences (viz., the gambler's fallacy), and misattributions of chance fluctuations to causal mechanisms are frequent. People are motivated and need to exercise control over their environment. Lack of understanding of random fluctuations clearly indicates unrealistic attempts to control, or at least to believe that one controls, events. However, if one considers that understanding of chance fluctuations cannot be perfect, which of the following two errors is more costly: excessive belief that one can control one's environment, or the belief that what happens is totally beyond one's control? The first position is characterized by excessive, and unrealistic confidence, the latter by helplessness. For creatures who need to master their environments to survive, the first form of delusion is clearly far less costly. In the world of business, for example, it is evident that policies that consist of making the future happen are more successful than 'submitting' to the actions of others. One may deceive oneself with the first policy, but this preferable to the latter.

A related source of judgemental bias concerns the general lack of appreciation of the concept of uncertainty. However, this too can have positive benefits. Uncertain events creat anxiety and can thus inhibit action. Furthermore, avoiding uncertainty is one way of reducing the complexity of the environment.

Inconsistency

As indicated in Chapter 8, inconsistency in judgement is one of the principal reasons that people should be replaced by models in repetitive judgemental tasks. People just do not seem to be capable of highly consistent judgement. Indeed, behaviour itself is often inconsistent and many people even argue that they should have the right to be inconsistent. From an evolutionary perspective, a certain level of inconsistency in behaviour has advantages. Indeed, in a hostile environment, perfectly consistent behaviour is a short-cut to destruction. The animal that always takes the same path to the same waterhole becomes an easy prey to its enemies. Inconsistency in behaviour therefore has the functional advantage of keeping opponents in a state of uncertainty concerning your actions. In a competitive market situation, for example, companies deliberately try to 'keep their competitors guessing' about their future actions. Furthermore, as most people know, in organizational politics people frequently avoid being consistent in order to keep others in suspense concerning their beliefs and/or goals.

A parenthetical point should be made here. It is functional to be inconsistent vis-à-vis one's 'enemies'. However, inconsistency in behaviour with oneself or those close to you is not to be recommended.

A commonly cited cause of inconsistency in repetitive judgement is boredom.

That is, one quickly becomes bored performing the same task in the same manner. Attention wanders and many different signals are picked up from the environment. However, boredom with repetitive tasks can have advantages. In a hostile environment it is necessary to keep aware of what is happening while engaged in a task, thus wandering attention can have positive value in monitoring potential sources of danger. Secondly, boredom induced through a repetitive task can lead one to question how to devise a system to do the task by other means. Necessity, induced by boredom, has clearly been parent to many inventions.

Learning

It was indicated that learning is frequently based on noting that events occur closely together—for example, in time. However, the observation of such joint occurrences can often give misleading information in respect of true relationships in the environment, and particularly when 'non-occurrences' cannot be observed. Nonetheless, the sheer power of the human body and mind to learn by noting positive covariations of events should not be underestimated. Consider, as an example, the ability of children to learn language and particularly the rules of grammar. By observation and experiment based on noting co-occurrences, children acquire schemes capable of generating quite complex behaviour. The same could be said of many motor skills, for example riding a bicycle or steering a car.

However, there are important distinctions between the learning of motor skills, the acquisition and use of language, and certain other conceptual skills, and many of the judgemental skills discussed in this book. These distinctions centre on (1) the conditions under which the skills were acquired, and (2) opportunities for testing and practising the skills. Most people underestimate the potential for learning inherent in situations where judgemental skills are acquired as well as the frequency, or more precisely lack of frequency, with which such skills are put to use.

As an example, contrast the situation where you might make a monthly forecast (in a business, say of sales), with that of using language, or possibly making a perceptual judgement to avoid bumping into an object while walking. The frequency of the first task is clearly far less than that of the second activities. Furthermore, feedback is both less rapid and can be confounded by other factors. Learning by observing or experiencing events that take place both frequently and with rapid feedback is efficient—memory, for example, does not need to be used heavily in the process. However, many important judgemental tasks of the type considered in this book are not of this nature. For example, how often do people make specific competence-based judgements (concerning, for example, revenue, personnel, administrative matters, etc.) compared to the judgements made to function simply as human beings? The proportion must be very small.

The point emphasized here is the following. Our learning processes are efficient for developing many skills necessary to our functioning as human beings. The environmental conditions for learning 'judgement' of more conceptual issues, however, are not so appropriate. We return to this point below.

Memory

Much has been made in this book of the deficiencies and limitations of human memory (see particularly Chapter 6). Whereas remembering is of great use to us in many situations, the efficiency of forgetting should not be overlooked. The amount of information with which a person is confronted is enormous. If we had to remember all that is perceived—through all our senses—the size of human memory would have to be far greater than it is. For example, there would have to be a quite complex process for retrieving information. As it is, human memory is imperfect. However, it is quite rapid (consider for example your ability to encode words and comprehend the meaning of speech), and it is quite adequate for dealing with many tasks we meet in our environment.

Computational capacity

Bias in judgement due to the limited 'computational capacity' of the human mind has been stressed frequently throughout the book. In particular, people avoid investing in 'mental effort' when other paths are open to them. Furthermore, much mental activity consists of 'simplifying' the judgemental situation. Once again, it can be argued that the human race has developed cognitive skills such that certain types of 'computational ability' are not necessary. A good example of this is the following:

> Consider the problem of predicting, before each shot, the direction of travel of a billiard ball hit by an expert billiard player. It would be possible to construct one or more mathematical formulas that would give the directions of travel that would score points and, among these, would indicate the one (or more) that would leave the balls in the best positions. The formulas might, of course, be extremely complicated, since they would necessarily take account of the location of the balls in relation to one another and of the cushions and of the complicated phenomena induced by 'english'. Nonetheless it seems not at all unreasonable that excellent predictions would be yielded by the hypothesis that the billiard player makes his shots *as if* he knew the formulas, could estimate accurately by eye the angles etc., describing the location of the balls, could make lightning calculations from the formulas, and could then make the ball travel in the direction indicated by the formulas.[17]

It is, of course, quite clear that the expert billiard player does not and cannot make the complicated mathematical computations described above when he plays each shot. However, he does manage to coordinate his movements as though he did. (Although he would probably be incapable of telling you *how*). The point being made here is that, despite lack of 'computational ability', people are capable of complex coordinated skills which they can achieve *without* computational ability *such as we understand it*.

Other aspects

There are other human judgemental biases which may also be the 'reverse side' of adaptive behaviour. One concerns the phenomenon whereby once a person has decided upon a course of action, there is a tendency to ignore information that could indicate that the action was ill-advised. However, once action has started, it may often be more costly to stop it before attempting to carry it out. In some cases, it may even be 'impossible' to stop an action once it has been engaged— consider a declaration of war. A second point related to the discounting of information concerns the preservation of a person's own self-image. If one allowed 'unpleasant' information to dominate one's self-image, this could be quite dysfunctional (see also comments above under 'Failure to appreciate randomness').

To summarize the above, I am suggesting the following. Many judgemental biases can be attributed to aspects of human behaviour which have done and still do provide adaptive responses to many situations. In the design of the present human system, Nature has determined a number of trade-offs between, on the one hand, different parts of the system (in order to co-ordinate the whole), and, on the other, different types of error. Until recently, human evolution has adapted to the environment. However, humans now have considerable powers to modify the environment. But in doing so, it must be seriously questioned whether unaided judgement is sufficient to meet the needs of this changing environment. In 'designing humans', natural selection has developed trade-offs between possible errors that were appropriate to the environment humans faced. However, if humans change the environment, they must also change the apparatus (i.e. the human system) for dealing with it. Otherwise, the trade-offs developed through natural selection will no longer be appropriate.

CONCLUDING COMMENTS

Despite the somewhat authoritative manner in which this book is written, it should be made clear that we know relatively little about how the human mind works and its influence on behaviour. The research done to date has only scratched the surface of these issues, and when I say 'scratch the surface', two meanings can be implied: first, existing research has, almost necessarily, dealt with surface phenomena. That is, inferences have been made about the human mind by examining behaviour (i.e. the end result of judgement) under different circumstances; and second, the range of conditions under which human judgement has been systematically examined remains small. Nonetheless, the findings revealed to date do constitute a fairly coherent view of human mental capabilities. Future research will, of course, determine the 'veridicality' of the present-day schema.

The importance of judgement on behaviour is, I believe, generally under-estimated. Few persons seem to be aware that they are continually making all kinds of predictive and evaluative judgements. Indeed, the activity is so common that most of us take it for granted. However, as is true in many other domains, it is precisely those things that we take for granted that should be questioned.

Underlying this book is the premise that it is important to learn the limits of one's judgemental ability. I believe this to be essential for two main reasons: first, because it helps avoid fantasies about the abilities of both oneself and others. The importance of this should not be overlooked. In their professional work, people are frequently evaluated and promoted or demoted as a consequence of actions based on judgements. If, as shown in this book, the relationship between judgement and outcomes is complex, one must question the process by which some persons rise or fall within organizational hierarchies.

Reputations can clearly be gained and lost through purely chance mechanisms. The moral for the individual is clear: whatever others think of you, don't fool yourself. Second, poor judgements can and do lead to disastrous outcomes. Understanding and improving judgement is consequently of great importance.

A few years ago, Paul Slovic made a comparison between a view of the human mind described by William Shakespeare, on the one hand, and that of Herbert Simon, the 1978 Nobel prize winner in economics, on the other.[18] Shakespeare said:

> What a piece of work is man! how noble in reason! how infinite in faculties! in form and moving how express and admirable! in action how like an angel! in apprehension how like a god! the beauty of the world! the paragon of animals!

Simon said:

> The capacity of the human mind for formulating and solving complex problems is very small compared with the size of the problems whose solution is required for objectively rational behavior in the real world—or even for a reasonable approximation to such objective rationality.[19]

The views, admittedly several centuries apart, are quite different. The student of human behaviour will also clearly agree with both men under different sets of conditions. Like Slovic, my own view is expressed by a contemporary of Shakespeare, Francis Bacon. He said: 'We do ill to exalt the powers of the human mind, when we should seek out its proper helps.' It is in precisely this spirit that this book has been written.

NOTES AND REFERENCES

1. Since much of this chapter represents a review of evidence and views expressed in earlier chapters, specific reference is made only to new references.
2. This example is adapted from H. J. Einhorn, Learning from experience and suboptimal rules in decision making. In T. Wallsten (Ed.), *Cognitive processes in choice and decision behavior*. Hillsdale, N.J.: Lawrence Erlbaum, 1980.

3. For an empirical demonstration see D. C. Dearborn and H. A. Simon, Selective perception: A note on the departmental identifications of executives. *Sociometry*, 1958, **21**, 140–144.
4. J. E. Russo, The value of unit price information. *Journal of Marketing Research*, 1977, **14**, 193–201.
5. J. S. Bruner and L. J. Postman, On the perception of incongruity: A paradigm. *Journal of Personality*, 1949, **18**, 206–223.
6. R. M. Hogarth, Cognitive processes and the assessment of subjective probability distributions. *Journal of the American Statistical Association*, 1975, **70**, 271–289.
7. E. J. Langer, The illusion of control. *Journal of Personality and Social Psychology*, 1975, **32**, 311–328.
8. See R. E. Nisbett and L. Ross, *Human inference: Strategies and shortcomings in social judgment*. Englewood Cliffs, N.J.: Prentice-Hall, 1980.
9. Table 9.2 is taken from R. M. Hogarth and S. Makridakis, *Forecasting and planning: An evaluation*. Unpublished manuscript, INSEAD, Fontainebleau, France, 1979.
10. R. P. Abelson, Script processing in attitude formation and decision-making. In J. S. Carroll and J. W. Payne (Eds.), *Cognition and social behavior*, Hillsdale, N.J.: Lawrence Erlbaum, 1976, 33–45.
11. I am indebted to Claude Michaud for this observation.
12. The actual frequency of different types of schemata is an empirical question on which I can hazard but pure guesswork.
13. See, for example, P. Wright, The harassed decision maker: Time pressures, distractions and the use of evidence. *Journal of Applied Psychology*, 1974, **59**, 555–561.
14. See the extensive review on this issue provided by I. L. Janis and L. Mann, *Decision-making: A psychological analysis of conflict, choice, and commitment*. New York: The Free Press, 1977.
15. The writing of this section was stimulated by conversation with Hillel J. Einhorn. Fascinating references on the topic discussed are: D. T. Campbell, Systematic error on the part of human links in communication systems. *Information and Control*, 1959, **1**, 334–369; D. T. Campbell, On the conflicts between biological and social evolution and between psychology and moral tradition. *American Psychologist*, 1975, **30**, 1103–1126; and M. Toda, The design of a fungus-eater: A model of human behavior in an unsophisticated environment. *Behavioral Science*, 1962, **7**, 164–183.
16. Toda, cited in Reference 15, p. 166.
17. M. Friedman and L. J. Savage, The utility analysis of choice involving risk. *Journal of Political Economy*, 1948, **56**, 279–304.
18. P. Slovic, *From Shakespeare to Simon: Speculations—and some evidence—about man's ability to process information*. Eugene, Oregon: Oregon Research Institute Monograph, Vol. 12, No. 12, 1972. The quotation from Shakespeare is from Hamlet, Act II, Scene ii. Whereas one could argue that Slovic took this quotation out of context, it does help indicate the range of qualities ascribed to human mental capabilities.
19. H. A. Simon, *Models of man: Social and rational*. New York: Wiley, 1957, p. 198.

APPENDICES

A. Rules of probability

B. Notes on probability assessment

C. Notes on assessing utility

D. A guide to further reading

APPENDIX A

Rules of probability*

The main text argued that predictive judgement is most usefully expressed in probabilistic form. For instance, instead of saying that there is a 'good chance' of, say, next year's sales exceeding budget, such predictions should be calibrated with an explicit probabilistic statement of the form 'There is a 0.30 probability of next year's sales exceeding target.' However, this type of statement immediately raises two problems: First, what is meant by probability—in this case of 0.30? Second, how are such probabilities assessed? A response to the first question is given below in the section headed 'The "meaning" of probability'. The second question is the subject of Appendix B.

A further use of probability theory referred to in the text concerned the rules governing the probabilities of 'combinations' of events. For example, how should a probabilistic prediction founded on a base-rate be modified by specific data? How does one moderate the predictive validity of a data source by considerations of its reliability? The rules of probability which govern these operations are the subject of this Appendix. Use of the word 'rules', however, requires some clarification. The principles to be enumerated below should be considered rules in the same manner as the rules of logic or arithmetic. You may or may not choose to follow them. But following them guarantees that the probabilities you estimate for combinations of events will be consistent with the assessment of probabilities of the different events of which the combinations are composed. Furthermore, use of the rules allows one to deduce probabilities of single events which may not be intuitively evident.

However, first consider the 'meaning' of probability.

THE 'MEANING' OF PROBABILITY

The 'meaning' of probability has been the subject of long debate and for many the issues are still far from settled. Nonetheless, one, and only one operational definition of probability is given here.

Definition: The probability a person assigns to an event represents his or her

---

* This appendix does not claim to be a complete statement of the intricacies of the rules of probability. It simply aims to provide some basic knowledge and principles to help the reader appreciate aspects of the main text.

subjective *degree of belief* that the event will occur and is expressed on a continuous numerical scale with end-points of 0 and 1.

In other words, a probability is a quantified opinion. The actual scale used is, of course, arbitrary; however, it should be noted that there is no implication that a person's subjective degree of belief is arbitrary. Furthermore, because it is subjective, this does not mean that different people will necessarily differ.

The end-points of the probability scale, 0 and 1, represent certainty. That is, in assigning a probability of 0 to an event a person is saying that he or she is certain that the event will *not* occur; by an assessment of 1, certainty that the event *will* occur is implied. Intermediate values represent different shades of uncertainty. For example, an assessment of 0.50 implies a belief that an event is as likely to occur as not.

For *repetitive* events, most people have a good intuitive feeling for probability based on considering the ratio of so-called 'favourable' to 'possible' occurrences, i.e. the number of times an event did occur divided by the number of times it could have occurred. Familiar gambling devices, such as tossing a coin or die, or observing a roulette wheel, are cases in point. From experience one 'knows' that in tossing a fair coin the chance of observing a 'head' on any throw is about one-half. Similar statements can be made, for example, about the observation of male or female births. The relative frequency of past occurrences of an event is often a useful indicator of probability. However, it is a mistake to equate probability and relative frequency unless one is willing to make a subjective judgement that all 'possible' cases are equally likely, i.e. probable. Hence, a subjective judgement of 'degree of belief' is involved in estimating probabilities on the basis of observed relative frequencies. This issue is discussed in greater detail in Appendix B.

Many important events are, of course, not repetitive. Consider, for example, the possibility of certain types of accident in nuclear power plants or an investment in a new industry. In these cases, subjective judgement—unaided by observation of past relative frequency—is necessarily the sole basis of probability.

People often baulk at the above notions. However, they must be faced squarely. The only comfort that can be given is that the expression of opinions in the form of subjective probabilities that conform to the rules of probability theory is consistent with several intuitively appealing principles of rational behaviour. In other words, if you behave rationally, your subjective opinions can be considered probabilities that conform to the rules of probability theory.

RULES OF PROBABILITY

Events

Probabilities are assigned to *events*, for example the observation of rain at a certain place tomorrow. Consequently, it follows that an event must be precisely defined. For example, if a bet is made conditional on the occurrence of an event it should not be possible for someone to avoid paying the bet on account of a loose definition. The event, rain tomorrow in a certain town, for instance, would have to be operationally defined by a given level of precipitation at a specific point where measurements can be taken.

Events belong to a class of events which make up a range of possibilities (often technically known as a *sample space*). Furthermore, events might themselves be subdivided. As an example, consider assessing probabilities for the level of a company's sales next year. The range of possibilities is from a theoretical minimum of zero to some maximum value. Events can be divisions of that range, for example, all values in excess of budget. This 'event', could be further subdivided into smaller ranges, and at the limit to actual values expressed at the level of dollars and cents.

The actual definition of events one works with in a particular problem must be made specific.

In using probability theory, people often refer to the *complementary event*. This covers all events in the range of possibilities other than the event you are considering. For example, the complementary event to sales exceeding budget is that of sales being equal to or less than budget.

In the sequel, events will be labelled by letters, for instance A, B, E, etc. The shorthand used to denote the probability of an event is given, for example, in the case of event A, by $p(A)$. Events also occur in different kinds of 'combinations'. The reader should therefore note the following:

$p(A \text{ or } B)$	:	the probability that either A *or* B occurs.
$p(A \text{ and } E)$	:	the probability that A *and* E occur.
$p(B\|E)$	:	the conditional probability of B given E (i.e., the probability of B occurring given that E has occurred or could be supposed to have occurred).

Two further points need to be made: (1) events are sometimes *mutually exclusive*, which means that if one occurs the other(s) cannot. Consider, for instance, a horse race with four horses, A, B, C, and D. The event of any one horse winning the race is mutually exclusive of the others—only one horse can win the race (excluding ties). By definition, an event and its complement are mutually exclusive; (2) events can be *independent* of each other. By this is meant that knowledge of the occurrence of one event does not affect the probability of the other, or vice versa. For example, the events of 'rain today' and 'your car breaking down tomorrow' could be independent if your assessment of the probability of both events were the same whether or not you knew the other event had occurred. That is, you assess the same probability of 'your car breaking down tomorrow' irrespective of whether it did or did not rain today. Note that although in many situations one may use data to assess whether two events are independent (for example, sunspots and stock-market prices), in the final analysis independence is a subjective judgement.

Properties and rules of probability theory

There are four properties:

(1) For any event A, $0 \le p(A) \le 1$.
(2) If the set of all the events within a range of possibilities is denoted by S, then

$$p(S) = 1.$$

(3) If A and B are mutually exclusive, then

$$p(A \text{ or } B) = p(A) + p(B).$$

(4) $p(B|C) = \dfrac{p(B \text{ and } C)}{p(C)}$

From these four properties, all the rules (and 'theorems') of probability theory may be derived. Two rules, of 'addition' and 'multiplication', are particularly useful in calculations.

Addition rule

The probability of either of two events, C and D, occurring is

$$p(C \text{ or } D) = p(C) + p(D) - p(C \text{ and } D).$$

In the special case that C and D are *mutually exclusive*, $p(C \text{ and } D) = 0$, and we have Property 3.
   The addition rule generalizes to more than two events.

Multiplication rule

The probability of two events, E and F, both occurring is

$$p(E \text{ and } F) = p(E)p(F|E) = p(F)p(E|F).$$

In other words, 'the probability of both E and F is the probability of E multiplied by the probability of F given E, or the probability of F multiplied by the probability of E given F'. The multiplication rule also generalizes to more than two events. A special case of the multiplication rule occurs when E and F are independent. In this case,

$$p(E) = p(E|F) \quad \text{and} \quad p(F) = p(F|E).$$

That is, knowledge of F does not affect the probability of E, and knowledge of E

does not affect the probability of F. If this is the case, then

$$p(E \text{ and } F) = p(E)p(F).$$

Examples of addition and multiplication rules

The following example may help the reader appreciate both rules. Imagine you are attending a race meeting. You have the opportunity of betting on two horses, G_1 and G_2, running in the same race, and on two horses, H_1 and H_2, running in different races.

In the first race, what is the probability that either G_1 or G_2 wins? Second, what is the probability that both H_1 *and* H_2 win their respective races?

The first question is a simple application of the addition rule for mutually exclusive events: $p(G_1 \text{ or } G_2) = p(G_1) + p(G_2)$. That is, if G_1 or G_2 wins the race, no other horse can win. You clearly have a better chance of picking the winner if you can bet on both G_1 and G_2.

The second question can be answered by the multiplication rule:

$$p(H_1 \text{ and } H_2) = p(H_1)p(H_2|H_1).$$

That is, the probability of both H_1 and H_2 winning is the probability that H_1 wins multiplied by the probability that H_2 wins given that H_1 won. [If H_1 and H_2 are independent, note that $p(H_1 \text{ and } H_2) = p(H_1)p(H_2)$.]

It should be noted that since the probability of an event is at most 1, joint probabilities, e.g. $p(H_1 \text{ and } H_2)$ must be equal to or less than the individual probabilities of which they are composed. Thus the joint probability of several events is frequently a very small number (which, by the way, explains why race tracks can pay such large sums for naming the winners of, say, three consecutive races—in France, the so-called 'tiercé'). People, incidentally, have been shown to overestimate systematically the joint probability of several events, and to underestimate the probability of one of several events occurring. That is, people's unaided intuitions do not appreciate the properties of the multiplication and addition rules.

Bayes' theorem

Property 4 provides the formula for calculating conditional probabilities and is known as Bayes' theorem (or rule). Recalling that

$$p(B \text{ and } C) = p(B)p(C|B),$$

note that Property 4 can be re-written as

$$p(B|C) = \frac{p(B)p(C|B)}{p(C)}$$

which, if both sides are multiplied by $p(C)$, reflects the fact that

$$p(B \text{ and } C) = p(C)p(B|C) = p(B)p(C|B).$$

Bayes' theorem is particularly useful for updating so-called *base-rate* probabilities by *specific* data (cf. Chapter 3).

X-ray problem

The information given is that the *base-rate* or *prior* probability of being ill is 1 out of 200, or 0.005. Denote this by $p(I) = 0.005$. You are also told that the reliability of the X-ray machine can be described as follows:

$$p(+|I) = 0.95$$

$$p(-|\overline{I}) = 0.95.$$

That is, the probability that the X-ray says you are ill ($+$) when you are ill (I) is 0.95; the probability of the X-ray saying you are not ill ($-$) when you are indeed not ill ($\overline{I}$) is also 0.95.

What you are required to estimate is $p(I|+)$, that is the probability that you are sick given that the X-ray indicates you are ill. In other words, how should the information from the X-ray modify your *prior* opinion of being ill—$p(I) = 0.005$—into a so-called *posterior* opinion, $p(I|+)$? From Bayes' theorem,

$$p(I|+) = \frac{p(I)p(+|I)}{p(+)}.$$

In the right hand side, the only quantity not provided in the problem is $p(+)$. However, this can be derived by use of the addition and multiplication rules. Specifically,

$$p(+) = p(I \text{ and } +) + p(\overline{I} \text{ and } +)$$

$$= p(I)p(+|I) + p(\overline{I})p(+|\overline{I}).$$

This equation is usually not intuitively evident. Consequently, Table A.1. may help.

Table A1

	Ill (I)	Not ill $(\overline{I})$	
Test indicates ill $(+)$	$p(+ \text{ and } I)$	$p(+ \text{ and } \overline{I})$	$p(+)$
Test indicates well $(-)$	$p(- \text{ and } I)$	$p(- \text{ and } \overline{I})$	$p(-)$
	$p(I)$	$p(\overline{I})$	

The cells of the table indicate joint probabilities, the totals in the margins represent the so-called marginal probabilities, e.g. $p(+)$. Note that $+$ can occur with either I or $\overline{I}$, thus

$$p(+) = p(+ \text{ and } I) + p(+ \text{ and } \overline{I}).$$

The same table completed with numbers from the problem is given in Table A2.

TABLE A2.

	I	$\overline{I}$	
$+$	0.004 75	0.049 75	0.0545
$-$	0.000 25	0.945 25	0.9455
	0.005	0.995	

Consequently,

$$p(I|+) = \frac{p(I)p(+|I)}{p(+)}$$

$$= \frac{0.005 \times 0.95}{0.0545}$$

$$= \underline{0.087}$$

The cab problem

The information given in the problem is as follows:

$p(G) = 0.85$ There is a base-rate or prior probability that a cab is Green. (Note, $p(B) = 0.15$).

$p(SG|G) = 0.80$ When testing witnesses, 80% of Green cabs were said to be green (SG). Consequently,

$$p(SB|G) = 0.20.$$

$p(SB|B) = 0.80$ When testing witnesses, 80% of Blue cabs were said to be blue (SB). Consequently,

$$p(SG|\overset{B}{\cancel{G}}) = 0.20.$$

The probability that the cab involved in the accident was blue is $p(B|SB)$. This is

$$p(B|SB) = \frac{p(B)p(SB|B)}{p(SB)}$$

Following the same procedure as above, the probability to be deduced from the data is $p(SB)$. Therefore, proceeding in the same manner as before,

$$p(SB) = p(B \text{ and } SB) + p(G \text{ and } SB)$$
$$= p(B)p(SB|B) + p(G)p(SB|G)$$
$$= (0.15 \times 0.80) + (0.85 \times 0.20)$$
$$= 0.29.$$

Therefore,

$$p(B|SB) = \frac{p(B)p(SB|B)}{p(SB)}$$
$$= \frac{0.15 \times 0.80}{0.29}$$
$$= \underline{0.41.}$$

It is unusual for people to be able to work out the correct answers to these problems without prior exposure to similar kinds of problems. The best advice for novices is to play with tables, as illustrated for the X-ray problem, as opposed to manipulating formulae. Bayes' theorem is the normative method for modifying *base-rate* opinion by *specific* data.

APPENDIX B

Notes on probability assessment

This appendix, which is written in tutorial fashion, provides guidelines to probability assessment and an introduction to some probabilistic ideas.* No prior knowledge of probability or statistics is assumed other than some definitions given in Appendix A.

The reader is advised to work through the appendix and, in particular *to do* the exercises which can also be supplemented by assessment tasks from the reader's own experience. The material has been found more useful if several persons work through the exercises together.

The appendix is organized in six sections:

- First experience with probability assessment.
- Graphical representation of probability assessment.
- Exercises in graphical representation.
- The method of successive subdivisions.
- Checking out probability assessments.
- Assessing probabilities from historical data.

FIRST EXPERIENCE WITH PROBABILITY ASSESSMENT

To appreciate what is involved in the assessment of probability, it is helpful to consider a concrete example. Specifically, I asked three friends the following question:

Do you believe that the population of the greater London area is:
    less than 11 million?
    between 11 and 13 million?
    greater than 13 million?

None of the three knew the answer for certain. However, note that I have defined three events which are both mutually exclusive and exhaustive (i.e. they cover the range of all possibilities). Thus one of the events must be true.

My three friends assigned probabilities—representing their *subjective degrees of belief*—to the events as given in Table B1.

* The notes are based on previously unpublished material developed by R. M. Hogarth and J. Téboul.

193

Table B.1

Event	Probabilities		
	Roger	Tom	Michael
Less than 11 million	0.10	0.70	0.30
11 to 13 million	0.80	0.20	0.50
Greater than 13 million	0.10	0.10	0.20
	1.00	1.00	1.00

First, note that my three friends had quite different opinions. Second, they are all consistent in the sense that in each case the sum of the probabilities assigned to the range of possibilities equals one.

But which of my friends was correct in his assessment? There is no answer to this since they all just said what they believed.*

The best way to consider probability assessment is to try it oneself. Therefore, please complete the following exercises:

(A) You see before you a picture of a person. How old do you think she is?

---

* Problems of determining the 'validity' of probability assessments are discussed further below.

Years

Less than 15	_____
15–20	_____
21–25	_____
26–30	_____
31–35	_____
36–40	_____
41–45	_____
Greater than 45	_____

Here age has been broken down into 8 mutually exclusive and exhaustive classes. Record your opinion in probabilistic form beside each age classification. For example, you think that the person is between 21 and 25 years of age with probability . . . . Remember that to be *consistent*, the sum of your probabilities must equal one.

Also, do not feel compelled to stick to your original assessments. Feel free to change assessments as you like. Simply record your opinion.

Take your time and do this task extremely carefully. Ask yourself, in particular, what knowledge you have concerning the issue at hand.

(B) You are presented with another picture. Once again, how old do you think this person is?

Do this exercise in the same manner as the last. However, whereas last time age groupings were provided, this time feel free to use whatever age groupings you deem appropriate.

(C) Why not try birth-dates of some well-known people?

Jimmy Carter,

Valéry Giscard d'Estaing,

Queen Elizabeth.

(In these cases it is possible to check your answers against records).

Evaluating the exercises

You have now just completed a task which many people find very difficult. The difficulty you may have experienced is probably due to the fact that although the task in itself was somewhat trivial (and you had some idea of the range in which the true replies must lie), you have probably never questioned yourself so precisely concerning such matters before.

Experience indicates that the most difficult facet of probability assessment is asking yourself what you really think. As you are the only person who can judge what this is, there is no single way to determine how this should be done. You may find it useful to try out these exercises with some friends. Ask them afterwards how they went about doing the exercises and compare your different approaches.

GRAPHICAL REPRESENTATION OF PROBABILITY ASSESSMENTS

Probability assessments are often usefully represented in the form of graphs. This section presents some basic material concerning the representation of probability assessments in graphical form.

1. Histograms

Consider the distribution shown in Table B2 of the age of a person known to be between 16 and 50 years of age, which has been assessed by considering seven class intervals of 5 years.

Table B.2

Age	Class interval (in years)	Probability
16–20	5	0.03
21–25	5	0.12
26–30	5	0.25
31–35	5	0.35
36–40	5	0.20
41–45	5	0.04
46–50	5	0.01
		1.00

It is possible to represent this distribution in the form of a graph known as a *histogram*, as shown in Fig B.1.

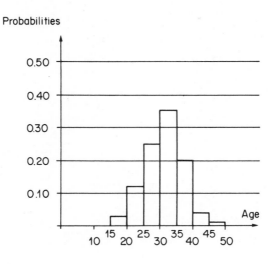

Figure B.1

The graph shows age on the abscissa (i.e. horizontal axis) and probability on the ordinate (i.e. vertical axis). The histogram gives a good indication of the general shape of the assessed probability distribution; however, its interpretation can be misleading in that the graph depends upon the fact that the variable—age—has been considered in seven intervals of 5 years.

Consider, for example, what happens if the assessed probabilities are broken down into *one* class interval of 5 years, and *three* of 10, as shown in Table B3.

Table B.3

Age	Class interval (in years)	Probability
16–20	5	0.03
21–30	10	0.37
37–40	10	0.55
41–50	10	0.05
		1.00

This distribution, which is entirely consistent with the preceding one, yields the histogram shown in Fig. B.2. This histogram is clearly different from the original one, a fact which is brought home when the first histogram is placed over the second (Fig. B.3).

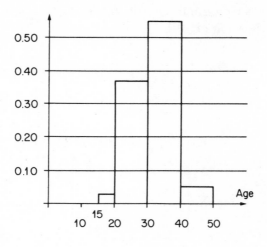

Figure B.2

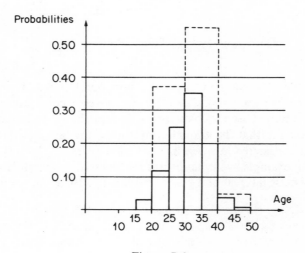

Figure B.3

It is evident that the form of the graph depends upon the class interval chosen, and this is a severe constraint. However, this problem can be overcome if, instead of representing *probability* on the ordinate, we use this axis to represent *probability per unit of measure* of the intervals—here 'years'.

2. Probability density

This probability per unit of measure is called *probability density*, and is calculated by dividing the probability of each class interval by the unit of measure (years), as shown in Table B.4.

Table B.4

Age	Class intervals (in years)	Probability	Probability density (× 1000)
16–20	5	0.03	6
21–25	5	0.12	24
26–30	5	0.25	50
31–35	5	0.35	70
36–40	5	0.20	40
41–45	5	0.04	8
46–50	5	0.01	2

(Note that the densities have been multiplied by 1000 to avoid decimals)

By way of example, consider the interval 16–20. The probability 0.03 divided by 5 yields 0.006 (which, when multiplied by 1000 gives 6).

For the second table of probabilities we obtain Table B.5. The resulting histograms are as given in Fig. B.4. Note that the histograms are now comparable.

Table B.5

Age	Class interval (in years)	Probability	Probability density (× 1000)
16–20	5	0.03	6
21–30	10	0.37	37
31–40	10	0.55	55
41–50	10	0.05	5

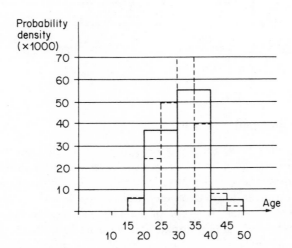

Figure B.4

3. Transforming histograms

In the example of the assessment of age considered here, it is difficult to ask someone to assess a probability for *each* age—i.e. the probability of 16, 17, 18, etc. It is far easier to consider intervals of age—in the example, *seven* intervals of 5 years. However, often what is ultimately desired is a more refined distribution than that given by the class intervals. This may be achieved by simply drawing a smooth line through the mid-points of the class intervals at the tops of the rectangles forming the histogram.

The second graph in Fig. B.5 is a subjective extrapolation by the assessor of his initial assessment. It may be considered as the graph he would have obtained had he been able to decompose the variable considered (age) into infinitely small subdivisions. It is known as the assessor's *probability density function*—or, for short, *PDF*.

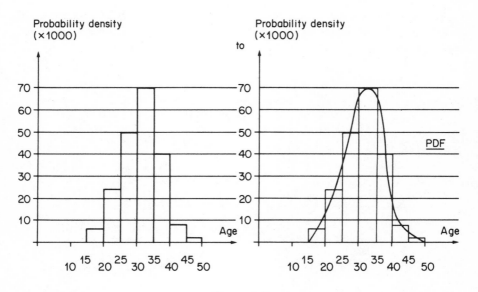

Figure B.5

4. Measuring probability by a PDF

On the graph of the *probability density function (PDF)* given in Fig. B.5, *probability density* is given on the ordinate (i.e. vertical axis), and the *variable*— age—on the horizontal axis (i.e. abscissa). How does one therefore measure the probability for a given interval of age—say, 29–33 years?

By the manner in which the graph of the *PDF* was constructed, the total area between the *PDF* and the horizontal axis *must* be equal to 1. Therefore, the probability of any given interval—in this case 29–33—must be the area under the *PDF* between the limits of the interval considered. An example is given in

Fig. B.6. However, calculating or measuring such areas is not easy. Therefore, consider an alternative route.

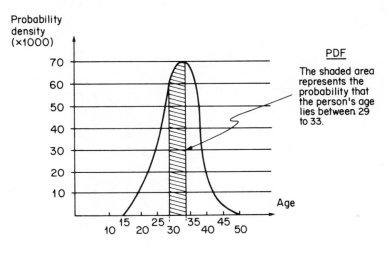

Figure B.6

5. Cumulative probabilities

Instead of asking what the probability is that the person's age lies within a certain interval (e.g. 29 to 33) first ask 'what is the probability that the person is younger than a given age?'. To answer this, reconsider the original distribution of age—with class intervals of 5 years—and construct a table of *cumulative* probabilities (Table B.6).

Table B.6

Age	Probability		Age	Probability that person is less than or equal to the given age
16–20	0.03		20	0.03
21–25	0.12		25	$0.03 + 0.12 = 0.15$
26–30	0.25		30	$0.15 + 0.25 = 0.40$
31–35	0.35		35	$0.40 + 0.35 = 0.75$
36–40	0.20		40	$0.75 + 0.20 = 0.95$
41–45	0.04		45	$0.95 + 0.04 = 0.99$
46–50	0.01		50	$0.99 + 0.01 = 1.00$

By way of example, note that the probability that the person is less than or equal to 25 is the probability of his age being in the interval 16–20, i.e. 0.03, *plus* that of the interval 21–25, i.e. 0.12: $0.03 + 0.12 = 0.15$ as indicated; the remaining figures are obtained in analogous manner.

A graph of the cumulative probabilities can be drawn as in Fig. B.7. Next, 'smooth' the graph by drawing a curve through the tops of all the lines. (Once again, this is a subjective extrapolation of the original probability assessment.) The graph so obtained (Fig. B.8) is known as a *cumulative distribution function* or, for short, *CDF*.

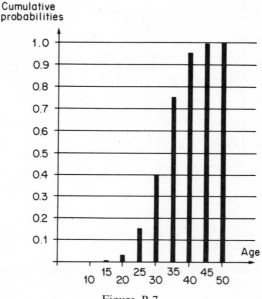

Figure B.7

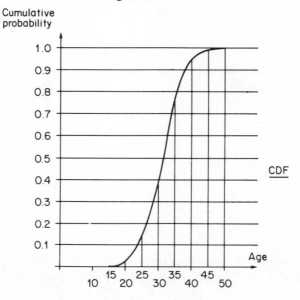

Figure B.8

6. Measuring probabilities with a CDF

The cumulative distribution function (CDF) permits easy calculation of any given interval of the variable. For example, consider the interval 29–33. From the *CDF* we can read:

(1) The probability that the person is younger than 33 is 0.64.
(2) The probability that he is younger than 29 is 0.30.

Thus the probability that the person's age lies in the interval 29–33 is 0.64–0.30 = 0.34.

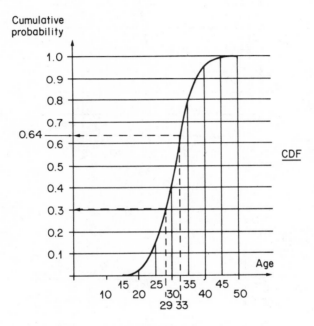

Figure B.9

7. Relationship between PDF and CDF

Mode—Median—Fractiles

It is illuminating to represent a *probability density function (PDF)* and *cumulative distribution function (CDF)* together, as in Figs. B.10 and B.11.

The distribution may be characterized by two measures of *central tendency*.

The *mode* is the value which corresponds to the greatest probability density— i.e. to the highest point on the *PDF*. In the example this is 33.

The *median* is the value for which there is as much probability that the person's age is equal to or less than this figure, as that it is above it. It thus corresponds to the 0.50 point on the ordinate of the *CDF*. In the example considered here, therefore, the median is 32. The median is the value which cuts the range of possible values of the variable into two equally likely subdivisions.

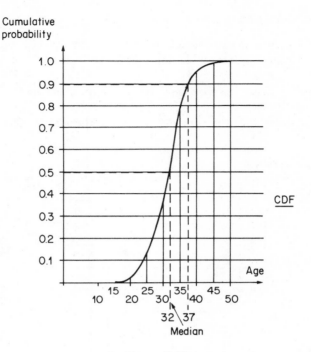

Figure B.10

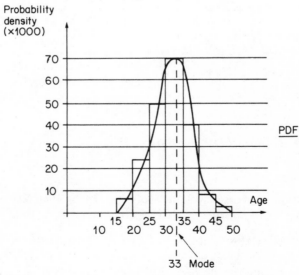

Figure B.11

The *median* is, in fact, a special case of any point on the scale of the variable (here age) corresponding to a point of the cumulative probability scale known as a *fractile*. The age 37, for example, is the 0.90 *fractile* (see previous *CDF*). Thus the median is the 0.50 *fractile*.

8. Summary

The key points to note from this section are:

(1) A *probability density function (PDF)* shows the relationship existing between probability density and the variable studied. (Probability density is probability per unit of measure and is thus independent of the size of class intervals considered initially).

(2) The area under the graph of a *PDF* is equal to 1 (reflecting allocation of probabilities to all possible values of the variable).

(3) The point corresponding to the highest point of the *PDF* is known as the *mode* of the distribution. It is *the most likely value*.

(4) Cumulative probabilities may be represented by a graph of the *cumulative distribution function (CDF)*.

(5) The points indicated on the vertical axis of the graph of the *CDF* (which show the cumulative probabilities) determine—through the *CDF*—the *fractiles* of the distribution of interest.

(6) The value of the variable represented by the 0.50 fractile is called the *median* of the distribution. This point signifies that one half of the assessed probability lies below it and one half above it.

Exercises on graphical representation

(A) (i) What is the *mode* of a distribution?
   (ii) What is the *median* of a distribution?
   (iii) What is meant by the statement: 'the median is the 0.50 fractile'?

(B) The variable 'age' considered in the text is an example of a *continuous* variable. That is, a variable which may take any one of an infinite number of values: for example, 25 years, 10 months, 5 days, 4 hours, 3 minutes, 10 seconds, 12 milliseconds, etc., is one possible value and there are clearly an infinite number of these. A *discrete* variable, on the other hand, is one that may take only a certain given number of values; for example, the number of goals scored in a soccer match (0, 1, 2, 3, 4, 5, 6, etc.). Whether we are dealing with *discrete* or *continuous* variables the principles enumerated above remain exactly the same, but with one exception: since we no longer have probabilities for intervals of the variable, we talk of probability *mass* instead of probability *density*.

Draw the probability *mass* function (*PMF*) and cumulative distribution function (*CDF*) for the assessed distribution shown in Table B.7.

(Note: Since discrete variables can often be treated *as though* they were continuous, in the rest of this appendix all variables are treated as continuous.)

(C) Take one of the distributions you assessed at the last exercise and draw both the *PDF* and *CDF* of this distribution. Try and do this in a manner such that you have a continuous distribution which satisfies you. To do this, you may be forced to modify your opinion concerning the characteristic studied. This does not matter so long as you still express your opinion.

(D) *Reading graphs* Try to have a friend work through this appendix with you. Exchange the graphs of your *CDF*s. These graphs represent your assessed opinions concerning the characteristics of interest—in the present example, ages of different persons. Read and try to understand the graph of your friend. In particular, ask your friend questions concerning the probabilities of events and see to what extent his or her answers agree with the opinions previously assessed on the graphs. For example, ask what the probability is that the girl in the picture is less than 31. Or, that she is between 21 and 23? Your friend has already implicitly given an answer to these questions in the graphs. See to what extent his or her opinions still agree with the graphs.

Table B.7   *Probability of the number of goals that will be scored in a certain soccer match*

Number of goals	Probability
0	0.30
1	0.20
2	0.20
3	0.10
4	0.10
5	0.05
6	0.05

ANSWERS TO EXERCISES ON GRAPHICAL REPRESENTATION

(A) (i) The *mode* is the point of the abscissa of a *PDF* corresponding to the highest point of that graph. It is the most probable value.
   (ii) The *median* is the point which divides all possible values of the variable into two equally likely subdivisions.
   (iii) The median is a specific fractile, namely the 0.50 *fractile.*
(B) See Figs. B.12, B.13.

THE METHOD OF SUCCESSIVE SUBDIVISIONS

1. Methods of probability assessment

So far you have assessed probability distributions by considering fixed intervals of the variable under study and then allocating probability to the intervals. For example, fixed intervals of five years were considered and then the likelihood of each of the intervals was estimated. This approach is called the *variable fixed* method.

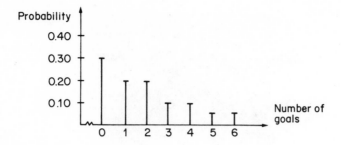

Figure B.12 Probability mass function for number of goals to be scored in a certain soccer match

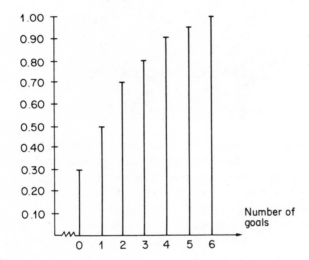

Figure B.13 Cumulative distribution function for number of goals to be scored in a certain soccer match

It is, however, also possible to attack probability assessment from another angle: specifically to consider *fixed intervals of probability* and then ask what values of the variable are covered by these fixed probability intervals. These methods are called the *probability fixed* approach. One such method is presented here.

2. The method of successive subdivisions

Once again, age is used as an example. Consider the accompanying picture of a person for whose age you are asked to assess a probability distribution.

The method presented is known as the *method of successive subdivisions*, for reasons that will become evident. This method enables one to record the assessed distribution directly onto a graph of the *CDF* (*cumulative distribution function*).

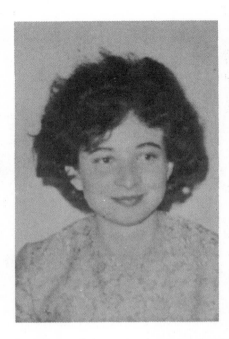

Age is recorded on the abscissa and cumulative probabilities on the ordinate. In the present example, assume that the person's age is assessed to lie between 20 and 45. That is, it is deemed impossible that the person's age is less than 20 or greater than 45. The reader will find the presentation easier to understand if he or she also attempts to assess a distribution as illustrated here.

The method of successive subdivisions consists of asking questions to determine particular fractiles of the distribution being assessed. The procedure is as follows:

Question 1

For which age do you deem it is equally likely that the person's age is above that age as it is below it? In other words, can you determine an age for which you deem there is as much probability that the person *is* that age, or *younger*, than that she is *older* than the given age? Another way of saying this is: Can you divide the range of possible ages into two equally likely subdivisions? What is the age which separates these two subdivisions?

On the abscissa of your *CDF* place a mark beside this age. Recall, however, what this age means for you. It means that you consider it equally likely that the person's age lies between 20 and the indicated age, as that it lies between that age and 45.

As you have no doubt already noticed, the point you have just determined is the *median* or 0.50 *fractile* of your distribution.

In short, *M*—the median—is the point for which you should be prepared to bet

that there is an equal chance that the person is older or younger than that age—
M. For example, the median age, M, was assessed by the author to be 29, and is
marked as shown in Fig. B.15.

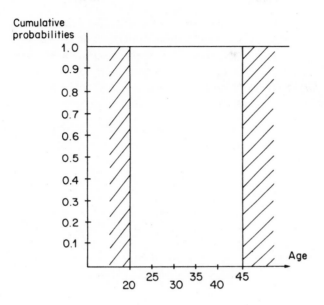

Figure B.14

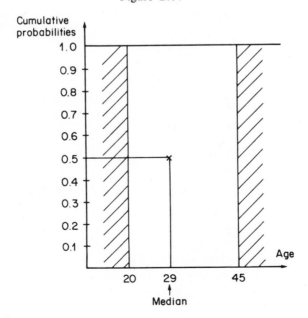

Figure B.15

Question 2

Now consider only ages *below* the median—*M*—you have just assessed. Can you determine a point on the interval from 20 to your previously assessed median—*M*—where you consider that it is equally likely that the person's age lies below that point (i.e. age) as above it? In other words, can you divide the interval from 20 to your previously assessed median into two intervals which have equal probability? When you find this point, mark it on the abscissa (i.e. age axis) of your *CDF*. To make this assessment, it may help you to *imagine that you have been told that the person is under M years of age*. Under this hypothesis, proceed exactly as in the first question.

The author considered the relevant age to be 27. This is marked on the graph of the *CDF*. As you will have noticed, the age 27 is the 0.25 *fractile* of the author's distribution.

Question 3

Now consider possible ages *above* the median of your distribution—*M*. Can you find a point between your 'median' and 45 years for which you consider it equally likely that the person is under that age as older than it? That is, can you divide the interval from the median to 45 into two equi-probable sub-intervals? Please mark the point which separates these subintervals on the abscissa of your *CDF*.

The author assessed the relevant age to be 33. This is marked on the graph in Fig. B.17. 33 is, of course, the 0.75 *fractile* of the author's distribution.

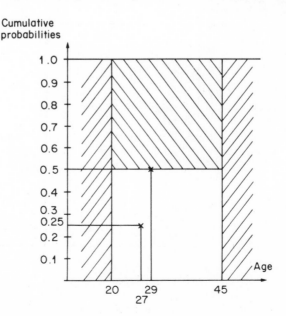

Figure B.16

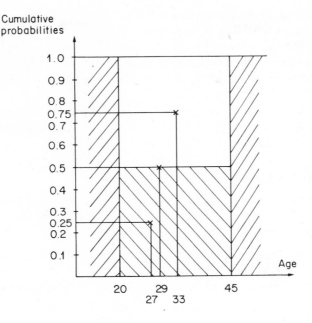

Figure B.17

3. Summary of questions

The range of possible ages was first delimited: 20 to 45. 20 therefore corresponds to the 0.00 *fractile*, and 45 to the 1.00 *fractile* of the distribution.

Then:

(1) A point was determined between 20 and 45 below and above which there was an equal probability of the person's true age being in either interval. That is, it was considered that the person could equally well be older than the given age as younger. The point so determined is the *median* or 0.50 *fractile* of the assessed distribution. For the author, this point was 29 years.

(2) Next, only ages below 29 (the assessed median) were considered possible, and the interval from 20 to 29 was divided into two equally likely subdivisions. This time the relevant age was assessed to be 27. Note that it has in effect been said that it is equally likely that the person's age lies:

between 20 and 27 on the one hand, and
between 27 and 29 on the other.

(3) Next, attention was restricted to ages above the median, 29; and the interval from 29 to 45 was divided into two equally likely subdivisions. On this occasion the assessed age was 33. This means that it is considered equally likely that the person's age lies between 29 and 33 as that it lies between 33 and 45.

Of course, certain specific ages were taken above, and there is no reason why the ages adopted here should correspond to the ages which you assessed.

Reconsider the assessed points. The age of 29—the first point assessed—was seen to be the *median* or 0.50 *fractile* of the distribution. The age 27 divided the interval between 20 and 29 into two equally likely subdivisions. Hence, since 29 was the 0.50 *fractile*, 27 must be the 0.25 *fractile*.

Similarly, the interval between 29 and 45 was divided into two equally likely subdivisions at the age of 33. Thus, as 29 is the 0.50 *fractile* and 45 marks the maximum possible age, 33 must be the 0.75 *fractile*.

4. Checking the points

Having marked these points on the graph (Fig. B.18), recall for a moment what they mean. For illustrative purposes, this is done using the figures assessed here. Your own figures will probably be different.

(1) It is considered equally likely that the person is above 29 years of age as that she is equal to or below that age.
(2) The following age intervals are considered to be equally likely:

   20–27   27–29   29–33   33–45.

   There is probability of 0.25 that the person's true age lies in each of these intervals.
(3) Furthermore, it is considered *twice* as likely that, for example, the person's age lies between 29 and 45 than that it lies between 20 and 27 or 27 and 29.

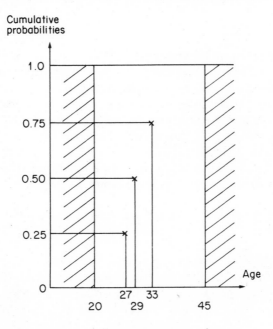

Figure B.18

Reconsider the three points which you have just assessed for the 0.25, 0.50 and 0.75 *fractiles* and see whether you are satisfied that the kinds of relationships discussed above also hold for your figures. For example, check that *for you* the interval between your 0.75 *fractile* and 45 is really only *half* as likely as the interval between 20 and your 0.50 *fractile* (median).

When you have finished checking out these relationships, mark any necessary changes on your *CDF*.

5. Drawing the CDF

There are now five points on the *CDF* and a line can be smoothed through the points to give an estimation of the *CDF* (Fig. B.19). Of course, there is no rule as to the number of points which are necessary to do this. One simply assesses as many points as are deemed necessary to estimate the distribution.

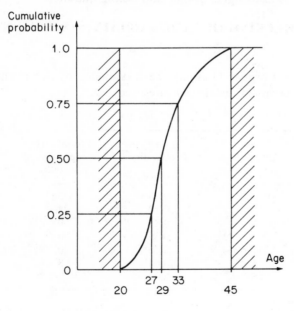

Figure B.19

6. Summary

The method of successive subdivisions consists of six steps:

(1) Determine the range of possible values the variable can take (i.e. the *fractiles* 0.00 and 1.00 of the distribution).

   In point of fact, in order to save yourself from too many 'surprises' (or the occurrence of events deemed *impossible*) it is often wiser to start out by assessing the 0.01 and 0.99 *fractiles* of the distribution. Delimiting the 0.00 and 1.00 *fractiles* may be too categoric.

(2) Determine the median or 0.50 *fractiles*.

(3) Determine the 0.25 *fractile*.
(4) Determine the 0.75 *fractile*
(5) Question yourself as to whether you are really satisfied with the assessed *fractiles*, and if so,
(6) Draw a smooth line through the assessed *fractiles*.

7. Exercises

Use the method of successive subdivisions to assess probability distributions for:

the population of your town;
the revenue of your organization next year;
the height of the building in which you work.

If you are working through the appendix with a friend, check out your distributions by exchanging graphs and asking questions.

CHECKING OUT PROBABILITY ASSESSMENTS

1. Summary

Up to this point probabilities have been estimated by two methods:
(i) Where intervals of the *variable* are fixed, viz.:

Table B.8

Age	Class intervals (*in years*)	Probability	Probability density (× 1000)	Cumulative probability
16–20	5	0.03	6	0.03
21–25	5	0.12	24	0.15
26–30	5	0.25	50	0.40
31–35	5	0.35	70	0.75
36–40	5	0.20	40	0.95
41–45	5	0.04	8	0.99
46–50	5	0.01	2	1.00

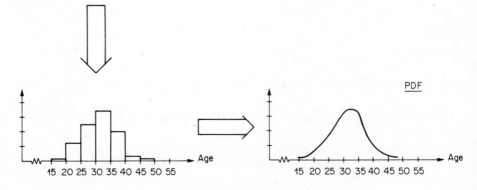

Figure B.20

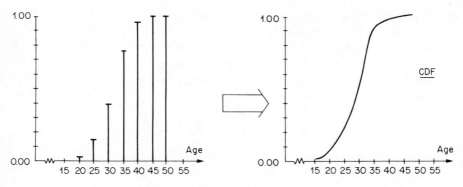

Figure B.21

(ii) Where intervals of *probability* are fixed, viz.:

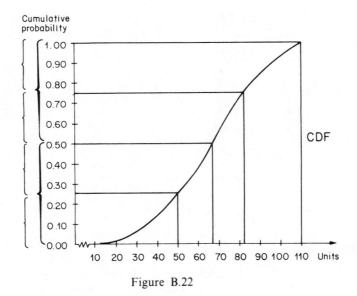

Figure B.22

2. Coherence

The basic requirement of a probability assessment is that it should be *coherent*, and more specifically, coherent in *two* respects:

(1) The assessed distribution should be coherent with the laws of probability, e.g. the probabilities assigned to a set of mutually exclusive and exhaustive events should sum to 1; and

(2) The assessed distribution should also be *coherent* with the assessor's state of uncertainty. For example, if we are fairly certain concerning the age of a person we might assign a *tight* distribution, as in Fig. B.23. However, if we are very uncertain, the distribution should be more spread out, as in Fig. B.24. But no matter *how* uncertain you are concerning a given event, you should always be able to assess a distribution which is *coherent* with your degree of uncertainty.

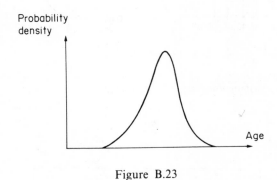

Figure B.23

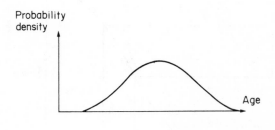

Figure B.24

3. Evaluation

Strictly speaking, a probability assessment cannot be 'evaluated' in that it is simply a statement of the assessor's personal 'degree of belief'. Indeed, the only case where one can say a particular assessment is 'wrong', is when after a categoric assessment (i.e. probability of 0 or 1), the 'impossible' happens.

However, in predictive situations it is legitimate to assess the extent to which a person's assessments are realistic. This may be done by considering, over a series of assessments, the degree to which the person's assessments are matched by the empirical relative frequency of the events assessed. For example, events for which probabilities of 0.60 are assessed should occur about 60% of the time. Occasionally, an assessor who is well *calibrated* should observe surprises. However, actual and expected surprises should be roughly equal. That is, in 100 assessments, a well-calibrated assessor should experience about:

- 2 true values falling outside the assessed 0.01 and 0.99 fractiles;
- 20 true values falling outside the assessed 0.10 and 0.90 fractiles;
- 40 true values falling outside the assessed 0.20 and 0.80 fractiles;
- 50 true values falling outside the assessed 0.25 and 0.75 fractiles; and so on.

A typical finding in many studies of probability assessment is that people experience too many surprises. Their distributions are often 'tighter' than is justified by subsequent reality. In other words, there is a strong tendency toward over-confidence in assessment.

4. Sources of surprises

As indicated in the main text, there are many judgemental biases and these affect probability assessment. Consider the following:

(a) *Avoidance of uncertainty.* The notion of uncertainty is uncomfortable. By failing to face up to uncertainty we do not acquire mechanisms for dealing with it explicitly.

(b) *Representativeness.* We tend to imagine that what we see or will see is *typical* of what can occur. We seldom give credence to the possibility of 'surprising' or 'unusual' events. Hence we tend to assess distributions which are too 'tight'.

(c) *Availability* When imagining what could happen, we remember similar past situations. Unfortunately, our memory search process for similar instances often stops after superficial recollection and may tend to be overly-biased by recent events (e.g. the last sales campaign).

(d) *Anchoring and adjusting.* In making any particular judgement, we tend first to 'anchor' on a specific value of the uncertain quantity (e.g. last year's revenue) and then make adjustments from this anchor point. Unfortunately, the anchor tends to dominate our judgement even though it may not be entirely relevant to the particular task at hand.

(e) *Internal coherence.* We like our judgements to be coherent with facts we have observed. Thus, if we do know of events which are inconsistent with our beliefs we tend to diminish their importance in formulating our judgements.

(f) *Unstated assumptions.* Our judgements are often made against a background of assumptions which are not made explicit (for example, our stated probability distribution may be conditional upon the premise that our competitors will *not* undertake a certain action).

5. Methodology bias

Different methods of assessing probabilities induce different stated probability distributions.

218

6. Avoiding surprises/biases

(1) Be sure that the variable for which you are to assess a distribution is *unambiguously* defined. What are your implicit and explicit assumptions concerning the task at hand?

(2) Ask yourself what you *know* about the task at hand and not just what you *think* you know.

(3) Is the judgemental 'heuristic' you are using susceptible to bias? Check the following:

   (a) Are you avoiding uncertainty?

   (b) Try to think in terms of ranges of values and not just one *typical* value (i.e. fight 'representativeness').

   (c) Have you considered *all* the information *available* to you and not just that which comes first to your mind?

   (d) To what extent does/did the first number you thought of determine your entire assessment?

   (e) Have you considered all *conflicting*—as well as coherent—evidence?

(4) Check out your distribution by different assessment methods:

   • Assess your distribution by probability fixed *and* variable fixed approaches.

   • Reconcile the sources of differences (don't just split the difference unless you know why!).

   • Have someone question you concerning the implications of your assessment.

   • In actually making an assessment, use *external random processes* in order to calibrate your judgements. For example, consider an example of age:

     (a) When assessing the median a useful reference is to consider the probability of observing—say, heads on the toss of a fair coin.

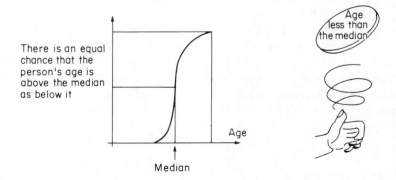

Figure B.25

(b) For assessing extreme fractiles, consider the possibility of randomly drawing, say, one black ball out of an urn containing 98 white and 2 black balls.

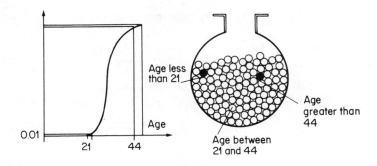

Figure B.26

(c) One may also usefully consider a roulette wheel to assess the chances of an event occurring.

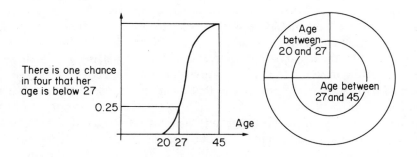

Figure B.27

7. Summary

Probability assessment is difficult. It is open to biases and there is *no one true method*. To be effective, we need to ask ourselves searching questions and to avoid biases. In practice, this means:

(1) use *different* methods for the same assessment task;
(2) develop means for questioning ourselves concerning our judgements, i.e. beware of human biases; have others question us; compare our judgements to external random processes, etc.

ASSESSING PROBABILITIES FROM HISTORICAL DATA

1. Definitions of probability

(a) Probability has been defined here as a *measure of a degree of belief* (see Appendix A).

(b) Another commonly used definition is the ratio of favourable to possible cases, i.e.

$$p = \frac{\text{number of 'favourable' cases}}{\text{number of possible cases}}$$

(where *p* stands for 'probability').

This is the so-called objective definition, although as will be shown below, it is but a *special case of the subjective* view.

2. Establishing the ratio *p*

A machine produces plastic caps for bottles at the rate of 200 per hour. In every hour, the machine produces a number of *defective* caps, and thus it is uncertain how long the machine should be run in order to produce 200 *good* caps. To answer this question, it would be useful to know the probability that any given cap produced by the machine is defective, and thus, how many good caps one could *expect* the machine to make in a given period of time.

One way to estimate the probability that a cap produced by the machine is defective is empirical observation. Assume, therefore, that you have observed the machine for a period of *five* hours during which time it produced 1000 caps. In Table B.9, column (1) records the hour of observation. Column (2) records the number of caps produced per hour; column (3) the number of good caps produced each hour; and finally column (4) shows the number of defective caps produced each hour.

Table B.9   *Caps produced by machine in 5-hour period*

(1) Hour	(2) Total number of caps produced	(3) Good caps	(4) Defective caps
1	200	190	10
2	200	185	15
3	200	170	30
4	200	195	5
5	200	187	13
Total:	1,000	927	73

From the table note that

(1) Although the total number of caps produced per hour is constant (200), the number of defective caps produced per hour varies. For example, in hour 3 there were 30 defectives, but only 5 in hour 4.
(2) In total there were 73 defectives among the 1000 caps produced.

We now ask: What is the probability that a given cap produced by the machine is defective?

3. Assumptions: identical and independent trials

The question is answered in the following manner. *First*, assume that each cap was produced *under identical circumstances*. For example, the machine was not adjusted or changed in any way during the time the caps were produced. *Second*, assume that the production of a given defective (or good) cap has no effect upon the fact that another cap produced is either good or defective.

In these circumstances—of *identical* and *independent* trials—it can be assumed that the proportion of defective to total caps produced by the machine is a fair estimate of the probability that the machine will produce a defective cap.

4. Ratio of favourable to possible cases

That is, *in circumstances which are deemed to be independent and identical*, ask how many times the event of interest—a defective cap—appears in the number of trials or occasions observed, i.e. the number of caps produced.

In the example, there are 73 defective caps on 1000 occasions when defective caps could have been produced, thus, it can be said that the probability of the machine producing a defective cap is 73/1000 or 0.073.

5. Definition

The argument implied by the example of the machine producing plastic caps leads to a definition. That is, the probability of an event may be taken to be equal to the ratio

$$\frac{\text{number of times the event occurs}}{\text{number of times the event could occur}}$$

or

$$\frac{\text{number of 'favourable' cases}}{\text{number of possible cases}}$$

when all *possible* cases have an *equal chance* or *likelihood* of occurring. Note, however, that this definition of probability is circular in that the words *chance* and *likelihood* (which are synonyms for probability) have been used to define probability.

In order to use the definition, a *subjective* judgement must be made that all cases are *equally probable*. In this sense, therefore, the so-called *objective* definition is but a special case of the *subjective* definition.

6. Long-run relative frequency

As you might already have observed, the estimation of probability in the above example was made by equating *probability* with the *relative frequency* of the event of interest in a given number of trials. In the case under consideration, the *relative frequency* of defective to total caps is defined by the ratio 73/1000 or 0.073. Note, however, that had we observed only the first hour of the machine, the relative frequency would have been 10/200 or 0.05. Thus, for the definition of probability adopted above to be useful, we should really think in terms of *long-run relative frequency*, which implies that we must observe a great number of trials. We could always *estimate* a probability based on a few trials. However, we will have greater *confidence* in our estimate the greater the number of trials. In many practical situations it is not possible to observe a large number of trials; nonetheless it can often be useful to consider the relative frequency of past events in order to *estimate* probabilities.

7. Estimating probabilities of sales

You are the manufacturer of a product for which the selling season is about to begin. You are uncertain as to how many units of your product will be demanded but have no reason to believe that the forthcoming season will be any different from its ten predecessors (for each of which, you had no reason to believe that any one would be different from the others). In the ten preceding seasons you sold your products in the quantities given in Table B.10. On the basis of these figures, and assuming that you have no other information, how would you assess demand for the forthcoming season?

An approach would be to calculate the relative frequencies of the observed quantities. Notice that a demand of:

- 17 000 occurred 2 times in 10 seasons;
- 18 000 occurred 4 times in 10 seasons;
- 19 000 occurred 3 times in 10 seasons;
- 20 000 occurred 1 time in 10 seasons.

Therefore, the relative frequencies of occurrence are as given in Table B.11. (Recall that relative frequency is defined as the ratio of observed to total cases. Thus, for example, the relative frequency of 17 000 units is 2/10 or 0.20).

These relative frequencies can, of course, also be represented in graphical form as in Fig. B.28, where relative frequency has been recorded on the ordinate and demand in thousands of units on the abscissa. In the absence of further

Table B.10

Seasons	Sales in 000's of units
1	19
2	18
3	18
4	20
5	19
6	17
7	18
8	19
9	17
10	18

Table B.11

Demand in 000's of units	Relative frequency
17	0.20
18	0.40
19	0.30
20	0.10
Total	1.00

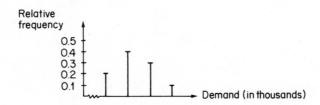

Figure B.28

information, this graph could well be used to represent a probability distribution over future demand. This could be done by simply replacing the words *relative frequency* by *probability*.

8. Estimating demand

It is unlikely that in practical situations demand for a given product would behave as 'nicely' as in the above example. Therefore, consider the following somewhat more complicated case.

A retailer wishes to assess his probability distribution for the demand of a certain product. He decides—somewhat arbitrarily—to examine demand for the product during the last 20 days. He considers that the pattern of demand observed during these 20 days will persist into the future and does not feel that on any one of the days there was any particular reason why demand should have been larger or smaller than demand on any other day.

He summarizes demand in the preceding 20 days as shown in Table B.12. In column (1) of the table, he records the different quantities that could have been demanded each day: from 0 to 10 or more. In column (2), he records the number of times different numbers of items were demanded during the 20-day period. For example, on only *one* occasion were *two* items demanded, but *three* items were demanded on *three* occasions. In column (3), the retailer notes the *relative frequency* with which each event—i.e. number of items demanded—occurred. For example, in 20 days 6 items were demanded on three occasions and thus the relative frequency of the event '6 items demanded' is 3/20 or 0.15. As you can readily observe, the entries in column (3) are obtained by dividing the corresponding entries of column (2) by 20.

Table B.12

(1) Number of items demanded	(2) Number of occasions	(3) Relative frequency
0	0	0
1	1	0.05
2	1	0.05
3	3	0.15
4	5	0.25
5	4	0.20
6	3	0.15
7	0	0
8	2	0.10
9	1	0.05
10 or more	0	0
	20	1.00

Our retailer may also represent his table of relative frequencies in the form of a graph, as shown in Fig. B.29, where the relative frequency is shown on the ordinate, and demand on the abscissa.

The graph shows a fairly symmetric pattern of demand, with one exception. In the 20-day period analysed, there was *no* day on which 7 items of the product were demanded. However, there were 3 days on which 6 were requested, and 2 days when 8 were requested. Does it seem reasonable, therefore, that in assessing his probability distribution over future demand the retailer should equate probability with relative frequency—that is, to have *zero* probability of having 7 units demanded but to have *non-zero* probability of having 6 and 8 units of demand? Given the present pattern of demand, and bearing in mind that the

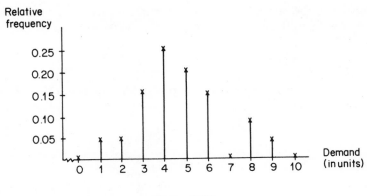

Figure B.29

distribution is based only on 20 observations, equating probability blindly with relative frequency in the observed sample seems unreasonable.

9. General principle

This example of estimating demand leads to the following general principle:

When using relative frequencies of past observations as a guide to assessing probabilities, past historical data should not be followed blindly. Rather, we should blend such past data with our own opinions and common sense.

The use of relative frequencies as probabilities is only really justified when there are a large number of observations. The retailer in the present example, for instance, finally assessed his distribution in a manner which allowed for what he considered to be an anomaly in the past data—i.e. no demand for 7 units of his product. Note that the retailer finally assessed what one could describe as a 'smooth' distribution (Fig. B.30). That is, he deemed it wiser to smooth out

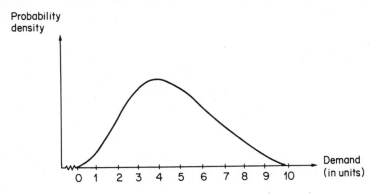

Figure B.30

irregularities in the sample data on the grounds that although the sample was very useful to him, the number of observations (20) was limited.

10. Summary

(1) A commonly used definition of probability ·is the ratio of so-called 'favourable to possible cases', i.e.

$$\frac{\text{number of favourable cases}}{\text{number of possible cases}}.$$

Estimating probabilities in this manner in practical situations frequently amounts to equating the relative frequencies of observations in a sample with probabilities. It was noted, however, that this procedure was only justified when
(a) all possible events (i.e. cases) are deemed to have an equal probability of occurring; and
(b) the total number of events under consideration is large.
(2) When other information is lacking, it is often possible to use historical data as a basis for estimating probabilities. When the sample size is small, however, the observed relative frequencies will only give a rough approximation of probabilities and the assessor may well prefer to *smooth* empirical distributions to account for irregularities in the observed data.

APPENDIX C

Notes on assessing utility

These brief notes are intended to supplement the discussion of 'assessing consequences' presented in Chapter 8. They do not purport to be a comprehensive guide to utility assessment.

The basic question addressed is how to assess *relative preferences* for possible outcomes of a decision that can be represented on several dimensions. Consider, for example, the selection of one of several job candidates who are evaluated on dimensions of, say, intelligence, motivation, and relevant prior experience. As further examples, Figure 8.3 of the text illustrated the dimensions by which Woodward–Clyde consultants intended evaluating different possible corporate strategies, and Figure 8.4 that of a company's scheme for evaluating training plans.[1]

Several methods for assessing relative preferences for multidimensional outcomes have been suggested in the literature. The basic features of these methods involve: (1) selecting dimensions on which the alternatives are to be evaluated; (2) determining the adequacy of the set of dimensions (see discussion in Chapter 8); (3) measuring each of the alternatives on scales which are comparable across dimensions; (4) weighting the dimensions according to their relative importance; (5) aggregating across dimensions to find a 'score' for each of the alternatives; and (6) choosing the alternative with the largest 'score'.

It should be noted that although the word *dimension* is used here to describe a given aspect of an alternative, the word *attribute* is frequently used in the literature. *Attribute* and *dimension* should therefore be considered interchangeable.

Edwards has presented a 10-step procedure for *multi-attribute utility* assessment.[2] This method is presented here for two reasons: first, it is a method that is both easy to understand and apply; and second, such 'simple' methods have been found to give results that are as satisfactory as those yielded by theoretically sounder but more complex methodologies.

In following the presentation, the reader is asked to imagine a choice between alternatives with multi-dimensional outcomes: for example, job candidates, different possible locations of a site for a new factory, alternative training plans for a company (cf. Figure 8.4), etc. One alternative which should also be kept in the set under consideration is that of not taking any action, i.e. the status quo.

Edwards' 10-step procedure can be subdivided into four phases:

(1) structuring the problem;
(2) determining the importance of dimensions;
(3) measuring alternatives on the dimensions; and
(4) choice.

A linear presentation of the Edwards' procedure is now made, although in practice there would be considerable 'recycling' between phases—in the same manner as the general decision analysis model presented in Chapter 8.

Structuring the problem

As discussed in Chapter 8, this is the most important phase. Indeed, in many cases it may not even be necessary to go beyond it since the best alternative could become evident simply by structuring the problem. There are four steps which are also covered by the general model indicated in Chapter 8.

Step 1

Identify the decision maker(s). Where an organization is *the* decision maker, it is particularly important to identify people who can speak for the organization.

Step 2

Identify the decision. It is important to note that value (i.e. relative preference for outcomes) depends not only upon (a) the identity of the decision-maker, but also on (b) what is being evaluated, and (c) the purpose for which it is being evaluated.

Step 3

Identify the alternatives to be evaluated.

Step 4

Identify the dimensions on which the alternatives are to be evaluated (cf. Tables 8.3 and 8.4).

Issues relevant to structuring problems, e.g. selection of a set of dimensions, were discussed in some detail in Chapter 8 and are therefore not considered further here.

Determining the importance of dimensions

The object of this phase is to determine the decision maker's attitudes toward the relative importance of the dimensions.

Step 5

Rank order the dimensions in terms of their importance. If there is more than one decision maker, Edwards recommends attempting to gain consensus on the rank ordering through group discussion. Consensus gained at this level can greatly facilitate the subsequent process.

Step 6

Translate the rankings to ratings. Edwards suggests that the lowest ranking dimension be given a score of 10. The next lowest dimension is then considered and it is asked how much more important it is than the lowest. This is then assigned a number to reflect its importance and one works one's way up the list of dimensions. In doing so, it is important to preserve ratios in the sense that if a dimension is allotted a score of 30, it should be considered three times as important as a dimension with a score of 10, but only half as important as a dimension with a score of 60, etc. In assigning numbers, one should not be reticent about changing previous assessments, re-arranging, etc. It is unlikely that the final assessments will be achieved at a first attempt and even more unlikely that a group will succeed in doing so.

Step 7

This is a computational step to convert the ratings to numbers that sum to 1. Simply add the weights assessed in Step 6, and divide each dimension's Step 6 assessment by the sum of all assessments to obtain a 'normalized' weight for each dimension.

Note that it is possible to go directly from Step 4 to Step 7. The intermediate steps simply serve to systematize the process.

Measuring alternatives on the dimensions

Step 8

Each alternative must now be measured on each of the dimensions. However, there is a problem in that the dimensions themselves are not expressed in commensurable units. Consider, for example, the dimensions/attributes at the base of the hierarchies in Figures 8.3 and 8.4. Rescaling is necessary.

Associate with each dimension a possible worth or value scale which goes from 0 to 100, the end points representing minimum and maximum *plausible* values. (Note *plausible*, not possible. The minimum plausible value does not necessarily indicate total absence of an alternative on a dimension). Given these comparable worth scales, the problem now consists of measuring the location of each alternative on the scales—for each of the dimensions. In some cases, all one can do is have an expert assess a value for each alternative. Consider, for example, dimensions such as Quality in Figure 8.4. In other cases, one may wish to define a relationship between a physical measurement, e.g. Person-hours in Figure 8.4, and a worth scale. Such relationships can clearly be assessed by substantive experts. Indeed, most evaluations of dimensions will require a high degree of subjective expert judgement; however, through this methodology one can obtain, and combine, assessments on the different dimensions by experts in each of their respective domains. For example, an expert in dimension A can assess all alternatives on this dimension; an expert in dimension B can make similar judgements in respect of dimension B; and so on.

Step 9

The overall worth of each alternative is calculated by summing each alternative's scores on the dimensions as weighted by the appropriate importance weights determined in Step 7.

Choice

Step 10

Step 9 yields a list of alternatives accompanied by their measures of relative worth. The normative rule is to choose the alternative with the largest assessment of worth.

Additional considerations

Chapter 8 discussed some important issues and assumptions involved in determining the set of dimensions (attributes) on which the mathematical operations are to be performed. In particular, for the procedures outlined here to be used with confidence, the assumption of *value independence* should be checked. Chapter 8 also considered the technique of *sensitivity analysis*. One should not believe the figures that emerge from an analysis. They are bound to be *wrong*. However, it is important to discover *how wrong* they are relative to the problem at hand. This can be achieved by varying the quantitative inputs to the problem and observing the extent of changes in overall preferences for alternatives to such variations.

Another important point is that there is no need to follow slavishly through the 10-step procedure outlined above. In some applications, it might be advisable to avoid Steps 5–7 (i.e. determining the relative importance of dimensions) since these value judgements can cause conflicts. It is possible to wait until the measurement procedure has been completed (Step 8) and then to see how the weights that might be given by different parties to the decision would affect the final rank-ordering of alternatives. This is also important in that the analysis of alternatives often takes place concurrently with policy formulation and the importance weights might simply not be available when the alternatives are first compared. In addition, some alternatives might easily be eliminated at an early stage of the analysis if it can be shown that no set of weights, or at least no reasonable set of weights, could ever make the alternatives acceptable. In many situations, assigning equal weights to the dimensions can be satisfactory.[3]

There are situations where the decision-maker is choosing between alternatives against a budget constraint. Consider, for example, the allocation of funds to different projects in R & D, differential allocation of resources in advertising or training and development, and so on. Since alternatives usually vary in cost, it is important to bring cost into the model. The simplest procedure is to calculate benefit-to-cost ratios for each of the alternatives. That is, divide the overall worth of each alternative (as determined by the model) by its cost and re-rank the alternatives by the resultant benefit-to-cost ratios. The optimal choice is then to allocate the budget to the alternatives with the largest benefit-to-cost ratios, since these yield the greatest benefit per unit of cost.

People sometimes feel diffident about bringing cost directly into an analysis, for example by treating it as a dimension with a negative value. Thus, although scaling a worth function for cost is no different conceptually from scaling worth functions for other dimensions, the following ploy of evaluating alternatives relative to the *status quo* can be useful.

Let b_i denote the benefit of alternative i and b_{sq} that of the status quo; represent the cost of alternative i by c_i and that of the status quo by c_{sq}. Calculate the index:

$$\frac{b_i - b_{sq}}{c_i - c_{sq}}.$$

This ratio gives a notion of the incremental benefit of alternative i over the status quo relative to the additional cost, i.e. incremental benefit per unit of cost (assuming $c_i > c_{sq}$). It can be used as a measure of the efficacy, or expected efficacy, of an alternative relative to the status quo.

Finally, a useful user-oriented tutorial of multi-attribute assessment methods has been provided by Johnson and Huber.[4]

NOTES TO APPENDIX C

1. These notes are based on a presentation made in R. M. Hogarth, *Evaluating management education.* Chichester, England: John Wiley & Sons, 1979, Chapter 12.
2. W. Edwards, Use of multiattribute utility measurement for social decision making. In D. E. Bell, R. L. Keeney, and H. Raiffa (Eds.), *Conflicting objectives in decisions.* Chichester, England: John Wiley & Sons, 1977, pp. 247–275. In this presentation, Edwards also indicates several empirical examples.
3. See a relevant empirical example in H. J. Einhorn and W. McCoach, A simple multiattribute procedure for evaluation. *Behavioral Science*, 1977, **22**, 270–282.
4. E. M. Johnson and G. P. Huber, The technology of utility assessment. *IEEE Transactions on Systems, Man and Cybernetics*, 1977, Vol. **SMC-7**, 311–325.

APPENDIX D

A guide to further reading

This appendix provides a guide to further reading. It contains eight sections:

I. Overviews/discussions of behavioural decision theory
II. More general approaches to the study of decision behaviour
III. Rationality and human limitations
IV. Biases in information processing
V. Models of decision behaviour
VI. Risk
VII. Creativity and problem solving
VIII. Decision aids

The bibliography includes items referenced in the footnotes at the end of each chapter, although not all. With the exception of Section IV, the references are organized in *chronological* order so that readers can acquire an indication of the manner in which knowledge in the field has developed. Section IV is the most detailed and is divided into sub-sections corresponding to the conceptual scheme of Figure 9.1 and Table 9.2 (Chapter 9). References within sub-sections of Section IV are presented alphabetically.

I. OVERVIEWS/DISCUSSIONS OF BEHAVIOURAL
DECISION THEORY

The field now known in psychology as 'behavioural decision theory' has been reviewed periodically over the last three decades. The following books and papers are quite complete in terms of references, but readers should be aware that they were written for psychological audiences.

1. Edwards, W. The theory of decision making. *Psychological Bulletin*, 1954, **51**, 380–417.
2. Edwards, W. Behavioral decision theory. *Annual Review of Psychology*, 1961, **12**, 473–498.
3. Becker, G. M., and McClintock, C. G. Value: Behavioral decision theory. *Annual Review of Psychology*, 1967, **18**, 239–286.
4. Kleinmuntz, B. (Ed.). *Formal representation of human judgment*. New York: John Wiley, 1968.
5. Lee, W. *Decision theory and human behavior*. New York: Wiley, 1971.

6. Rapoport, A., and Wallsten, T. S. Individual decision behavior. *Annual Review of Psychology*, 1972, **23**, 131–175.
7. Newell, A., and Simon, H. A. *Human problem solving*. Englewood Cliffs, N.J.: Prentice-Hall, 1972. (For an overview of this book see H. A. Simon and A. Newell. Human problem solving: The state of the theory in 1970. *American Psychologist*, 1971, **26**, 145–159.)
8. Rappoport, L., and Summers, D. A. (Eds.), *Human judgment and social interaction*. New York: Holt, Rinehart & Winston, 1973. This volume includes the long overview paper by P. Slovic and S. Lichtenstein. Comparison of Bayesian and regression approaches to the study of information processing in judgment. *Organizational Behavior and Human Performance*, 1971, **6**, 649–744.
9. Rapoport, A. Research paradigms for studying dynamic decision behavior. In D. Wendt and C. A. J. Vlek (Eds.), *Utility, probability, and human decision making*. Dordrecht, Holland: Reidel, 1975.
10. Slovic, P., Fischhoff, B., and Lichtenstein S. Behavioral decision theory. *Annual Review of Psychology*, 1977, **28**, 1–39.
11. Vlek, C. A. J., and Wagenaar, W. A. Judgment and decision under uncertainty. In J. A. Michon, E. G. J. Eijkman, and L. F. W. de Klerk (Eds.), *Handbook of psychonomics, Vol. 2*, Amsterdam: North-Holland, 1979.
12. Einhorn, H. J., and Hogarth, R. M. Behavioral decision theory: Processes of judgment and choice. *Annual Review of Psychology*, 1981, **32,** in press.

II. MORE GENERAL APPROACHES TO THE STUDY OF DECISION BEHAVIOUR

The following references provide a broader perspective on human decision behaviour than those contained in Section I.

1. Bruner, J. S., Goodnow, J. J., and Austin, G. A. *A study of thinking*. New York: John Wiley, 1956.
2. Simon, H. A. Theories of decision-making in economics and behavioral science. *American Economic Review*, 1959, **49**, No. 3.
3. Cohen, J. *Chance, skill and luck*. Harmondsworth, Middlesex: Penguin Books, 1960.
4. Gore, W. J., and Dyson, J. W. (Eds.), *The making of decisions: A reader in administrative behavior*. Glencoe: The Free Press, 1964.
5. Kogan, N., and Wallach, M. A. *Risk taking: A study in cognition and personality*. New York: Holt, Rinehart & Winston, 1964. (One of the few studies of effects of personality on decision making.)
6. Simon, H. A. *The sciences of the artificial*. Cambridge, MA: M.I.T. Press, 1969.
7. Coombs, C. H., Dawes, R. M., and Tversky, A. *Mathematical psychology: An elementary introduction*. Englewood Cliffs, NJ: Prentice-Hall, 1970. (Chapters 5, 6 and 7 provide good introductions to theories of individual decision making, the theory of signal detection and game theory.)

8. Johnson, D. M. *A systematic introduction to the psychology of thinking.* New York: Harper & Row, 1972.
9. Cohen, J. *Psychological probability: Or the art of doubt.* London: George Allen & Unwin, 1972.
10. Wason, P. C., and Johnson-Laird, P. N. *Psychology of reasoning: Structure and content.* London: Batsford, 1972.
11. MacCrimmon, K. R., and Taylor, R. N. Decision making and problem solving. In M. D. Dunnette (Ed.), *Handbook of Industrial and Organizational Psychology.* Chicago: Rand-McNally, 1976.
12. Janis, I. L., and Mann, L. *Decision making: A psychological analysis of conflict, choice, and commitment.* New York: The Free Press, 1977.
13. Nisbett, R. E., and Ross, L. *Human inference: Strategies and shortcomings in social judgment.* Englewood Cliffs, NJ: Prentice-Hall, 1980.

III. RATIONALITY AND HUMAN LIMITATIONS

Much of this book is concerned with the notion that people cannot exercise rational choice because of limitations of the human information processing system. The following papers are pertinent to this issue.

1. Simon, H. A. A behavioral model of rational choice. *Quarterly Journal of Economics,* 1955, **69**, 99–118.
2. Miller, G. A. The magical number seven, plus or minus two: Some limits on our capacity for processing information. *Psychological Review,* 1956, **63**, 81–97.
3. Simon, H. A. Rational choice and the structure of the environment. *Psychological Review,* 1956, **63**, 129–138.
4. Toda, M. The design of a fungus eater: A model of human behavior in an unsophisticated environment. *Behavioral Science,* 1962, **7**, 164–183.
5. Toda, M. The decision process: A perspective. *International Journal of General Systems,* 1976, **3**, 79–88.
6. Russo, J. E. The value of unit price information. *Journal of Marketing Research,* 1977, **14**, 193–201.
7. Russo, J. E. Comments on behavioral and economic approaches to studying market behavior. In A. A. Mitchell (Ed.), *The effect of information on consumer and market behavior.* Chicago: American Marketing Association, 1978.
8. March, J. G. Bounded rationality, ambiguity, and the engineering of choice. *Bell Journal of Economics,* 1978, **9**, 587–608.
9. Simon, H. A. Rationality as process and as product of thought. *American Economic Review,* 1978, **68**, 1–16.
10. Simon, H. A. Rational decision making in business organizations. *American Economic Review,* 1979, **69**, 493–513.
11. Hogarth, R. M. Beyond static biases: Functional and dysfunctional aspects of judgmental heuristics. University of Chicago, Graduate School of Business, Center for Decision Research working paper, 1980.

12. Toda, M. What happens at the moment of decision? Meta-decisions, emotions and volitions. In L. Sjöberg, T. Tyszka, and J. A. Wise (Eds.), *Human decision making, Vol. II*, Bodafors, Sweden: Doxa, 1980.
13. Toda, M. Emotion and decision making. *Acta Psychologica*, in press.

IV. BIASES IN INFORMATION PROCESSING

In Chapter 9, Table 9.2 lists biases in information processing indicating that bias can occur at different stages of information processing: (a) acquisition; (b) processing; (c) output; and (d) feedback. Selected (but not exhaustive) references to these biases/sources of bias are provided here and organized according to the scheme given in Figure 9.1 and Table 9.2.

A. Acquisition

(i) Availability

1. Lichtenstein, S., Slovic, P., Fischhoff, B., Layman, M., and Combs, B. Judged frequency of lethal events. *Journal of Experimental Psychology: Human Learning and Memory*, 1978, **4**, 551–578.
2. Maier, N. R. F. Reasoning in humans: II. The solution of a problem and its appearance in consciousness. *Journal of Comparative Psychology*, 1931, **12**, 181–194.
3. Tversky, A., and Kahneman, D. Availability: A heuristic for judging frequency and probability. *Cognitive Psychology*, 1973, **5**, 207–232.

(ii) Selective perception

1. Bruner, J. S., and Postman,· L. J. On the perception of incongruity: A paradigm. *Journal of Personality*, 1949, **18**, 206–223.
2. Dearborn, D. C., and Simon, H. A. Selective perception: A note on the departmental identification of executives. *Sociometry*, 1958, **21**, 140–144.
3. Wason, P. C. On the failure to eliminate hypotheses in a conceptual task. *Quarterly Journal of Experimental Psychology*, 1960, **12**, 129–140.
4. Webster, E. C. *Decision making in the employment interview*. Industrial Relations Centre, McGill University, Montreal, 1964.

(iii) Frequency

1. Estes, W. K. The cognitive side of probability learning. *Psychological Review*, 1976, **83**, 37–64.
2. Smedslund, J. The concept of correlation in adults. *Scandinavian Journal of Psychology*, 1963, **4**, 165–173.
3. Ward, W. C., and Jenkins, H. M. The display of information and the judgment of contingency. *Canadian Journal of Psychology*, 1965, **19**, 231–241.

236

(iv) Concrete information

1. Bar-Hillel, M. The base-rate fallacy in probability judgments. *Acta Psychologica*, in press.
2. Borgida, E., and Nisbett, R. E. The differential impact of abstract vs. concrete information on decisions. *Journal of Applied Social Psychology*, 1977, **7**, 258–271.
3. Lyon, D., and Slovic, P. Dominance of accuracy information and neglect of base rates in probability estimation. *Acta Psychologica*, 1976, **40**, 287–298.
4. Nisbett, R. E., Borgida, E., Crandall, R., and Reed, H. Popular induction: Information is not necessarily informative. In J. S. Carroll and J. W. Payne (Eds.), *Cognition and social behavior*. Hillsdale, NJ: Lawrence Erlbaum, 1976.

(v) Illusory correlation

1. Chapman, L. J. Illusory correlation in observational report. *Journal of Verbal Learning and Verbal Behavior*, 1967, **6**, 151–155.
2. Chapman, L. J., and Chapman, J. P. Illusory correlation as an obstacle to the use of valid psychodiagnostic signs. *Journal of Abnormal Psychology*, 1969, **74**, 271–280.
3. Golding, S. L., and Rorer, L. G. Illusory correlation and subjective judgment. *Journal of Abnormal Psychology*, 1972, **80**, 249–260.
4. Shweder, R. A. Likeness and likelihood in everyday thought: Magical thinking in judgments about personality. *Current Anthropology*, 1977, **18**, 637–658.

(vi) Data presentation

1. Dickson, G. W., Senn, J. A., and Chervany, N. L. Research in management information systems: The Minnesota experiments. *Management Science*, 1977, **23**, 913–923.
2. Fischhoff, B., Slovic, P., and Lichtenstein, S. Fault trees: Sensitivity of estimated failure probabilities to problem representation. *Journal of Experimental Psychology: Human perception and performance*, 1978, **4**, 330–344.
3. Jenkins, H. M., and Ward, W. C. Judgment of contingency between responses and outcomes. *Psychological Monographs: General and Applied*, 1965, **79**, 1–17.
4. Lathrop, R. G. Perceived variability. *Journal of Experimental Psychology*, 1967, **73**, 498–502.
5. Ronen, J. Effects of some probability displays on choices. *Organizational Behavior and Human Performance*, 1973, **9**, 1–15.

B. Processing of information

(i) Inconsistency

1. Bowman, E. H. Consistency and optimality in management decision making. *Management Science*, 1963, **10**, 310–321.
2. Brehmer, B. Social judgment theory and the analysis of interpersonal conflict. *Psychological Bulletin*, 1976, **83**, 985–1003.
3. Einhorn, H. J. Expert measurement and mechanical combination. *Organizational Behavior and Human Performance*, 1972, **7**, 86–106.
4. Kunreuther, H. Extensions of Bowman's theory of managerial decision making. *Management Science*, 1969, **15**, B-415-439.

(ii) Conservatism

1. DuCharme, W. M. A response bias explanation of conservative human inference. *Journal of Experimental Psychology*, 1970, **85**, 66–74.
2. Edwards, W. Conservatism in human information processing. In B. Kleinmuntz (Ed.), *Formal representation of human judgment*. New York: Wiley, 1968.
3. Phillips, L. D., and Edwards, W. Conservatism in a simple probability inference task. *Journal of Experimental Psychology*, 1966, **72**, 346–357.
4. Phillips, L. D., Hays, W. L., and Edwards, W. Conservatism in complex probabilistic inference. *IEEE Transactions on Human Factors in Electronics*, 1966, **HFE-7,** 7–18.

(iii) Non-linear extrapolation

1. Bar-Hillel, M. On the subjective probability of compound events. *Organizational Behavior and Human Performance*, 1973, **9**, 396–406.
2. Cohen, J., Chesnick, E. I., and Haran, D. A confirmation of the inertial Ψ - effect in sequential choice and decision. *British Journal of Psychology*, 1972, **63**, 41–46.
3. Wagenaar, W. A., and Sagaria, S. D. Misperception of exponential growth. *Perception and Psychophysics*, 1975, **18**, 416–422.
4. Wagenaar, W. A., and Timmers, H. Intuitive prediction of growth. In D. F. Burkhardt and W. H. Ittelson (Eds.), *Environmental assessment of socio-economic systems*. New York: Plenum, 1978.
5. Wagenaar, W. A., and Timmers, H. The pond-and-duckweed problem: Three experiments on the misperception of exponential growth. *Acta Psychologica*, 1979, **43**, 239–251.

(iv) 'Heuristics' used to reduce mental effort

1. Gettys, C. F., Kelly, C. W. III, and Peterson, C. R. The best guess hypothesis

238

in multistage inference. *Organizational Behavior and Human Performance*, 1973, **10**, 364–373.

2. Kahneman, D., and Tversky, A. Subjective probability: A judgment of representativeness. *Cognitive Psychology*, 1972, **3**, 430–454.
3. Kahneman, D., and Tversky, A. On the psychology of prediction. *Psychological Review*, 1973, **80**, 237–251.
4. Knafl, K., and Burkett, G. Professional socialization in a surgical speciality: Acquiring medical judgment. *Social Science of Medicine*, 1975, **9**, 397–404.
5. Slovic, P. Choice between equally-valued alternatives. *Journal of Experimental Psychology: Human Perception and Performance*, 1975, **1**, 280–287.
6. Tversky, A., and Kahneman, D. The belief in the 'law of small numbers'. *Psychological Bulletin*, 1971, **76**, 105–110.
7. Tversky, A., and Kahneman, D. Judgment under uncertainty: Heuristics and biases. *Science*, 1974, **185**, 1124–1131.

(v) The decision environment

1. Asch, S. E. Effects of group pressure on the modification and distortion of judgments. In H. Geutzkow (ed.), *Groups, leadership and men*. Pittsburgh: Carnegie Institute of Technology Press, 1951.
2. Einhorn, H. J. Use of nonlinear, noncompensatory models as a function of task and amount of information. *Organizational Behavior and Human Performance*, 1971, **6**, 1–27.
3. Janis, I. L. *Victims of groupthink*. Boston: Houghton Mifflin, 1972.
4. Pollay, R. W. The structure of executive decisions and decision times. *Administrative Science Quarterly*, 1970, **15**, 459–471.
5. Wright, P. The harassed decision maker: Time pressures, distractions and the use of evidence. *Journal of Applied Psychology*. 1974, **59**, 555–561.

(vi) Information sources

1. Oskamp, S. Overconfidence in case-study judgments. *Journal of Consulting Psychology*, 1965, **29**, 261–265.
2. Slovic, P. Toward understanding and improving decisions. In W. Howell (Ed.), *Human performance and productivity*, Hillsdale, NJ: Lawrence Erlbaum, in press.

C. Output

(i) Response mode

1. Grether, D. M., and Plott, C. R. Economic theory of choice and the preference reversal phenomenon. *American Economic Review*, 1979, **69**, 623–638.

2. Hogarth, R. M. Cognitive processes and the assessment of subjective probability distributions. *Journal of the American Statistical Association*, 1975, **70**, 271–289.
3. Lichtenstein, S., and Slovic, P. Reversals of preference between bids and choices in gambling decisions. *Journal of Experimental Psychology*, 1971, **89**, 46–55.
4. Lichtenstein, S., and Slovic P. Response-induced reversals of preference in gambling: An extended replication in Las Vegas. *Journal of Experimental Psychology*, 1973, **101**, 16–20.

(ii) Wishful thinking

1. Cyert, R. M., Dill, W. R., and March, J. G. The role of expectations in business decision making. *Administrative Science Quarterly*, 1958, **3**, 307–340.
2. Morlock, H. The effect of outcome desirability on information required for decisions. *Behavioral Science*, 1967, **12**, 296–300.
3. Slovic, P. Value as a determiner of subjective probability. *IEEE Transactions on Human Factors in Electronics*, 1966, **HFE-7**, 22–28.

(iii) Illusion of control

1. Langer, E. J. The illusion of control. *Journal of Personality and Social Psychology*, 1975, **32**, 311–328.
2. Langer, E. J., and Roth, J. The effect of sequence of outcomes in a chance task on the illusion of control. *Journal of Personality and Social Psychology*, 1975, **32**, 951–955.
3. Perlmutter, L. C., and Monty, R. A. The importance of perceived control: Fact or fantasy? *American Scientist*, 1977, **65**, 759–765.

D. Feedback

(i) Outcome irrelevant learning structures

1. Einhorn, H. J. Learning from experience and suboptimal rules in decision making. In T. Wallsten (Ed.), *Cognitive processes in choice and decision behavior*. Hillsdale, NJ: Lawrence Erlbaum, 1980.
2. Einhorn, H. J., and Hogarth, R. M. Confidence in judgment: Persistence of the illusion of validity. *Psychological Review*, 1978, **85**, 395–476.
3. Fischhoff, B., Slovic, P., and Lichtenstein, S. Knowing with certainty: The appropriateness of extreme confidence. *Journal of Experimental Psychology: Human Perception and Performance*, 1977, **3**, 552–564.

(ii) Misperception of chance

1. Cohen, J. *Psychological probability: Or the art of doubt*. London, England: George Allen & Unwin, 1972.

2. Jarvik, M. E. Probability learning and a negative recency effect in the serial anticipation of alternative symbols. *Journal of Experimental Psychology*, 1951, **41**, 291–297.
3. Langer, E. J. The psychology of chance. *Journal for the Theory of Social Behaviour*, 1977, **7**, 185–207.
4. Wagenaar, W. A. Appreciation of conditional probabilities in binary sequences. *Acta Psychologica*, 1970, **34**, 348–356.

(iii) Success/failure attributions

1. Miller, D. T. Ego involvement and attributions for success and failure. *Journal of Personality and Social Psychology*, 1976, **34**, 901–906.
2. Ross, L. The intuitive psychologist and his shortcomings: Distortions in the attribution process. In L. Berkowitz (ed.), *Advances in experimental social psychology*, *Vol. 10*. New York: Academic Press, 1977.

(iv) Logical fallacies in recall

1. Buckhout, R. Eyewitness testimony. *Scientific American*, 1974, **231**, 23–31.
2. Loftus, E. F. Leading questions and the eyewitness report. *Cognitive Psychology*, 1975, **7**, 560–572.
3. Snyder, M., and Uranowitz, S. W. Reconstructing the past: Some cognitive consequences of person perception. *Journal of Personality and Social Psychology*, 1978, **36**, 941–950.

(v) Hindsight bias

1. Fischhoff, B. Hindsight ≠ foresight: The effect of outcome knowledge on judgment under uncertainty. *Journal of Experimental Psychology: Human Perception and Performance*, 1975, **1**, 288–299.
2. Fischhoff, B. Perceived informativeness of facts. *Journal of Experimental Psychology: Human Perception and Performance*, 1977, **3**, 349–358.
3. Fischhoff, B., and Beyth, R. 'I knew it would happen'—Remembered probabilities of once-future things. *Organizational Behavior and Human Performance*, 1975, **13**, 1–16.

V. MODELS OF DECISION BEHAVIOUR

There has been much interest in modelling how people make judgments and choices in given circumstances. These can be conceptualized under three headings: (a) linear models of judgment; (b) the lens model (see Chapter 1, Figure 1.1); and (c) heuristic combining models.

A. Linear models of judgment

1. Meehl, P. E. *Clinical versus statistical prediction*. Minneapolis: University of Minnesota Press, 1954.
2. Hoffman, P. J. The paramorphic representation of clinical judgment. *Psychological Bulletin*, 1960, **57**, 116–131.
3. Yntema, D. B., and Torgerson, W. S. Man–computer cooperation in decisions requiring common sense. *IRE Transactions on Human Factors in Electronics*, 1961, **HFE-2**, 20–26.
4. Shepard, R. N. On subjectively optimum selection among multi-attribute alternatives. In M. W. Shelly and G. L. Bryan (Eds.), *Human judgments and optimality*. New York: John Wiley, 1964.
5. Sawyer, J. Measurement *and* prediction, clinical *and* statistical. *Psychological Bulletin*, 1966, **66**, 178–200.
6. Goldberg, L. R. Simple methods or simple processes? Some research on clinical judgments. *American Psychologist*, 1968, **23**, 483–496.
7. Hoffman, P. J., Slovic, P., and Rorer, L. G. An analysis-of-variance model for assessment of configural cue utilization in clinical judgment. *Psychological Bulletin*, 1968, **69**, 338–349.
8. Slovic, P. Analyzing the expert judge: A descriptive study of a stockbroker's decision processes. *Journal of Applied Psychology*, 1969, **53**, 255–263.
9. Goldberg, L. R. Man versus model of man: A rationale, plus some evidence, for a method of improving on clinical inferences. *Psychological Bulletin*, 1970, **73**, 422–432.
10. Dawes, R. M. A case study of graduate admissions: Application of three principles of human decision making. *American Psychologist*, 1971, **26**, 180–188.
11. Dawes, R. M., and Corrigan, B. Linear models in decision making. *Psychological Bulletin*, 1974, **81**, 95–106.
12. Libby, R. Man versus model of man: Some conflicting evidence. *Organizational Behavior and Human Performance*, 1976, **16**, 1–12.
13. Dawes, R. M. The robust beauty of improper linear models. *American Psychologist*, 1979, **34**, 571–582.
14. Einhorn, H. J., Kleinmuntz, D. N., and Kleinmuntz, B. Linear regression *and* process-tracing models of judgment. *Psychological Review*, 1979, **86**, 465–485.

B. The lens model

1. Hammond, K. R. Probabilistic functioning and the clinical method. *Psychological Review*, 1955, **62**, 255–262.
2. Hursch, C., Hammond, K. R., and Hursch, J. L. Some methodological considerations in multiple cue probability studies. *Psychological Review*, 1964, **71**, 42–60.
3. Hammond, K. R., Hursch, C. J., and Todd, F. J. Analyzing the components

of clinical inference. *Psychological Review*, 1964, **71**, 438–456.

4. Tucker, L. R. A suggested alternative formulation in the development of Hursch, Hammond, and Hursch, and by Hammond, Hursch, and Todd. *Psychological Review*, 1964, **71**, 528–530.

5. Hammond, K. R. New directions in research in conflict resolution. *Journal of Social Issues*, 1965, **21**, 44–66.

6. Dudycha, L. W., and Naylor, J. C. Characteristics of the human inference process in complex choice behavior situations. *Organizational Behavior and Human Performance*, 1966, **1**, 110–128.

7. Hammond, K. R., and Summers, D. A. Cognitive control. *Psychological Review*, 1972, **79**, 58–67.

8. Hammond, K. R., and Adelman, L. Science, values, and human judgment, *Science*, 1976, **194**, 389–396.

9. Hammond, K. R., Mumpower, J. L., and Smith, T. H. Linking environmental models with models of human judgment: A symmetrical decision aid. *IEEE Transactions on Systems, Man, and Cybernetics*, 1977, **SMC-7** (5), 358–367.

10. Hammond, K. R., Rohrbaugh, J., Mumpower, J., and Adelman, L. Social judgment theory: Applications in policy formation. In M. F. Kaplan and S. Schwartz (Eds.), *Human judgment and decision processes in applied settings*. New York: Academic Press, 1977.

C. Heuristic combining models

1. Dawes, R. M. Social selection based on multidimensional criteria. *Journal of Abnormal and Social Psychology*, 1964, **68**, 104–109.

2. Kleinmuntz, B. The processing of clinical information by man and machine. In B. Kleinmuntz (Ed.), *Formal representation of human judgment.* New York: Wiley, 1968.

3. Tversky, A. Intransitivity of preferences. *Psychological Review*, 1969, **76**, 31–48.

4. Einhorn, H. J. The use of nonlinear, noncompensatory models in decision making. *Psychological Bulletin*, 1970, **73**, 221–230.

5. Tversky, A. Elimination by aspects: A theory of choice. *Psychological Review*, 1972, **79**, 281–299.

6. Hogarth, R. M. Process tracing in clinical judgment. *Behavioral Science*, 1974, **19**, 298–313.

7. Russo, J. E., and Rosen, L. D. An eye fixation analysis of multi-alternative choice. *Memory and Cognition*, 1975, **3**, 267–276.

8. Abelson, R. P. Script processing in attitude formation and decision making. In J. S. Carroll and J. W. Payne (Eds.), *Cognition and social behavior*, Hillsdale, NJ: Lawrence Erlbaum, 1976.

9. Payne, J. W. Task complexity and contingent processing in decision making: An information search and protocol analysis. *Organizational Behavior and Human Performance*, 1976, **16**, 366–387.

10. Simon, H. A., and Hayes, J. R. The understanding process: Problem isomorphs. *Cognitive Psychology*, 1976, **8**, 165–190.
11. Tversky, A. Features of similarity. *Psychological Review*, 1977, **84**, 327–352.
12. Nisbett, R. E., and Wilson, T. D. Telling more than we can know: Verbal reports on mental processes. *Psychological Review*, 1977, **84**, 231–259.
13. Smith, E. R., and Miller, F. D. Limits on perception of cognitive processes: A reply to Nisbett and Wilson. *Psychological Review*, 1978, **85**, 355–362.
14. Payne, J. W., Braunstein, M. L., and Carroll, J. S. Exploring predecisional behavior: An alternative approach to decision research. *Organizational Behavior and Human Performance*, 1978, **22**, 17–44.
15. Tversky, A., and Sattath, S. Preference trees. *Psychological Review*, 1979, **86**, 542–573.

VI. RISK

How do people make choices in the face of risk? The following readings provide some clues.

1. Tversky, A: Additivity, utility, and subjective probability. *Journal of Mathematical Psychology*, 1967, **4**, 175–202.
2. Slovic, P., and Lichtenstein, S. The relative importance of probability and payoffs in risk taking. *Journal of Experimental Psychology Monograph Supplement*, 1968, **78**, (3), Part 2.
3. Starr, C. Social benefits versus technological risk. *Science*, 1969, **165**, 1232–1238.
4. Howard, R. A., Matheson, J. E., and North, D. W. The decision to seed hurricanes. *Science*, 1972, **176**, 1191–1202.
5. Payne, J. W. Alternative approaches to decision making under risk: Moments versus risk dimensions. *Psychological Bulletin*, 1973, **80**, 439–453.
6. Slovic, P., and Tversky, A. Who accepts Savage's axiom? *Behavioral Science*, 1974, **19**, 368–373.
7. Coombs, C. H. Portfolio theory and the measurement of risk. In M. F. Kaplan and S. Schwartz (Eds.), *Human judgment and decision processes*. New York: Academic Press, 1975.
8. Kunreuther, H. Limited knowledge and insurance protection. *Public Policy*, 1976, **24**, 227–261.
9. Slovic, P., Fischhoff, B., and Lichtenstein, S. Cognitive processes and societal risk taking. In J. S. Carroll and J. W. Payne (Eds.), *Cognition and social behavior*. Hillsdale, NJ: Lawrence Erlbaum, 1976.
10. Slovic, P., Fischhoff, B., Lichtenstein, S., Corrigan, B., and Combs, B. Preference for insuring against probable small losses: Insurance implications. *Journal of Risk and Insurance*, 1977, **44**, 237–258.
11. Coombs, C. H., and Avrunin, G. S. Single-peaked functions and the theory of preference. *Psychological Review*, 1977, **84**, 216–230.
12. Karmarkar, U. Subjectively weighted utility: A descriptive extension of the

expected utility model. *Organizational Behavior and Human Performance*, 1978, 21, 61–72.

13. Aschenbrenner, K. M. Single-peaked risk preferences and their dependability on the gambles' presentation mode. *Journal of Experimental Psychology: Human Perception and Performance*, 1978, **4**, 513–520.

14. Kahneman, D., and Tversky, A. Prospect theory: An analysis of decisions under risk. *Econometrica*, 1979, **47**, 263–291.

15. Karmarkar, U. Subjectively weighted utility and the Allais paradox. *Organizational Behavior and Human Performance*, 1979, **24**, 67–72.

16. Payne, J. W., Laughhunn, D. J., and Crum, R. Levels of aspiration and preference reversals in risky choice. Unpublished manuscript, Duke University, 1979.

17. Schoemaker, P. J. H. *Experiments on decision under risk: The expected utility hypothesis.* Hingham, MA: Nijhoff, 1980.

18. MacCrimmon, K. R., and Larsson, S. Utility theory: Axioms versus 'paradoxes.' In M. Allais and O. Hagen (Eds.), *Rational decisions under uncertainty*, special volume of *Theory and decision*, in press.

VII. CREATIVITY AND PROBLEM SOLVING

Much research has been done on creativity; unfortunately, the topic is difficult and results are somewhat discouraging. This short list should, however, prove useful.

1. Ghiselin, B. (Ed.), *The creative process.* Berkeley, California: University of California Press, 1952. (Reprinted by Mentor Books, New York.)

2. Osborn, A. F. *Applied imagination.* New York: Scribner, 1953.

3. Wertheimer, M. *Productive thinking* (enlarged edition). New York: Harper, 1959.

4. Campbell, D. T. Blind variation and selective retention in creative thought as in other knowledge processes. *Psychological Review*, 1960, **67**, 380–400.

5. Gordon, W. J. J. *Synectics.* New York: Harper & Row, 1961.

6. Bruner, J. S. *On knowing: Essays for the left hand.* Cambridge, Mass.: The Belknap Press of Harvard University Press, 1962.

7. Ogilvy, D. *Confessions of an advertising man.* New York: Atheneum, 1963.

8. Barron, F. The psychology of creativity. In T. M. Newcomb (Ed.), *New directions in psychology*, Vol. 2. New York: Holt, Rinehart & Winston, Inc., 1965, 1–134.

9. Guilford, J. P. *The nature of human intelligence.* New York: McGraw-Hill, 1967, Ch. 14.

10. Maier, N. R. F. *Problem solving and creativity in individuals and groups.* Belmont, Cal: Wadsworth, 1970.

11. de Bono, E. *Lateral thinking.* New York: Harper, 1973.

12. Koestler, A. *The act of creation.* New York: Dell, 1973.

13. Adams, J. L. *Conceptual blockbusting: A pleasurable guide to better problem solving.* San Francisco, Cal: San Francisco Book Co., 1976.

14. Stein, M. I. *Stimulating creativity*, *Vols. I and II*. New York: Academic Press, 1974–75.
15. Whitfield, P. R. *Creativity in industry*. Penguin: Harmondsworth, Middlesex, England, 1975.
16. Souder, W. E., and Ziegler, R. W. A review of creativity and problem solving techniques. *Research Management*, 1977 (July), 34–42.
17. Ackoff, R. L. *The art of problem solving: Accompanied by Ackoff's fables*. New York: John Wiley, 1978.

VIII. DECISION AIDS

A. Texts on decision analysis

1. Raiffa, H. *Decision analysis*. Reading, Mass: Addison-Wesley, 1968.
2. Schlaifer, R. *Analysis of decisions under uncertainty*. New York: McGraw-Hill, 1969.
3. Lindley, D. V. *Making decisions*. Chichester, England: John Wiley, 1971.
4. Brown, R. V., Kahr, A. S., and Peterson, C. R. *Decision analysis for the manager*. New York: Holt, Rinehart & Winston, 1974.
5. Keeney, R. L., and Raiffa, H. *Decisions with multiple objectives: Preferences and value tradeoffs*. New York: John Wiley, 1976.
6. Moore, P. G., and Thomas, H. *The anatomy of decisions*. Harmondsworth, England: Penguin, 1976.

B. Examples of decision analysis

1. Howard, R. A., Matheson, J. E., and Miller, K. E. *Readings in decision analysis*. Menlo Park, CA: Stanford Research Institute, 1976.
2. Bell, D. E., Keeney, R. L., and Raiffa, H. (Eds.). *Conflicting objectives in decisions*. Chichester, England: John Wiley, 1977.
3. Kaufman, G. M. and Thomas, H. (Eds.). *Modern decision analysis: Selected readings*. Harmondsworth, Middlesex: Penguin, 1977.
4. Hogarth, R. M. Judgement, drug monitoring and decision aids. In W. H. W. Inman (Ed.), *Monitoring for drug safety*. Lancaster, England: MTP Press, Ltd., in press.

C. Views on multi-attribute methods

1. MacCrimmon, K. R. An overview of multiple objective decision making. In J. L. Cochrane and M. Zeleny (Eds.), *Multiple criteria decision making*. Columbia, SC: University of South Carolina Press, 1973.
2. von Winterfeldt, D., and Fischer, G. W. Multi-attribute theory: Models and scaling procedures. In D. Wendt and C. A. J. Vlek (Eds.), *Utility, probability and human decision making*. Dordrecht, The Netherlands: Reidel, 1975.
3. Gardiner, P. C., and Edwards, W. Public values: Multiattribute-utility

measurement for social decision making. In M. F. Kaplan and S. Schwartz (Eds.), *Human judgment and decision processes.* New York: Academic Press, 1975.

4. Fischhoff, B. Cost benefit analysis and the art of motorcycle maintenance. *Policy Sciences,* 1977, **8**, 177–202.

5. Einhorn, H. J., and McCoach, W. A simple multi-attribute procedure for evaluation. *Behavioral Science,* 1977, **22**, 270–282.

6. Johnson, E. M., and Huber, G. P. The technology of utility assessment. *IEEE Transactions on Systems, Man and Cybernetics,* 1977, *Vol.* **SMC-7** (5), 311–325.

7. Humphreys, P. Application of multi-attribute utility theory. In H. Jungermann and G. de Zeeuw (Eds.), *Decision making and change in human affairs.* Dordrecht-Holland: Reidel, 1977.

D. Other aids

1. Einhorn, H. J., and Hogarth, R. M. Unit weighting schemes for decision making. *Organizational Behavior and Human Performance,* 1975, **13**, 171–192.

2. Linstone, H. A., and Turoff, M. *The Delphi method: Techniques and applications.* Reading, Mass: Addison-Wesley, 1975.

3. Beach, B. H. Expert judgment about uncertainty: Bayesian decision making in realistic settings. *Organizational Behavior and Human Performance,* 1975, **14**, 10–59.

4. Spetzler, C. S., and Staël von Holstein, C.-A. S. Probability encoding in decision analysis. *Management Science,* 1975, **22**, 340–358.

5. Axelrod, R. (Ed.). *Structure of decision: The cognitive maps of political elites.* Princeton, NJ: Princeton University Press, 1976.

6. Kahneman, D., and Tversky, A. Intuitive prediction: Biases and corrective procedures. In *TIMS Studies in Management Science, Vol. 12,* 1979, pp. 313–327.

7. Social judgment theory aids are exemplified in the references numbered 8, 9, and 10 under the 'lens model' sub-section (B) of Section V.

Index